Also by Eswyn Lyster:

Lyster Pioneers of Lower Canada and the West, the story of the Lysters of Queen's County, Ireland who settled in Canada early in the nineteenth century. Cartwright Printers, Courtenay, British Columbia, 1984. (Under the name Eswyn Ellinor-Lyster) ISBN 0-9691833-05

Most Excellent Citizens

Canada's War Brides of World War II

A History

by

Eswyn Lyster

Order this book online at www.trafford.com
or email orders@trafford.com

Most Trafford titles are also available at major online book retailers.

Printed in Victoria, BC, Canada.

ISBN: 978-1-4269-0250-5 (Soft)
ISBN: 978-1-4269-1000-5 (e-book)

*Our mission is to efficiently provide the world's finest, most comprehensive
book publishing service, enabling every author to experience success.
To find out how to publish your book, your way, and have it available
worldwide, visit us online at www.trafford.com*

Trafford rev. 11/13/2009

www.trafford.com

North America & international
toll-free: 1 888 232 4444 (USA & Canada)
phone: 250 383 6864 • fax: 812 355 4082

Dedicated to the war husbands,
without whom there would be no story,
and to all the brave men who fought to save Britain
and free the world, 1939 - 1945.

Bill Lyster (circled) with members of the Calgary Highlanders, arriving in Halifax, Nova Scotia late August 1940. They are about to board the *Pasteur* en route to England. The regiment returned to Canada in the summer of 1945.[1]
Credit: author's collection

Dr. David Bercuson, who kindly provided the Introduction, is a Historian and the Director of the Centre for Military and Strategic Studies, University of Calgary. Among his many books is "Battalion of Heroes: The Calgary Highlanders in World War Two".

Cover:
Mother wanted this photograph of Ted and Joan Bowles, taken October 14, 1944, to be used on the cover of Most Excellent Citizens. She loved their resolutely optimistic expressions saying "Don't use my wedding pictures, there is already enough of me in this book".

The poppy, by a Cree beader, is from Robertson's Trading Post, La Ronge, SK.

Terry, Jane & Stuart Lyster
Executors of Coral Eswyn Lyster's Testamentary Trust
Canada, 2009

30 May, 1943.

Dear Mother and All,

... I have found myself a very, very lovely little English girl and have gotten myself engaged. At present she is in the services with the Wrens. She is 19 years of age and will be 20 in September. Her name is Eswyn Ellinor, and her people are very nice and good to me. They have a store in the town where we are at present. I have known Eswyn and her people since February and have been more or less making myself a frequent visitor ever since.

Eswyn is a very good partner and can really cook. She isn't the common ordinary sort that is usually about, but very clever and extremely sensible. I know that you will like her very much and I am sure that she will fit into our family quite well, and I am looking forward to the day when you can put your own stamp of approval on her, and verify my choice.

However we don't plan on being married until this war is either over or until there is some definite assurance that we can be married and not be separated. I couldn't see any sense in being a married man and being away from her, perhaps in another part of the world altogether.

We plan on going back to Canada and starting our own home there ...

Well folks, I must close now and I do hope you are pleased with this bit of news as I think I am a very fortunate fellow, so
      Cheerio for now,
              Loads of love,
              Bill.

Opposite:

Extract from the letter my Canadian fiancé wrote home to Alberta when we became engaged. Although ostensibly addressed to his whole family it is evident he is really reassuring his mother. In doing so he painted a very rosy picture of my almost non-existent domestic talents, knowing that she, a hard-working prairie housewife, would be interested in them. It should come as no surprise that in subsequent years Bill became a very successful sales manager and head of his own sales agency, a job that depended wholly on this talent.

ACKNOWLEDGEMENTS
AND THANKS

Deepest thanks to my children, Terence, Stuart, and Elizabeth Jane, and my daughter-in-law, Carolyn, for their invaluable assistance with this project and for their encouragement when it seemed never-ending. My special appreciation to Jane for her photographs of sites in London, England; Terry for making the trip on the *Mauretania* to Halifax with me back in 1946 (and in reverse, from Qualicum to Halifax in 2006, The Year of the War Bride), for becoming my Project Manager and for supplying maps and sketches; Stuart for designing and maintaining my web site, and for making sure the book was backed up at all times. Gratitude to Carolyn for her sharp eye for a misprint, muzzy construction or misplaced sentence fragment. Also to my granddaughter, Suzy Lyster, for permission to use her photograph taken with John Ralston Saul in Santiago, Chile. Thanks to my friends for sticking by me while I took eleven years off my social calendar and was so often unavailable. Special thanks to my late friend, Ruth Holt, for her help with early research.

I must single out Melynda Jarratt, BA, MA (History), for her generosity in sharing so much of her research, expertise, and advice on this complicated subject, and for reading and correcting an early version of my manuscript, Annette Fulford for her many contributions, and Bev Tosh for her encouragement and insight, and for including my portrait in her collection of war bride paintings, "One Way Passage".

Special thanks to the late Ben Wicks, Harry Palmer, Calgary photographer; singer/composer Shari Ulrich, and poet Dianne Hicks Morrow. Gratitude to Newfoundland war bride, Margaret Rowe, who distributed *sixty* "War Bride Project forms", and to Mary Rand and all those close friends who gave moral support during and after recovery from the stroke that hampered things back in 1999-2000. Nor could I have completed this journey without the tremendous support of Spindrift Writers, Parksville, BC. Salut!

The staff of Qualicum Beach Branch of the Vancouver Island Regional Library have been exceptionally helpful in making out-of-the-way material available. My thanks as well to the other librarians and archivists in Canada and Britain, far too numerous to list.

Above all, my deep appreciation to the hundreds of war brides who opened their hearts and shared their stories with me, and particularly to Betty Ramshaw who supplied the last chapter. I'm delighted that the voices of these women have come through so vividly, even when describing experiences common to us all. Back in 1998 I could not have imagined the abundance of submissions. This bounty has given me the luxury of choice, but has also meant that a multitude of worthy stories could not be fitted into the available space. We have remembered, we have laughed and have wiped away the odd tear together, and I salute you all.

Eswyn Lyster, Qualicum Beach, 2009

CONTENTS

INTRODUCTION

This is the story of Coral Eswyn (Ellinor) Lyster, 1923-2009, Canadian War Bride - and of so many others like her. Eswyn was very proud of her "war bride" status, an official status created by the Government of Canada in the First World War to designate those women, like Eswyn, who married Canadian servicemen in the course of the war and who subsequently came to Canada to rejoin their husbands.

In both wars Canada paid the war brides' sea and rail passage and allowed them to take a limited amount of their personal items with them aboard ship. The vast majority of the war brides in both wars were women from the United Kingdom; some 48,000 of them had arrived in Canada by the end of 1946 but others kept coming for several years after. In the Second World War many were also from the low countries, especially the Netherlands, where Canadian troops wintered in 1944/45 and occupied the entire country for about a year after the Nazi surrender in May, 1945.

War brides came to Canada alone (with their children if they had them) and not with their husbands. The Canadian Army had worked out an elaborate system for repatriation which took into account factors such as length of service, time in combat, family emergencies, and so on. Some able bodied men were actually returned to Canada beginning in early 1945. Wives had to stay put, largely because of the anticipated huge shortage of shipping after the fighting ended. Many of them waited until 1946 before being able to board ship.

Eswyn's experience – and that of tens of thousands of others – was mixed. The good part was re-unification with their husbands – in Eswyn's case Bill, a former officer in the Calgary Highlanders – and a new, and in many ways better, life in a country untouched by war and thriving with post-war prosperity. In Britain life remained hard and bleak with rationing continuing for years and shortages in basic foods and energy supplies such as coal lasting until the early 1950s. But the war brides also ended in a place where they were strangers, for all the warmth that Canadians might have felt for their erstwhile allies, competing for scarce apartments, appliances and just about everything else. Their friends and relatives were a world away in the days before instant mass communication and there was every prospect they would never see family or friends again.

Canada was a very British country then, with Union Jacks everywhere and almost everyone in English-speaking Canada seeming to have a relative back in the "old country." But Canada was not the UK and everything from grocery shopping to radio, to the denomination of Canadian money was different. The Canadian winter was especially hard and seemed to last forever.

Some war brides couldn't take it in the long run and went home but the vast majority stayed and became Canadians, contributing to all walks of life raising families, working farms, and increasingly entering the workplace. They became singers and artists and broadcasters and added their energy and talent to a growing young country. Eswyn and her sisters made a huge contribution to Canada and Eswyn's book will be one small reason why they will never be forgotten.

D.J. Bercuson

PROLOGUE

What is a war bride? World War II gave the world's gene-pool a mighty stir, producing alliances between men and women who would otherwise never have met. During the nearly six years of war, marriages of servicemen while away from their home country became a world-wide phenomenon. Literally millions of these marriages took place. Charts (next page) cover only the known marriages within the Allied Forces.

DEFINITION OF A CANADIAN WAR BRIDE

When chartered war bride associations were organized in Canada in the 1970s a definition of "war bride" was necessary to identify eligibility for membership. Kathleen (Reed) Garside of Regina, Saskatchewan, the driving force behind the Associations, sought an official definition. She received the following information from Colonel Robert L. Martin, Director of Personnel, Legal Services, Department of National Defence (DND), Ottawa, in a letter dated October 1983:

> (A war bride is any) person who was referred to as a 'dependent spouse' of a member of Military Forces of Canada, and Auxiliary bodies or services designated by the Governor General in Council, as forming part of the Military Forces overseas, and who became a Dependent Spouse during the period 10th September 1939 – 30th September, 1947. Exceptions to this rule may be in instances whereby due to the exigencies of War (e.g. P.O.W.'s) or medical reasons marriage could not take place until arrival in Canada on or before the 30th September 1947. In some cases P.O.W. husbands were brought directly to Canada, and in some cases some engaged girls were brought to Canada ahead of their P.O.W. husbands-to-be, but still had to have arrived on or before the 30th September, 1947 and have had their way paid by the Government. If they arrived here and the husband paid their way, they are not classified as a War Bride.

Colonel Martin had obviously consulted late 1940s DND files concerning transportation to Canada of servicemen's dependents. A cut-off date had been necessary for that operation. Maintaining staff in Britain and on the continent for this task was not only expensive, but the Canadian personnel who had been away from Canada for a long time were anxious to return and get on with their lives.

The date given by Colonel Martin referred only to *the deadline when eligibility for conducted passage to Canada ceased*. Marriages continued to take place as late as 1949, usually after fiancées arranged and financed unescorted passages themselves.

A careful study of the process from Permission to Marry to arrival at the final Canadian destination confirms that *marriage* was the only qualification required for a woman to become a dependent war bride. The Canadian Army and the Canadian Wives Bureau both demanded proof of marriage before granting Dependent's Allowances or arranging escorted passages. Arrival before or after certain arbitrary dates has nothing to do with it. (There is evidence in Department of Immigration files that a few common-law wives applied for transportation, but were refused.)

Having sought an official definition, the Saskatchewan Association accepted it (indeed, considering the source, why would it be questioned?). Colonel Martin's definition became an integral part of their Articles of Association. Other provincial war bride associations followed suit. In Saskatchewan's case the "closing" date was later amended to December 30, 1947.[1]

Recently a wife who arrived after December 1947 asked me if she was "really a war bride". She had been told by an Association member that because of her late arrival in Canada she was not! I assured her that she was. It seems that in practice Associations usually admitted those who did not fit the date of arrival criteria. The "Boat Boards" of the now defunct Vancouver Island War Brides Association certainly listed three members who arrived in the nineteen fifties: Florence (Weston) Drury, *Samaria,* 1951, Alice (Stachura) McGough, *Iveria,* 1952, and Mabel (Dewen) Czuboka, *Georgic,* 1953.

Not long after I began researching this book I realised that in Canada the words "war bride" had another informal definition: "arrival in Canada and assimilation into a community". However, there were many war brides who did not come to Canada, instead settling with their husbands in their own country. The tidal wave of publicity that greeted the 1946 arrivals obscured this fact. For instance Annie (Fisher) Ottewell had been widowed when her Canadian husband was killed in an accident in 1944 while he was stationed at England's Camp Bordon, Hampshire.[2] Annie remained in England. She received a Silver Cross from Canada, as well as a life-long widow's pension, confirmation that marriage alone, made the war bride.

A broader definition than Colonel Martin's was needed. I came up with the following and have found no reason to change it:

A Canadian war bride is a woman of any nationality other than Canadian who met a Canadian serviceman serving overseas in World War II, and subsequently married him.

CHART 1, WAR BRIDES *OTHER* THAN BY MARRIAGES TO CANADIAN FORCES: nk=not known

COUNTRY OF ORIGIN, WIVES	COUNTRY OF ORIGIN, HUSBANDS	NUMBER OF MARRIAGES IF KNOWN
Britain	USA (GIs stationed in Britain)	. . . more than 100,000 married British women.[3] (a much disputed figure) . . . the total British war bride immigrant population was 70,133[4]
Algeria, Australia, Belgium, Canada, China, Czechoslovakia, Denmark, Eire, Finland, France, Great Britain,	USA (GIs serving overseas other than in Britain)	One million (This figure is for all GI war brides **including** Britain)[5]

Holland, Hungary, Italy, Japan, Latvia, Morocco, Newfoundland, New Guinea, New Zealand, Philippines, Poland, Russia, Sweden, and Switzerland.		
Britain	Free France, Norway, Holland, Poland, etc. (Servicemen who fled to Britain in 1940 from German-occupied countries)	nk These war brides spent the Cold War years trapped behind the Iron Curtain
Unidentified overseas countries.	Britain (men serving outside mainland Britain)	nk
Canada (women's divisions of Canada's armed services, nurses, Red Cross volunteers, etc. stationed in Britain and Continental Europe) e.g., matron of a hostel married a Scotsman	Britain	nk
Canada (civilian or service-women serving in Canada).	Britain, New Zealand, Australia, Norway, etc. training in Canada with the British Commonwealth Air Training Plan (BCATP)	Approximately 3,750 [6]

CHART 2, CANADA'S WAR BRIDES

COUNTRY OF ORIGIN, WIVES	COUNTRY OF ORIGIN, HUSBANDS	NUMBER OF MARRIAGES IF KNOWN
GREAT BRITAIN: England, Scotland, Wales, Northern Ireland, Channel Islands, Isle of Man.	Canada (men serving in Great Britain)	44,886 [7]

Algiers, Australia, Belgium, France, The Caribbean, Chile, Denmark, Ireland (Eire), India, Italy, France, Germany, Greece, Holland, Hungary, Jamaica, Newfoundland, Norway, North Africa, South Africa, Russia.	Canada (men serving overseas other than in Great Britain. Also in Newfoundland)	2,897 ibid.

Total marriages:	**47,783**

Marriages continued to take place after eligibility for the Canadian government supervised sailings ceased, so the true total would be slightly higher.

Not included in the above:

The United States	Marriages between American women and Canadian servicemen previously unrecorded are coming to light from published obituaries.	nk
Newfoundland. Before 1949 Newfoundland was Britain's oldest colony. After Confederation with Canada their war brides became Canadian war brides, but too late to be in the above total.	Wives of Newfoundland servicemen who served with British forces in Britain and Continental Europe (and of men in Newfoundland Forestry Units who served in Scotland). Newfoundland women who married Canadian Servicemen stationed in Newfoundland who usually settled in Canada post-war.	800 (Estimation by Memorial University, St. John's.)

The true total of Canada's war brides? As elusive as most statistics, but probably 50,000.

CANADA'S SUPPORT

In writing *Most Excellent Citizens* I've learned a lot. Without Winston Churchill and his unshakable determination we would have lost the war. Without the support of the United States we could not have won it. Those 61 Divisions did the trick. Lend Lease and Bundles for Britain increased our meagre food rations and clothed the survivors of Hitler's bombs. Another thing about the Americans is their genius for publicity. Canada, however, just went about doing much the same thing, but didn't shout it from the rooftops.

British historian, Richard Holmes, Professor of Military and Security Studies at Cranfield University and the Royal Military College of Science, has this to say about Canada's contribution, in his book *In the Footsteps of Churchill, a Study in Character*.

> In 1940-1 Britain would not have survived as an independent nation had it not been for the agricultural, industrial and financial aid received from Canada. Had the Germans invaded, in all probability, the royal family and the government, along with the other British-based governments in exile, would have been transferred to Canada along with the Royal Navy.
>
> Canadian assistance included tanks and aircraft produced free of charge under the Canadian Mutual Aid programme; in terms of manpower it produced over a million volunteers for the Allied armed forces, of which 368,000 served in Europe and 42,000 were killed, from a population of only 11 million. . . . As usual only the squeaking wheels get the grease: the quietly competent Canadians and their low-key Prime Minister deserve much more credit than they received, or that I can give them here.

The story of Canada's war brides, despite tragedies, traumas and the occasional petty-mindedness of government departments, minor officials and others, is in most instances a love story. Sometimes even a "they-lived-happily-ever-after" love story, and is in all respects a complicated and therefore a fascinating one. I sincerely hope I have done it justice.

Eswyn Lyster,
"Sussex Downs", Qualicum Beach, British Columbia.
2009

A word to the reader:

While the author's experience and perspective shapes this book, the broader war bride story is told in large measure through the words of the participants. Their quotes are easily distinguished because they are indented and rendered in smaller print. For instance early in the first chapter Sheila Anketel-Jones is introduced and then quoted:

> I was still at school when war was declared and can to this day recall the feeling of utter panic which seized me as I heard the Prime Minister's dreadful words. The white, strained faces of my parents terrified me even more.

The author's words and those of Betty Ramshaw in Chapter 23 are not indented and are in larger print.

The *Oxford Canadian Dictionary* has been consulted to determine spelling except where usage and jargon of WWII seemed more appropriate.

Part I:
British War Brides

War changes everything.
    Anon.

The nine o'clock news announced the discovery of the German blacklist. Among the people to be dealt with when England was invaded were Winston, Vic Oliver, Sybil Thorndyke, Rebecca West and me. What a cast!

    Noel Coward's Diary, 13 September, 1939

In the 1930s, Mrs. Dearden, a family friend whose life had been radically changed by World War I, was notorious for her gloomy predictions for the future. 'They'll come!' she would say, 'they'll come!' Her words haunted me even though I had no idea who it was she thought would come. They haunted me even more during the summer and autumn of 1940 when Hitler threatened to invade England. Years later I was astonished to read the Dictator's words quoted in Peter Fleming's book, *Invasion 1940*: (p. 131) 'When people are very curious in Great Britain and ask: "Yes, but why doesn't he come?" we reply: "Calm yourselves! He is coming! He is coming! " '

    the author

Chapter 1: Future War Brides:
The Phoney War and the Battle of Britain

The British war bride story began September 3, 1939. We weren't aware of it yet, but the old adage is true, war does change everything. The 1939 British teenager was very different from the new millennium version. Makeup, inspired by close-ups of our favourite movie stars, was usually forbidden by our fathers. Sometimes we could get away with a touch of palest pink lipstick. Our daydreams about blue chiffon gowns with diamanté straps evaporated, to be replaced with uniforms in three dull shades of serge, drab factory overalls, or civilian "make do and mend" clothing. If we were in uniform hair had to be above the collar. If we were in a factory it had to be confined in a hairnet or "snood".

In 1939 some future war brides didn't know anyone who had died – this too would soon change. These were the "innocents" who went to war, not knowing what the future might hold, including the marriages that would bring about the greatest changes of all.

WAR DECLARED!

The words on the placards were printed in the largest available font, and the skinny British newsboys and down-at-heel men shouting the words would seem strange to twenty-first century eyes. There being no truly informal dress in 1939, these messengers of doom wore crumpled suits, shirts, and ties, with cloth caps or Trilby (Fedora) hats, the cast-off clothing of those slightly higher in the scheme of things who could afford to buy replacements. Everyone gathered around the radio that Sunday morning to hear Prime Minister Neville Chamberlain announce that his latest effort to avoid war with Germany had failed. The world was about to go into a horrendous convulsion that would displace, mutilate and obliterate millions of its inhabitants.

Only 21 years previously the Great War, the "war to end all wars", had ended in an Armistice. (Until 1939 nobody had reason to call it "the *First* World War".) For the older generation this new war was a nightmare, for us it was a frightening yet strangely exhilarating development. We so often complained that "nothing ever happened", and now something had!

War bride Sheila Ankatel-Jones wrote to me from Sussex, England, where she has lived for many years with her Canadian husband:

I was still at school when war was declared and can to this day recall the feeling of utter panic which seized me as I heard the Prime Minister's dreadful words. The white, strained faces of my parents terrified me even more.

A few minutes after the Prime Minister's broadcast air raid sirens sounded across southern England, including those in the village of Aldwick, Sussex where my parents owned a shop that sold newspapers, cigarettes, confectionery and other items. Not knowing it was a false alarm we were frightened. I know I waited in silent panic to be blown to bits. Absolutely nothing happened and then the All Clear sounded. Never again would I be so terrified, not even the following year when sirens were followed by the drone of enemy bombers and the "crump" of exploding bombs.

War bride Joan (Ibbs) Bowles, of Victoria, British Columbia was one of thousands of children evacuated from city areas:

On September 3, a bright, sunny day, I was in church. The preacher told us that England had just declared war on Germany. By the time I got home my mother had my bag packed and with my friend we were hurried on to a train to Worthing. We were both so homesick that we were back in London after just six weeks.

Catherine (Kier) Macdonald, Qualicum Beach, British Columbia remembers the awful feeling in her chest as she watched children boarding evacuation trains. Joyce (Harrison) McLennan, Whitehorse, Yukon Territory lived in Bedale, a small market town in Yorkshire, and remembers distributing lunch bags to arriving evacuees.

Fast on the heels of the false air raid alarm and the evacuation of children, Winston Churchill, newly appointed as First Sea Lord, announced to the House of Commons the torpedoing of the British passenger liner, *Athenia*. The ship had left Glasgow for Montreal just before the declaration of war. Passengers learned Britain was at war from the ship's notice board.

The commander of the submarine U-30, Fritz-Julius Lemp, fired three torpedoes at what he thought was an armed warship. Two hit the *Athenia* before Lemp realized his mistake. Passenger liners were off limits even for German U-boats. He neither informed Berlin, nor surfaced to take. on survivors. Thus, because of a gross error in judgment, the longest and bloodiest battle of the war, the Battle of the Atlantic, began on day one.

Hitler is said to have learned of the sinking and of the 30 Americans among the 112 lost, from radio reports. He must have been furious for he hoped Britain would warm to his peace overtures, and the last thing he wanted to do was provoke the United States.[1]

Barbara Bailey was one of two future Canadian war brides to survive the sinking. After a harrowing night in a lifeboat she was taken to Galway, Ireland and spent the rest of the war in England where she met and married a Canadian. As Barbara (Bailey) Durant she embarked for Canada on the *Aquitania*, and was understandably shocked when some war brides on board didn't bother to attend lifeboat drills. Barbara and her husband farmed in the Ottawa region of Ontario.[2] A second future war bride was rescued from the *Athenia*, but sadly my informant was taken seriously ill before she could give me any details.

In 1941 Oberleutnant Lemp was involved in an event even more damaging to Germany's cause. It was from submarine U-110, under Lemp's command, that the British Navy captured an Enigma cipher machine not from U-571, and not by the American Navy, as the Hollywood film *U-571* would have us believe. Prime Minister Tony Blair called the film an affront to the British sailors who lost their lives in the action.[3] The influence of Enigma on the outcome of the war is too well-known to be repeated here. Gwladys (Rees) Aikens, a member of the Queen Alexandra's Imperial Military Nursing Service/Reserve (QAIMNS/R), was also rescued from a torpedoed ship. Her story is told in a later chapter.

WARTIME MINISTRIES IN BRITAIN

Ministries of all kinds sprang up: War, Defence, Labour and National Service, Food, Agriculture, Fuel, Transport, Information, Supply, Aircraft Production, Health, Works, Home Security, etc. There were even sub-departments in charge of those British necessities, tea and sugar. The Emergency Powers (Defence) Act enabled the Government to introduce regulations without reference to Parliament, which they proceeded to do ad infinitum. Censorship was imposed on overseas mail.[4]

Hanging over everything was the ominous-sounding Mass Observation, that had been in operation since 1937. Ordinary citizens were recruited to report on public reaction to certain events. These methods, so dangerous in the hands of dictatorships, seem in Britain to have had an English spin to them. (Some women treated their reports as a kind of confessional, if the recently published *Love and War in London, A Woman's Diary, 1939-42,* based on Olive Cockett's contributions, is anything to go by.) In order to fight totalitarianism Britain itself became a totalitarian country.

After that first false alarm, and for the rest of the Phoney War, we had no more air raid warnings. Future war brides, still in school or starting our first jobs, helped sew blackout curtains, and stick trellis patterns of brown paper tape on windows to control flying glass. Our brothers and cousins left for overseas, part of a six-year game of Musical Chairs in which millions all over the world travelled far from home, often never to return.

Joan (Ibbs) Bowles' brother trained as a pilot in the United States:

(My brother) was in Dallas and sent letters home saying how wonderful people were to the British boys. They were not in uniform as at that time America was not in the war. My brother went with two others to get me an engraved bracelet. That was January 3 and he was killed January 18. It was fate. He wasn't supposed to fly that night but somebody else couldn't go . . . it was their last night flying before leaving as they had received their wings. The other two boys visited us when they got back to London and brought me the bracelet. Neither of them survived the war.

We had a dreadful time with my mother after my brother died. As she was only 40 our doctor suggested she have another child. Dallas, named for the city my brother had visited, was born December 12, 1942, and my youngest sister, Linda in 1945. My dear mother had a very sad life. Linda became very ill. She was in one hospital and my Dad in another miles away. My mother spent the whole day on buses to visit them. On the way to visit us in Canada after the war, Linda died. Now, being a mother myself, I realise how hard it must have been for my parents see me move so far away.

The Local Defence Volunteers, the LDV or "Look, Duck and Vanish" Brigade (Churchill quickly renamed them the Home Guard) seemed to be our only defenders. Each Sunday morning Aldwick's detachment paraded outside *The Ship Inn*. Foreshadowing the 1940 hit song, *They're Either Too Young or Too Old*, they were older men, some in semi-military garb, and spotty youths too young to be called for military service. When dismissed the seniors stashed their improvised weapons and headed for the pub while the boys went home for Sunday dinner. We made nervous jokes about this makeshift army, hardly realizing that Canada's First Division (Army) had arrived in Britain just before Christmas 1939, and would be followed over the next months and years by four more Canadian Divisions.

Saucepans were donated to scrap metal drives, iron railings were taken, including over a mile of them from London's Hyde Park. When those around Manchester's public parks disappeared, the gates were left and for weeks after ceremoniously locked at sundown. We contributed to local "Buy a Hurricane" and "Buy a Spitfire" Weeks, we bought war bonds, dug trenches and were issued gas masks.

Ethel "Jo" (Goodwin-White) Sherrin, who came to Edmonton, Alberta served with Air Raid Precautions (ARP):

> My father and I immediately joined the ARP. We spent the next year measuring people for gas masks and staking out their gardens for air raid shelters. The English take pride in their gardens and it took a lot of persuasion to get some people to agree. My mother was the last to capitulate and only agreed because it was the law.

British children, in a time-honoured tradition, sang a playground ditty:

> Under the spreading chestnut tree
> Neville Chamberlain said to me
> 'If you want to get your gas mask free
> Join the blinkin' ARP.'

In Aldwick our newspaper delivery boys took better paying jobs and my father, mother and I inherited their paper routes, not exactly what my parents had in mind when they purchased the business in 1938. Even the Phoney War wasn't safe. The Blackout was total and buses, army lorries and the few private cars still on the roads had ninety percent of their headlights masked. After dark drivers could neither see nor be seen. Many pedestrians were killed or injured before the "real" war began.

A photograph in the British press showed the first women to fill jobs left vacant by departing men. They were two bus "conductresses", a name that quickly evolved into "clippies", from the little machine hanging from their necks that went "ping!" as it punched your destination on the bus ticket.

In October 1939 a National Register of all citizens was completed. Everyone in the land was issued a numbered identity card.[5] At first single women and childless widows, 19-31, were required to *register* for National Service. Only later would they be called up:

> In conscripting women, Britain went further than any other nation – further than Russia and Germany . . . (by mid 1941) it was calculated that among those between eighteen and forty, nine single women out of ten, and eight married women out of ten were in the forces or in industry. Those left over were mostly looking after the nation's young children.[6]

If before the declaration of war job choices for women had been severely limited, now only armed combat was unavailable to us. Civilian jobs essential to the war effort were styled "reserved occupations". Some married women, formerly childless, had rushes of maternal instinct and needed extra clothing coupons to buy maternity smocks. Motherhood was also a reserved occupation.

Gwendolyn (Harms) Keele, later Zradicka, of Richmond, British Columbia sent in this little-known exemption:

> I heard via the grapevine that if you had the nerve to say that your occupation was 'prostitute' no more was said, as it too was regarded as an essential occupation!

Under the National Service (No. 2) Act, December 1941, all women aged 18 to 60 had to register and the schedule of Reserved Occupations was abandoned.

The Phoney War came to an abrupt end on April 9, 1940 when Hitler attacked Norway and Denmark. On May 10 he invaded France and the Low Countries. In Britain a dizzying sequence of events saw Prime Minister Chamberlain step down to be replaced by Winston Churchill at the head of a coalition government:

> (Churchill) was Prime Minister at last at the age of sixty-five . . . It was almost forty years after he had first been elected to Parliament. He took over in the most perilous circumstances in which any Prime Minister has ever come to office. And there were political as well as military perils. He was not the choice of the King. He was not the choice of the Whitehall establishment, which reacted with varying degrees of dismay.[7]

The fate of Britain and much of the western world would depend on the strength and single-mindedness of this man, yet he barely survived in office to the end of the month. Between May 24 and May 28 the War Cabinet debated whether or not to accept Hitler's overtures for peace. Only Churchill stayed firm. On June 4 we heard his never-to-be-forgotten words: "We shall fight them on the beaches . . . We shall never surrender!" Our known world was falling apart. By mid-May Holland's Queen Wilhelmina was the Royal Family's personal evacuee at Buckingham Palace. Other refugees in England included The Grand Duchess of Luxembourg and the kings of Norway, Greece, Yugoslavia and Albania. They joined Emperor Haile Selassie of Abyssinia (Ethiopia) who had fled there with his several wives when Mussolini attacked and occupied his country in 1936.

The 72-year-old Queen Mary, widow of King George V, was moved to Badminton, Gloucestershire. She is said to have enjoyed her six years as an "evacuee". Her parting words before returning to London in 1945 were, "Oh, I *have* been happy. Here I've been anybody to everybody, and back in London I shall have to start being Queen Mary all over again!" [8]

At the end of May the rescue of the British Expeditionary Force from the beaches of Dunkirk, France began. Many were killed. Many, including the son of our next-door neighbour, were taken prisoner and spent the next five years in prison camps, but the 338,000 men who were rescued were welcomed in Britain with such rejoicing that Churchill reminded us wars are not won by retreats. The war in France had ended, the Battle of Britain, he warned, was about to begin.

Churchill described the German invasion barges waiting in French ports just across the Channel where sixty thousand, battle-hardened troops who had already defeated so much of Europe were ready to invade southern England. My family no longer lived in peaceful Sussex-by-the-Sea. Overnight our barbed-wired, mined and military-guarded beach had become the Front Line. When the Prime Minister had growled "We shall fight on the beaches" my first thought was "He can't possibly mean our beach!" Surprisingly he did, but I didn't find out until years later when I read of the German invasion plan (code named Sea Lion): "All landings in the Deal-Ramsate area were abandoned, but the front was extended from Folkestone to Bognor Regis." [9] Aldwick was a mile or so west of Bognor Regis. I had nightmares in which invasion troops, still dripping English Channel water, scaled the Sussex flint wall at the bottom of the garden behind the shop. My only weapon in these dreams was a kitchen spatula which I waved about ineffectively. Strangely, these nightmare troops wore World War I spiked helmets.

If I'd been privy to the government's secret discussions I might have been even more alarmed. At a June 29 Cabinet meeting Alexander Cadogan, Permanent Undersecretary of the Foreign Office, discussed Anthony Eden's recent tour of Sussex and Kent. " . . . certainly makes it seem that the Germans can take a penny steamer to the coast and stroll up to London! . . . (we are) completely unprepared!" [10]

One Londoner's reaction to the invasion threat was interesting:

> (It's going to) make a fine shumuzzle. The Germans drive on the right and we drive on the left. There'll be a jolly old mix-up on the roads if the Germans do come.[11]

Eighteen-year-old Joy (Hicks) Loveridge, who lives in Qualicum Beach, was a WAAF at Debden RAF Station, Essex. Because of her secretarial skills she was assigned to the Orderly Room. Her shorthand may have been first class, but she typed on "a very ancient Oliver". Joy spoke of the RAF personnel arriving at Debden after escaping from France:

> I will never forget their faces. It was then we began to realise our situation was precarious. I first saw Peter Townsend when he reported to the Group Captain. I was immediately and completely infatuated. Some time later he was shot down and nothing

8

was heard of him for several days. We were all shattered, but he turned up in clothes some sailor had given him. I had to take down his report and read it back to him. I can still remember how hot and clammy my hands were.

Peter Townsend was the man Princess Margaret in later years decided she would not marry. Joy may have been smitten with him, but Canadian airman, Doug Leveridge, was the man of her choice.

Catherine (Munro) Mahon, also of Qualicum Beach, spoke of the changes in Durnoch, Scotland after war broke out:

The town was full of troops as the 51st Highland Division were followed by some of the 52nd Lowland, even some Gurkhas trained there. The hotels and large private summer homes were taken over by the War Department. Many Norwegians escaped and came over in boats and were trained there too.

War being an untidy business, dates are not easily defined but are required for history books and battle honours. The official dates for the Battle of Britain are July 10 to October 31, 1940, however Edith Kup, a plotter at Debden, Essex (she was not a war bride) did not agree:

(the ground crews) were fantastic, working round the clock . . . to keep the aircraft in the air and looking after their pilots like fathers . . . The history books have it that the Battle ended on 31 October but not to us; certainly the aerodromes were not being attacked so regularly, but the boys were always in the air.[12]

Betty (Barber) Fouchard, writing from Nepean, Ontario recalled her duties as a WAAF:

The Operations Room consisted of a huge table divided into sections, and mapped out was south east England, the English Channel, and part of France, Holland and Belgium. We were in #11 Fighter Sector which protected south east England, and London. Our main job was plotting the course of our fighters and bombers and enemy aircraft. The position or plot was relayed to us by phone from Radar Stations on the coast and overland plots from the Royal Observer Corps.[13]

The plot gave us position and direction the planes were flying, height and number of aircraft in the group. The information was for the Operations officers who sat high above the table. They were responsible for alerting the aerodrome when enemy aircraft were in the air, and would order pilots to scramble in order to intercept. If we received a new plot and it was an enemy aircraft we yelled 'Rats!' to make everyone aware of their

WAAF 'C' Watch, Operations Room, Biggin Hill RAF Station, Kent, 1943. Back row: Margaret, Jean, Dorothy, Anne, Front Row: Betty, Joan, Ivy.
Credit: Betty (Barber) Fouchard

approach. I also worked at a smaller table in an adjoining room. Usually there were at least four people with headsets on. This was RDF (Radio Direction Finding, an early form of Radar). We were given bearings on a plane's direction of flight from Royal Observer Corps for planes that had been shot down or were in trouble, mainly off the coast. May Day messages had been picked up from radio signals. Each person was given a bearing and used a string to place the info on the table. Where the strings intersected was the position of the aircraft. Air Sea Rescue then used the information for rescue attempts.

Through their headsets these Operations Room WAAFs sometimes had to endure hearing the screams of pilots trapped in burning planes.

Bob Carswell wrote about his mother, Pat (Leonard) Carswell, who came to Montreal, Quebec:

When my mother arrived in Canada to Canadians she was just another war bride; to us she was our mother. In later years we found out that she was on plotting tables during the Battle of Britain at Biggin Hill (RAF Fighter Station), which was bombed fifty times. She took shelter during one bombing in a bunker under an unexploded bomb, and survived a direct hit on her building that killed a soldier on the other side of the wall. She later trained as a cypher officer, kept a logbook, and flew some 60 hours as crew-in-training in RAF planes of all descriptions because her Wing Commander wanted all his officers to have flying experience so they would know what the pilots experienced. When she retired her commission at age twenty-two she was commanding 250 women. She retired only because she could no longer fit into her uniform due to pregnancy. Her rank as Section Officer in the WAAF was equivalent to that of Flight Lieutenant in the RAF.

Hitler's planned invasion of England was first postponed and then cancelled, but the air raids crept closer to London. On August 15, 1940, about 6:20 pm Croydon was bombed, despite Hitler's orders that it (just ten miles south of the capital) and London itself were off limits. Brenda (Clapham) Carriere witnessed the raid:

. . . from our house on the top of a hill, we saw some planes approaching Croydon aerodrome. At first we thought they were ours, until they started dropping their bombs.

The raids continued and the Bourjois scent factory was hit. Only a fence separated it from the airfield. Lilian (Ball) Goulding, (later Goulden) of Shelbourne, Nova Scotia worked in the factory:

I stamped all kinds of facial soap. The specialty was 'Evening in Paris'. My brother came into the house one night in August 1940 and said there was an air raid. I said there can't be as no siren had sounded. Luckily we made it to our Anderson Shelter where we were safe. Next morning my girl friend and I cycled to work only to find the factory had been dive bombed and other factories in the area had been hit too.

Marie-Louise (Newry) Snider was living in nearby Bromley:

We lost our house in the raids . . . a land-mine destroyed half our road. We were able to move into a requisitioned house with the few bits and pieces we had left.

By the end of the war Croydon had suffered more bombings than any other area in Britain.

On August 16, 1940 I was leaning from my third floor bedroom window, enjoying the warm sunshine and the view over *The Ship Inn* and the paddocks beyond to the low curves of the Sussex Downs. Suddenly the peace was shattered by the whine of Stuka dive-bombers. RAF Fighter Station Tangmere, tucked into the foot of the Downs about four miles away, was under attack. Black smoke and dust rose high into the sky. I ran downstairs to tell my father who was a fire warden. He said not to discuss what I had seen and I don't recall anything more than a slight buzz in the village: "They say Tangmere caught it this morning!" It was not until years later when memoirs began to be published that I was able to piece together what had happened. The hangers (built, ironically, by German prisoners in World War I) burned fiercely, destroying Hurricanes undergoing repairs and the few held in reserve. Among WAAF and RAF personnel there were thirteen dead, and many badly wounded. Jack Boret, the station commander, brought things under control, and the station remained active. Air Vice Marshal Sandy Johnstone has left an indelible picture of Boret:

> He was covered in grime, his pet parrot on his shoulder screeching its head off and trying to imitate the diving Stukas.[14]

At the height of the raid Billy Fiske, an American RAF volunteer who need not have been in the Battle at all, landed to refuel. Within moments his plane was engulfed in flames:

> . . . the remains of Billy Fiske's Hurricane still smoulders on the airfield and I gather Billy himself is gravely injured in the station hospital.[15]

Fiske died two days later in Chichester Hospital, the first American airman to die in World War II. A plaque in his memory in the crypt of St Paul's Cathedral was unveiled by the American Secretary of State the following year. It reads:

PILOT OFFICER
WILLIAM MEADE LINDSLEY
FISKE III
ROYAL AIR FORCE
AN AMERICAN CITIZEN
WHO DIED
THAT ENGLAND MIGHT LIVE
AUGUST 18th 1940

Another valiant defender that day was 23-year-old British pilot James Nicolson of 249 Squadron, who took off from Boscombe Down with two other Hurricanes. None of the three pilots had been in action before. They came under attack from German fighters and all too soon Nicolson was the only one still aloft. His foot wounded, splinters of Perspex (used for cockpit windows) in his left eye, his Hurricane on fire and the dashboard "dripping like treacle", Nicolson somehow managed to shoot down an Me 110 before jumping clear. In agony from his wounds he floated down over the village of Millbrook, Hampshire. An overzealous member of the Home Guard decided Nicolson was a German paratrooper, and began shooting. Nicolson landed with a Home Guard bullet in his behind and a definitely hostile attitude towards his co-defender of the Realm. He survived to win the only Victoria Cross awarded a fighter pilot in the Battle of Britain.[16] Of such were the men of Churchill's "Few".

There is a sad postscript. Flight Lieutenant Nicolson did not survive the war. His widow had a long struggle to bring up their son on an inadequate pension. Eventually, faced with old age, she made the difficult decision to sell her husband's Victoria Cross. It was auctioned in London in 1983 for the world record sum of £110,000.[17]

In August 1940 Nan (Phillips) Pullin, of Edmonton, Alberta was living on a farm next to Tangmere airfield. She wrote to me in November 2001:

> We must have been neighbors if you too watched the attack on Tangmere. My brother, Peter, had just gone out into the pasture next to the airport to get the cows when the attack occurred. Some of the cows were killed and Peter came home crying.

Gladys (Bauley) Armstrong, Etobicoke Ontario, was at Tangmere after the raid:

> After training as WAAF transport drivers my sister and I were posted to RAF Station Tangmere. The station had been badly bombed so we were billeted a few miles away in the tote (Totalizer: a betting machine) of the Fontwell Race Track.

Doreen "Dawn" (Layfield) Simpson of Edmonton, Alberta also joined the WAAF, travelling from Dublin to Belfast to enlist:

> After 'square-bashing' (parade square drill) and Radar School I was posted to the Isle of Man. I ended up on a top secret Radar called '7000'. I served all over, from the far north at Dunnet Head to Land's End in Cornwall.

GEE (or 7000) NAVIGATIONAL DEVICE

GEE became operational early in 1942. According to an internet discussion of Dunnet Head, Scotland (the northernmost point of Britain; John O'Groats is nearby) "the remains of a once-secret radar installation known simply as 'Gee' rise from long grass whispering with wartime ghosts".

Jill (Hunter) Forbes wrote of her mother, Marguerite (Lee) Hunter, who came to Toronto, and in wartime had worked with Radar:

My parents were very happy together and gave the four of us a really wonderful upbringing. My mother was determined that we see all provinces and territories in Canada. It was a super experience and I have always been grateful for the opportunity she gave us to get to know this country. My mother died in August 1973 from a rare blood disorder. We heard from a visiting British doctor that he had seen similar cases in Britain among Radar Operators who had worked during the war.

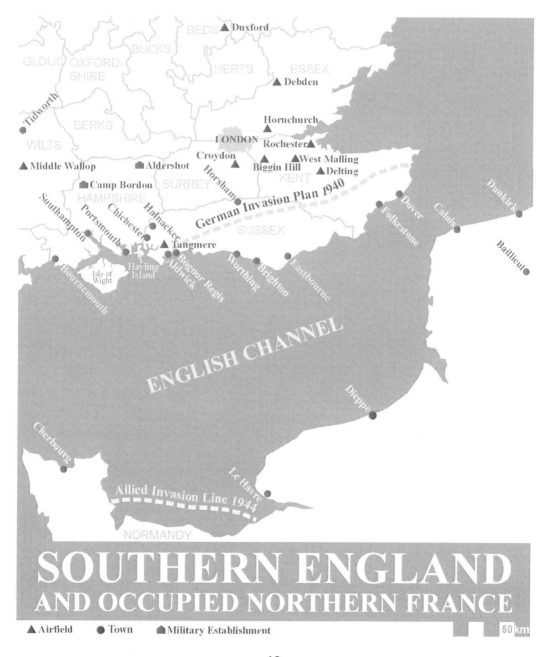

SOUTHERN ENGLAND AND OCCUPIED NORTHERN FRANCE

▲ Airfield   ● Town   ⛫ Military Establishment   50 km

Nineteen-forty was a very bad year, all the boys I had ever known had been killed and I wondered if there would be anyone left to marry when it all ended. I had always wanted to marry and have children . . . very unambitious for nowadays, I'm afraid.

P. Anne (Bourke) Risley

The thought of my mother going to work was unbelievable, but she did – she had no option.

Sheila Anketel-Jones

(In an effort to ease the paper shortage 5.5 million books were collected in London for salvage.) The haul turned up a first edition of Gibbon's *Rise and Fall of the Roman Empire* . . . It is unlikely that the paper recycled outweighed the value of what was lost.

Philip Ziegler, *London at War*

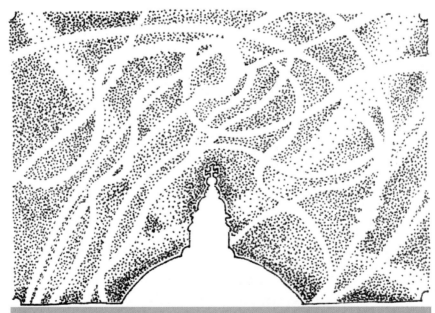

Dogfight contrails over St. Paul's.
Credit: Terry Lyster

Chapter 2: Future War Brides:
The Dark Centre of the Tunnel

In September 1940, the blitz on London began. Peggy (Fiddimore) O'Hara of Airdrie, Alberta worked for the Ministry of Labour, Red Lion Street, Holborn, London:

On that infamous Saturday afternoon, September 7, 1940, the London Docks were bombed. We didn't usually work on Saturdays, but important work had to be done and we were right in the middle of it. Buildings burning, water all over the place, gas and water mains hit. No trains running because of time bombs. A double-decker bus ambled along going to London Bridge Station and I ran for it. As I stepped into the road to board the bus I saw to my horror somebody's bloody arm lying in the gutter. I must have looked awful, because the bus conductor stepped down and put his arm around me. 'It's all right, love' he said, 'come and sit down.' Bless his heart, he had a flask of tea and insisted I drink some. I arrived home to find Mom and Dad looking up and down the street for me. More bombers were headed our way, so we went to the Anderson shelter, Mum had the pot of tea ready to take with her . . . and we stayed all night while London and the docks were blasted again. Next morning the train stopped outside Balham Station and everyone had to take the bus into Victoria. Balham Station had been bombed and people sheltering there had been drowned from burst water and sewer pipes. When I finally reached Holborn I found our office building down to the ground along with many others.

That evening in Aldwick, seventy miles south of London, we watched the red glow from the burning city.

Ethel (Goodwin-White) Sherrin was an Air Raid Warden in Walthamstow, London:

I'll never forget our first destructive bomb. It was a beautiful moonlit night and Father and I were on duty, singing as we walked. Over the Monoux School grounds we saw a plane caught in the searchlights. 'Good grief,' said Father, 'they're dropping parachutes. Run back to the Post and report the Germans are invading.' When I got back to the street most of the houses were gone. I knew we had been standing outside Mrs. Draper's at Number 14, but I couldn't find Number 14. I clawed away bricks and junk, calling Father all the time. The rescue squad arrived and had us all keep quiet. Then we heard Father's voice, calling 'I'm over here!' We pulled away the debris and there was Father sitting serenely under Mrs. Draper's door. He had ducked into the doorway when he realized the parachute was not attached to a man but to a land mine, the first to be dropped on London. I grew up a lot that night.

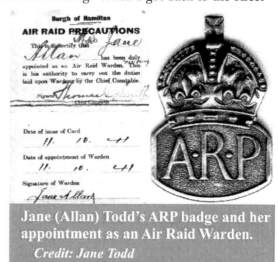

Jane (Allan) Todd's ARP badge and her appointment as an Air Raid Warden.
Credit: Jane Todd

Land mines were enormous sea mines that were dropped by parachute from a plane. They drifted down silently, exploding on contact with the ground to cause maximum damage. On September 30, 1940 one of them landed between two houses in Ashstead, Surrey where Eileen (Bailey) Blackburn, now of Burnaby, British Columbia was living:

> The blast completely demolished our neighbour's house killing four people. It blew the side of our house away, leaving the upper rooms hanging. Dad dug himself out and searched for my Mom, who had fallen with the walls and was trapped under a burning beam. When Dad got her out her legs were badly burned. I was buried under the roof. Dad called me and I said, 'I'm here, you're walking on me!'

In 1941 a land mine fell on Aldwick somewhere behind *The Ship Inn*. Luckily the ground had been ploughed allowing the mine to bury itself in the soft soil before exploding, saving my family and our neighbours from swift extinction. The surrounding buildings were damaged, and for the first, but not the last time our shop window shattered.

M. Jane Tarr was one of four English war brides who came to Empress, Alberta. She too was from Sussex, but whereas I left Empress at the end of 1946, Jane stayed there the rest of her life. She grew up in Horsham, Sussex where she worked at Christ's Hospital School, the Bluecoat School south of the town. In Jane's day the boys wore the quaint long blue coats, with knee breeches and stockings as they had since the 16th century.

While on ARP duty Jane was caught in a bomb blast, and knocked unconscious against a stone wall. She suffered severe nerve damage and hearing loss. Her husband Melvin died after she had been in Canada only sixteen years. Jane's daughter wrote in 1998:

> My mother provided room and board to many young people over the years, worked as a hotel chambermaid and babysat children to make ends meet. She spoke many times of returning to Britain, the land she loved, but when she had the freedom to go she never did take the opportunity. She lived in Empress until her death in August 1987.

Winifred (Hawkes) Rose is active in the North Vancouver war brides group. In 1940 she made shells in Bleeca's factory, Brighton, Sussex:

> Time lost going to air raid shelters was soon saved by working through the raids. Later I was transferred to Ben William's textile factory in High Wycombe, Buckinghamshire making soldier's uniforms, and later still to the Royal Electrical Mechanical Engineers (REME) workshops assembling V8 engines for army vehicles. At home, when the first bombs fell, we had no shelter. Later we were issued a Morrison table shelter which was put in the living room. There wasn't enough room for everybody so the youngest in the family slept there. We never knew whether we would be alive tomorrow so we lived day-to-day, as normally as possible. One Saturday I planned to take my nephew to the Odeon cinema Mickey Mouse show. Thankfully I decided not to go which may have saved our lives. The cinema had a direct hit.

As a young schoolgirl Sheila Anketel-Jones rode her bicycle past roped-off areas marked "Unexploded Bomb", and was exposed to the most dreadful sights:

> I saw the remains of six people, two mothers and four small children, dropped into a bucket from the end of a spade. I watched the boys I had grown up with take themselves off, one by one, to join the armed forces, some never to return. Ordinary, everyday life went on, it had to. I continued riding my bicycle to school despite the fact that I had probably spent half the night in the air raid shelter. There was no thought that one might stay home and catch up on one's sleep . . . everybody simply carried on. My mother was called up. The thought of my mother going to work was unbelievable, but she did – she had no option. She came home one day with a pair of trousers. We were horrified. Ladies simply did not wear trousers, certainly not ladies like my mother. In the appalled silence that followed she very quietly and with difficulty and dignity, explained that if by any chance during an air raid she should be thrown into an ungainly position it would be better to be wearing trousers. A second episode also illustrates the kind of woman she was – once the guns started firing our door-knocker would continuously knock. It was eerie and terrifying. I begged Mother to do something, such as tying a rag around it. She was adamant. There may have been a war on, but one had one's standards, and tying a rag on the door-knocker was not one of them.

Nancy (Etches) Fussell, of Delta, British Columbia had just left school when the war broke out:

> Despite everything it was a most exciting time to be a teenager. I grew up overnight. We thought we would never die and took far too many chances during the war years.

When Dorothy (Kent) Hartland, of Creston, British Columbia was a file clerk with the Navy, Army and Air Force Institute (NAAFI) naval accounts office in Claygate, Surrey she lived through a frightening experience:

> One Sunday morning in September 1940 I was talking with a friend outside a shop when the air raid warning sounded. Before we knew it there were a hundred or more planes nearly overhead, flying at a fairly high altitude. Some left formation and started bombing and machine gunning. The warden was yelling through a megaphone, 'Get to the shelter', but the shelter was across a very wide road so my friend and I attempted to drop to the ground. We were caught in the blast from a 1,000 lb. bomb that had dropped to the side of the shelter. We were lifted up about 20 feet and through the plate glass window of the store. Miraculously when the glass finished raining down there we sat, our clothing in shreds, and our stockings seemed to have been drawn from our legs, but relatively unhurt. I was driven to the First Aid Post to have stitches in my left shin.

Dorothy Kerby of Mississauga, Ontario came to Canada as a pregnant war widow. Her war work had been in a NAAFI canteen where she was promoted to manager:

> One of my first customers was a young Cockney lad who asked me for 'A cup of Rosie Lee and a wad.' I figured out that what he wanted was a cup of tea and a rock bun. I often think of how great a bunch those NAAFI girls were. They came from all walks of life,

worked extremely hard, and endured all the vicissitudes of wartime Britain with good humour. [1]

Dorothy's husband, Wing Commander Hal Kerby, 403 Squadron, had been killed in a raid over Hamburg seven months after they were married. Their son was born in Toronto General Hospital the following March. Dorothy remained in Canada eventually marrying "another fine Canadian".

Joyce (Bird) Smith, who came to Victoria, British Columbia worked with people who had lost their homes:

> My first job was issuing permits to people who had been bombed out so they could get vouchers for food, go to the local bathhouse, and get clothing from the WVS (Women's Voluntary Service). It was very sad, seeing the bewilderment and despair in the faces of people who only had the clothes they were wearing when the bomb hit.

Buckingham Palace was bombed nine times between September 13, 1940 and July 1944. The swimming pool, chapel, roof, ground floor, the West Front, balcony, the North Lodge and the gardens were all damaged. Winston Churchill records that during that first September raid six bombs hit the Palace and gardens. Had the windows not been open in the room where they were, the glass would have splintered into the faces of the King and Queen. [2]

After the September raid censors at the Ministry of Information deleted the name of the target from Associated Press reports to New York. "Dolts, idiots, stupid fools!" cried Churchill, "Let it be broadcast everywhere. Let the humble people of London know they are not alone." It was after this attack that an unruffled Queen Elizabeth made her famous comment, "Now I can look the East End in the face." Is it any wonder that the woman Hitler called "The most dangerous woman in Europe," was so widely admired? Canadian Pilot Officer Keith "Skeets" Ogilvie won a commendation for shooting down the bomber responsible for the September attack on the Palace.

On March 8, 1941 Stephen Robertson, a member of the Metropolitan Police, was busily extinguishing incendiary bombs in the grounds near the North Gate when the Palace was hit again. He was buried under rubble when a wall collapsed, not found for half an hour, and died on his way to hospital. Stephen's girl friend, Irene Barrett, was devastated, believing she could never love anyone again, but in 1942 she met Canadian Joseph William Hunt of the Queen's Own Rifles. He was sympathetic and understanding, having just been jilted by his Canadian girl friend. They married and despite Joe's problems with post-traumatic stress and the premature death of a daughter, enjoyed a good life together. Irene never forgot her first love, and in correspondence with Queen Elizabeth (by then The Queen Mother) learned that in the Royal Archives Stephen was described as 'an unknown policeman'. In June 1998 Irene was present in the Palace garden when The Queen Mother unveiled a plaque in remembrance of Constable Stephen Robertson.

When Eleanor Roosevelt stayed at the Palace in 1942 she found the huge rooms were, to use her word, 'freezing'. Shattered windowpanes had been fitted with temporary covers and in every way wartime restrictions were as strictly observed as in the humblest home in the land.

In 1942 notices about a new restriction appeared in hotel bathrooms:

As part of your personal share in the Battle for Fuel you are asked NOT to exceed five inches of water in this bath.
                    The Ministry of Fuel

The same ruling applied to private homes. The baths often had a painted black line to mark the five inch level.

The American reporter, Edward R. Murrow, who had been in Britain since before the war began, sent daily "This is London" broadcasts to the United States. He was an effective voice counteracting the defeatism of America's Ambassador to Britain, Joseph Kennedy, and the isolationism of Charles Lindbergh. In his pushed-back Fedora, oversized fawn raincoat with gun patches and tied belt, Murrow set the style for a generation of war correspondents. He never put personal safety ahead of a good story, causing American poet Archibald MacLeish to write "You burned the city of London in our houses and we felt the flames that burned it. You laid the dead of London at our doors and we knew that the dead were our dead . . . " [3]

Murrow had many Canadian listeners, as evidenced by his May 29, 1940 broadcast:

Those of you who live in Canada may care to know that another contingent of Canadian airmen arrived in England yesterday. They report an uneventful crossing.

Because Murrow made the situation in Britain so real to his listeners in the United States he was probably responsible for the "Bundles for Britain", clothing sent by generous American women to replace items lost by bomb victims. These were followed by donations of wedding dresses from Mrs. Roosevelt, Mrs. Eisenhower and many other well-placed American women. Intended primarily for GI brides, they were occasionally made available to Canadian brides. Murrow endeared himself to British listeners when he reported "Occasionally one hears in London comments such as: 'Protect us from a German victory and an American peace.'" [4]

The dreadful air raid of Sunday, September 8, 1940 on London blocked every rail line to the south. Next morning my father waited for hours at Bognor station for the London newspapers. Back at the shop my mother and I fielded telephone calls, not the usual, "The paper-girl left the gate open," (a complete fiction), but complaints about undelivered papers. One I've never forgotten: "Why hasn't my husband's newspaper been delivered? He cannot eat breakfast without his copy of the Times!" I wanted to say "Don't you know there's a war on?" but my father had drilled in me the need to be polite to paying customers. I got my own back, though. On my very last day as a paper-girl I made a point of leaving all their gates open!

On September 9 Harold Nicolson wrote in his diary: "If we are to be saved we shall be saved by our own optimism." Ten days later he recorded that there were still 32 unexploded bombs on the Southern Railway lines. Nicolson's interest was because he left Sissinghurst Castle each Monday morning and took the London train from Staplehurst station. Luckily he was safely at Sissinghurst when a Spitfire crashed into the station and demolished it.

SIGN OF THE TIMES
Wreaths and crosses, no tomatoes.

outside a Yorkshire shop, c 1942

Jean Spear had intimate knowledge of the hazards of railway travel:

> The railway line between Surrey where I lived and London's Waterloo Station, my daily destination, was hit by bombs 92 times. It was only a distance of 20 miles but it was the most bombed section of railway line in the London area. So speedy and efficient were the repair crews, supported by the Royal Engineers, that seldom were these great inconveniences for thousands of commuters like me. But there were no repair crews or Royal Engineers to replace my building in Covent Garden which literally disappeared overnight. When I arrived one morning the firefighters and air raid wardens were digging for the bodies of the night staff of the magazine (*Woman*) for which I worked.

Wartime visitors to London believed that the boards covering the statue of Eros in Piccadilly Circus were for its protection. In truth the boards, that in happier times had protected the God of Love from New Year's Eve revellers, hid an empty plinth. Eros had been evacuated to the country. (It is ironic that this Angel of Christian Charity usually presides over a London site notorious for its "Ladies of the Night" - 1930s-speak for "prostitutes". The Ladies were not evacuated, and in wartime became universally known as "Piccadilly Commandos".)

Mary Soames wrote in *Clementine Churchill* of her own time in the Auxiliary Territorial Service (ATS). In 1941, as "Private M. Churchill" she was paid 1 shilling and 8 pence (less than 50 cents) a day, and after training in "the mysteries of anti-aircraft instruments" was responsible to a senior, usually a lance corporal. Her book gives a unique view of the demands placed by the war on the whole Churchill family. (Mary's sister, Diana, served in the Women's Royal Naval Service [WRNS]; her sister Sarah in the Women's Auxiliary Air Force [WAAF] Intelligence Branch.) Mary rose in the ranks and was posted to 481 Heavy Mixed Anti-aircraft Battery located in the middle of Hyde Park, where her father would occasionally drop in, often during an air raid. "The gun-teams are men," Mary said in an interview, "but women work the instruments controlling the guns and serve in the control room. Sometimes it's dull, and we don't do much, but often we make a lot of noise and feel very excited and important." [5] She was on duty Sunday, June 18, 1944, witnessing the Flying Bomb fall on the nearby Guard's Chapel during morning service.[6]

A hundred and twenty-one officers (among them several Canadians) and civilians were killed and almost as many were severely injured.

Joyce (Driver) Spence, of Prince Albert, Saskatchewan served with Mary Churchill:

> I was an ATS Radar Operator stationed in London, Mary Churchill being one of my officers. Knowing I went to Communion every Sunday she asked if she could come with me. Each Sunday I would run to the officers' quarters, Mary would come out, pulling on her coat, and off we'd go to a little church in Kensington. (Unless, of course, she had been out late the night before, in which case she would mumble sleepily, 'You go on without me.')

HYDE PARK GOES TO WAR

In addition to losing its iron railings, and hosting Mary Churchill's gun site (countless wartime books speak of "Hyde Park's big guns opening up" during air attacks), the Park held vast amounts of bomb debris in 400-yard long dumps near Rotten Row.[7]

After the United States came into the war the debris was moved to East Anglia to become the base material for the many landing strips built in anticipation of the arrival of the United States Army Air Force (USAAF). Tons of sand were excavated for sandbags and for smothering incendiaries from a Park site that in 1851 had housed the Great Exhibition's Crystal Palace. Local police raised Hyde Park pigs in a sty made from wood reclaimed from the bomb debris pile. The Canadian Broadcasting Corporation's "Big Betsy" (a mobile recording studio) was often in the Park recording the sounds of the Battle of Britain for Canadian listeners. The operator inside the van was reportedly more scared of shrapnel from Mary Churchill's anti-aircraft guns, than a direct hit from one of Hitler's bombs.[8] The park was often used as a temporary overnight bus "garage" to save on the fuel needed to get them to the depot.[9]

Future war brides in the services found the experience of having to mix with all kinds of people a good preparation for their journey to Canada. It was often the girls who had never left home who were immediately and so badly affected by homesickness. Mary (Paterson) Robinson, of Dawson Creek, British Columbia took her basic WRNS training in Leeds and her training as a Writer (a Specialized category) in London:

> I was posted to Evanton, Rosshire, a repair depot for the Fleet Air Arm planes. We were taught many valuable things, one of them being how to live happily with many other types of women.

Some of the service jobs seemed to belong to World War I. In 1941 Catherine (Kier) Macdonald, was a WAAF at RAF Station Kenley, Surrey where aircraft still had fabric coverings. Her job was to patch and "dope" damaged areas after planes had been in an air battle.

In May 1941 the first consignment of Lend-Lease food arrived from the United States.[10] Dried eggs and dried milk made all the difference to our nutrition, but I remember trying someone's recipe for peppermint candy that called for dried milk, crushed saccharine tablets and peppermint flavouring . . . it was awful. The meat ration was augmented by the occasional can of Spam® that allegedly could be cooked fifty-nine different ways.

By June 1942 my friend Doris "Tiger" [11] Timms and I had finished our basic training at WRNS Port Training Depot, HMS *Victory III* (Portsmouth). We were drafted to HMS *Mercury IV* (H.M. Signal School) at East Meon, Hampshire, a large establishment where Naval ratings and officers were trained in radio communications and the highly secret radar, as well as more traditional flag and lamp signalling and Morse Code. At first our Wren hats were the stitched-cotton navy-blue jobs, a style more suited to Christopher Robin. It was a great day when we were issued navy serge, flat-topped sailor caps. Our wartime tallybands (cap bands) proclaimed an anonymous "HMS" (His Majesty's Ship), full names of ships or shore bases being banned for the duration. It wasn't until Tiger and

"I had neither the wit nor the where-withal to have my uniform tailored..."
Credit: author's collection

I revisited East Meon in the nineteen-eighties that we obtained tallybands with "HMS MERCURY" emblazoned on them. We discovered that WRNS personnel on the base were the last of the breed. The very next week they were to become women members of the Royal Navy. What would our old Chief Petty Officer have said!

The wartime Wren uniform was relatively smart, although the serge used for the lower ranks was coarse. Also, you were lucky if jacket and skirt were a good fit. I had neither the wit nor the wherewithal to have mine tailored so was stuck with an oversized jacket and undersized skirt.

We hated the standard-issue black bloomers known as "blackouts". (WAAF's endured them in Air Force Blue, ATS personnel wore khaki.) In all three services they were also nicknamed "passion killers". Our black-cotton-stockinged legs were thrust into heavy black Oxfords, and how we envied Canadian and American servicewomen their medium heel court shoes (pumps) and their skin-toned nylons.

Tiger was drafted overseas and spent her war as a Wren Petty Officer in the Royal Navy Post Office, New York City. Her tailored uniform, with its dashing tricorne hat made her a stand-out among the many uniforms in town where she seems to have been constantly wined and dined. All things considered she had a very good war, and I used to tease her that she didn't even know there was a war on! However she pointed out that she was privy to deaths at sea and had the sad job of returning mail to the sender. Many times they were boys she had met while they were in New York.

HM SIGNAL SCHOOL (HMS *Mercury* or HMS *Victory IV*)

At the Signal School, we were inspected by the Duchess of Kent, and later by King George VI. His Majesty asked our First Officer, in his hesitant manner, "Do the Wrens do . . . er, everything?" Somebody tittered and the First Officer turned bright red. We did not catch her answer. It was a different age, and most of us didn't "do everything", but we could laugh merrily at a bit of innuendo.

My group was billeted in Hambledon, with *The Bat and Ball* pub a couple of miles away, across from the field where the first game of English cricket was alleged to have been played. It was a rite of passage to have a beer or shandy at *The Bat and Ball* and walk back to Hambledon the short way, across the fields. In those light summer evenings of wartime double-daylight-saving-time Wrens would gather huge mushrooms for breakfast the next morning. It was autumn when I made the trip, and in the dark I slipped on cow pats and was terrified of bumping into a live cow. Our billets were Georgian houses stripped of anything that made them home-like. But the long windows set in the thick walls could not be removed nor the views of the still lovely gardens. Naval language was mandatory, we stood on the deck, the kitchen was the galley, the biffy the head, and our bedrooms cabins. Our wooden bunks had straw-filled mattresses (palliasses) and pillows, and our blue and white cotton coverlets sported the WRNS insignia. We were told we could name our cabin for one of His Majesty's ships, and some wit in ours came up with "HMS *Impregnable*"! The First Officer was not amused.

NAVAL TERMS

When first we joined up in the Wrens
We learnt a thing or two,
We learnt to drill like sailors drill
And talk like sailors do.
We learnt the ropes, and other things
That we had never known,
We found out that the Navy has
 A language of its own.

We're taught to say we've "gone ashore"
If we have been in town,
 And when its time to go to bed

23

We "turn in" and "pipe down".
We never have a grumble, but
Instead we sometimes "drip"
And if we take French leave – well, then
We're told we've "broken ship".

We talk about the "Starboard Watch"
Instead of "Evening Shift"
And if we stay out late we say
We must have "gone adrift".
We call our bedrooms "cabins" and
A bed we call a "bunk"
We talk of being "bottled" * - but
It doesn't mean we're drunk.

The kitchen's called a "Galley" and
The dining room's the "Mess".
We call our Officers – oh well,
We'd better let you guess.
A waitress is a "Steward" and
A clerk is called a "Writer",
The Cook is sometimes called a "B",
We mean, of course, a "blighter".

We say we've had a "Friday while"
When on weekend leave we've been.
We talk of leave as "Liberty"
And washing as "dhobying".
And since we've joined the Wrens we find
It's no good being haughty,
For Naval terms are nautical
And sometimes – oh so naughty!

We are not made to wash the floors
Instead we "swab the decks",
We call the soldiers "Pongos"
And marines are "Leathernecks".
A sailor is a "matloe", but
Don't think cadets are men.
An officer in training is
A male, sea-going, "Wren".

We would not dare to say aloud
Nor write it with our pens,
But we'll leave you to imagine
What the sailors call the Wrens.
                                    Anonymous

Received from WRNS Petty-Officer Doris (Timms) Adams, c 1943
* fed up

Iris (Turner) Page came from Stoke-on-Trent, and lives in Qualicum Beach:

I volunteered for the WRNS out of fear of being called into another service. Our local industry was and still is the pottery and china business. They supported the British Pottery Research Association, and were prepared to sponsor my further education. Meanwhile in the Navy I had chosen to study meteorology, but they enrolled me in a Radio Mechanics course. We constructed our own one-tube radio receiver from scratch, and I mean scratch. We started by making our own screwdriver and spanner and worked from there. We used the old soldering iron, Bunsen burner, separate solder and flux. Only after we mastered all this were we given an electric soldering iron and allowed to use the solder with flux. During all this we were drilled at lunch hour by a Petty Officer (PO). Small children gathered at the fence and sang to us: 'We are the Ovaltineys . . . ' [12]

We had regular exams and at the end of six months our numbers had dwindled by about 85%. The remaining 15% were sent to study actual Navy communication equipment at HM Signal School, Leydene House, East Meon, Hampshire, the family home of comedienne Bea Lillie, (Lady Peel). I was then sent to Glasgow and each day travelled to various naval bases, mostly Greenock (HMCS *Niobe*), and went aboard HM ships (Carriers, etc.) to service their radio equipment. My next posting was to Orkney where I was introduced to the Chief Petty Officer (CPO) telegraphist. He had made the Navy his career and told me he hated Wrens. To him they were: 'Like a boil on the back of my neck.' However my boss was a Lieutenant who told me he knew nothing of my job and was relying on me completely.

The late Georgina (Bates) Burton was with The First Aid Nursing Yeomanry (FANY) a branch of the nursing service that has a particularly distinguished history. Many of the brave women who were parachuted into France to contact the Resistance were commissioned into the Corps. Twelve FANYs died in concentration camps, three: Odette Hallowes, Violette Szabo and Noor Inayat Khan, were awarded the George Cross, the last two posthumously. Georgina, better known as Joan, was a driver with the 2nd Hampshire Women's Transport Company, FANY, and was pleased that even after amalgamation with the ATS, members were allowed to wear their FANY flashes:

I have to mention the very fine women I worked with. Oftentimes word came that their husbands were killed, missing or taken prisoner. These were difficult times for them, but they carried on. I found the work very stimulating. Ambulance duties kept us busy transporting patients. There were night duties at the hospitals. I shall always remember driving at night in the blackout, limited vision, nasty fogs. The ambulance orderlies did a fantastic job and to this day I find the experience still useful. In 1942 I met John Burton. We had much in common and we had many good times in London during the blitz. My mother was very fond of him. 'Such a nice Canadian,' she used to say.

John Burton also sent a note:

I met my wife in Aldershot on Valentine's Day, 1942. She was baptized Georgina Mary, but was known as Joan by her British Army friends when I met her, so she has always been Joan to me.

For Mary (Mitchell) Vankoughnett, of St. Thomas, Ontario, a factory worker, the war began when she and fellow women workers filled sandbags to reinforce trenches. All this was accomplished after working hours, and without pay. Mary had a remarkable mother:

> Our weekly rations per person were two ounces of butter, four ounces of margarine, two ounces of tea, four ounces of sugar, four ounces of meat, two ounces of cheese, one pint of milk and four ounces of bacon. We were allowed one egg each a week. My mother had the foresight to stock up on staple foods for some time prior to the war. When that ran out she bought food on the black market. We were not short of clothing because she used her black market connections to buy clothing coupons. She seemed to know who to contact, and could afford the price. After my father died his relatives instructed Mother in the art of making money. She became a money lender. She also bought pawn tickets from people who could not afford to redeem their valuables, then sold them for a profit. She bought clothing from a warehouse and sold it 'on time' to those who could not afford to pay the full price. These enterprises were very profitable for my mother. She was thrifty, but could be very generous too.
>
> My mother was terrified of the bombing; this surprised me because I had considered her fearless. She explained that her fears were mostly for me. She reasoned that if the Nazi's conquered Britain, they would round up people with Jewish blood, declaring she would kill me herself rather than let them take me. I couldn't see how the Germans would know I had a part-Jewish father, so I dismissed it from my mind.

1942 was the worst year for Allied losses on the Atlantic. We were now eating far less meat and far more vegetables than we had before the war.

There was Woolton Pie, named for Lord Woolton, the Minister of Food. This concoction was publicised in our two-page national newspapers which showed the Minister "enjoying" a serving.

WOOLTON PIE

1 pound each diced potatoes, cauliflower, swedes and turnips
3-4 spring onions
1 tsp. vegetable extract .
1 tbsp. oatmeal
chopped parsley.

Cook vegetables for ten minutes in just enough water to cover. Save 200 ml of the water and set aside the rest for making soup. Cool vegetables and turn into pie dish, add reserved cooking water and oatmeal. Cover with wholemeal pastry or mashed potatoes.
Bake in a moderate oven until browned. Serve with brown gravy. Serves 5 or 6.

Modern readers could be forgiven for thinking this very odd "pie" was a side dish to serve with a main course. It *was* the main course.

In an effort to jolly us along jingles, which were neither poetic nor particularly persuasive, were circulated by the Food Ministry. One example:

> Those who have the will to win
> Cook potatoes in their skin,
> Knowing that the sight of peelings
> Deeply hurts Lord Woolton's feelings.

With less and less imports reaching Britain, the Women's Land Army (and its Women's Timber Corps division) came into its own. Their hours were long and their jobs were difficult, dirty and strenuous. Dorothy (Kent) Hartland's assignment was dangerous:

> I joined the Women's Land Army (WLA), and was at Blindley Heath, Godstone, Surrey. Thus began four years of planting, hoeing, and harvesting potatoes and turnips, threshing, haying and manure spreading, all in the beautiful Surrey countryside. We moved to Redhill and closer to the air raids. One day as I walked down the furrow, planting a potato with each step, I happened to glance 6 feet ahead and there was a salvo of unexploded bombs, just sitting there. The whole area had to be checked out and we were sent on another job.

When Ethel (Cunliffe) Tryon volunteered for the Women's Land Army, her Lancashire father commented, "You will have to clean out the shippens (barns)", to which she replied "I thought I was going to make butter!" Earlier Ethel was with a dance troupe that entertained at Blackpool's famous Tower Ballroom. She came to Parksville, British Columbia in early 1946. Her sister-in-law, Dutch war bride Josta Tryon, did not arrive in Parksville until 1949.

The Woman's Timber Corps (WTC) was formed in 1942. Lottie (Wallwork) Gillis of Tyne Valley, Prince Edward Island was a Timberjill:

Ethel Cunliffe in Land Army uniform.
Credit: Ethel (Cunliffe) Tryon

> As was the custom in Lancashire I left school the first holiday after my fourteenth birthday. I worked in a shoe factory but I had a sister in the Women's Land Army who transferred to the Timber Corps, so that decided what I would do. I trained at Bryn Cothi, Glamorganshire, South Wales. We were billeted on private families and paid 25 shillings per week. I sent 10 shillings a week home to help out. The uniform was the same as the WLA except we wore green berets. When training I had to make a road on the side of a hill wide enough to support a tractor and trailer. That was to toughen us up. We learned to name all the species of trees, even from a piece the size of our thumb.

THE WLA TIMBER CORPS SONG (Tune: "Lili Marlene"):
The Foresters

They're tramping through the forests,
They're trudging through the mire,
They're brushing past the undergrowth
They have but one desire,
Their greatest thought their highest aim
To see in England peace again.
They have no tanks or rifles,
They have no stripes or drill,
They have no ships or aeroplanes,
But England needs them still.
They're fighting hard with axe and saw
They're Britain's Women's Timber Corps.
They're proud of their profession,
Bad weather does not count,
They bring the tall trees crashing down
The pile of pit props mount.
They're doing their bit to win the war,
This almost unknown Timber Corps.

J.I. Helluin

Credit: Lottie Gillis.

By 1943 90% of single and 80% of married British women were involved in war work. [13]

Twenty-year-old Sonia Butt, daughter of an RAF Group Captain, was already in training with the Special Operations Executive (SOE) when she met and married the dashing French-Canadian Captain Guy D'Artois. A month later they both parachuted into German occupied France. Sonia's work was to instruct members of the French underground in the use of explosives. Despite many alarming clashes with the Gestapo, Sonia survived to rejoin her husband and settle in the province of Quebec.

SCOTLAND AND SCOTTISH WAR BRIDES

The first air raid on Britain in October 1939 was against naval vessels in the Firth of Forth, Scotland. The first British civilian to be killed on land by a Nazi bomb, March 16, 1940, was James Isbister a young Scotsman living in Orkney. He left a wife and newborn baby. [14]

Scotland's war was different enough to warrant special mention. Many young Scottish women married Newfoundlanders whose logging skills were put to good use felling

Scottish trees. These Newfoundland Foresters were in non-military units, unlike Canada's Forestry Units that were part of the Canadian Army.

Of all the countries that made up Great Britain, only Scotland had the excitement of a high-ranking German officer landing on its territory. Rudolph Hess was the Deputy Führer of Germany, third only to Hitler and Goering. He piloted a Messerschmitt from Germany to Scotland on May 10, 1941, with the idea of speaking to the Duke of Hamilton about a peace agreement. At least he had good navigation skills. He landed by parachute quite near the Duke's estate letting his plane crash land, but broke his ankle on impact. Scottish nurse and ambulance driver Ann Biles was called to the scene where she found a farmer guarding the prisoner with a pitchfork. She brought Hess to Mearnskirk Hospital where his injury was treated. Hitler washed his hands of his former Deputy, declaring him to be insane. Hess was confined to a Scottish castle, and ended his days in Spandau Prison, Germany.

Some years later Ann Biles met Ralph Lawrence, a First Lieutenant in the RCN, when he was a patient in Mearnskirk. They were married in 1944 but sadly, twelve days after their honeymoon he went down with the *Athabascan* in the English Channel.[15] Ann came to Canada as a widow and later remarried.

Jane "Jean" (Clark) Atkinson, of Port Mouton, Nova Scotia was a "clippie" on a Greenock, Scotland bus that ran to HMCS *Niobe,* the Royal Canadian Navy Headquarters:

> I met hundreds of the Canadian Navy that were billeted there - how could I escape marrying one of them? My mum nearly had a fit when I told her I was marrying Leading/Stoker Donald Atkinson. My Dad's sister told her it was *awful* letting me go away to Canada.

Jean and Don booked a small dance hall for Jean's going-away party:

> We invited the sailors from *Niobe* and all the girls I knew. What a great party! But that very day I received a summons to be in Liverpool, England next day for my departure for Canada.

It was late March 1944. Jean caught the train for Glasgow, then the overnight train to Liverpool:

> A woman met me, boarded me for the night and next morning put me on a bus with the windows boarded up that took me to the ship. I had never been in England before and here I was going all the way to Canada. We were ten days at sea, stopped twice and all the lights were darkened. U-boats were following us. Don was stationed in Halifax at HMCS *Stadacona.* We stayed in Halifax for almost a year where I learned the money, the right side of the street to catch a bus, and to be careful crossing the street.

Homesickness was the most hidden, least confessed malady of the soldier. For one thing, its ravages seemed impossible to describe. And of course for the distant family it was a compliment.

Ronald Blythe, *Private Words, Letters and Diaries from the Second World War*

I suppose you will be wondering how I am getting along; how I like England. England isn't as good as our country. I don't think there is any place like our fair Canada.

Walter E. Ottewell, Royal Canadian Engineers, Camp Bordon, England

It was a beautiful country, this south of England where the Canadians were stationed.

Peter Stursberg, CBC Radio war correspondent, *The Sound of War*

If you Canadians were to leave England I could not sleep at night.

Winston Churchill [1]

A Calgary Highlander (Second Division) leaving the *Pasteur*, the liner that brought his regiment from Halifax to Gourock, Scotland.
Credit: Farran, The History of the Calgary Highlanders 1921-54.

Chapter 3: The Canadians in Britain: "We've come here to do a job . . ."

CANADIAN AIRMEN

On May 31, 1945 Air Chief Marshal Sir Arthur Harris, Commander-in-Chief Bomber Command, arrived at Middleton St. George RAF Station, Yorkshire. He was there to bid farewell to those who were going to Canada. They were leaving the airfield from which so many had flown on hazardous raids over Germany. In his speech, the Air Marshal said:

> The Canadian Bomber Group and the Canadians in the Royal Air Force have won a reputation the equal of any and surpassed by none.[3]

The airmen leaving that day were the first of eight veteran squadrons of the Group to fly the Atlantic route home. It took them to Yarmouth, Nova Scotia via Cornwall, the Azores and Newfoundland.

The term 'airmen' describes Canadians who served overseas in Britain and other postings as pilots and ground crew in World War II. They can be divided into three groups:

- Canadians who went to Britain before the war and were accepted into the RAF.
- Members of the RCAF who were posted to Britain after the war began, and served with the RAF (60%).[4]
- Members of the RCAF who went to Britain and served in RCAF units.

The first group consisted largely of young men who had their imaginations fired by the epic flights of pioneer aviators. In the 1930s the word "aviation" was as evocative to them as the word "space" would be to another generation thirty years later. Global depression meant that only a privileged few could take flying lessons and only the very wealthy could own planes. For most, the route to a cockpit was through their nation's air force. In Canada the RCAF demanded that candidates have a very high educational standard, but Britain's Royal Air Force accepted volunteers with high school diplomas, who were healthy, and came with good references. In the 1930s young Canadians began travelling to Britain to join the RAF. Capt. Henry Seymour-Biggs, a British naval officer who had retired to Victoria, British Columbia helped this process by vetting young men and providing them with letters of introduction to the Air Ministry. He offered no

financial assistance, reasoning that the right sort of man would earn the cost of the trip (about $180) Those who couldn't come up with the whole amount worked their passage to Britain. Ken Stofer of Victoria, himself a Biggs' boy, has written *The Biggs' Boys* about the Captain and the young men he sponsored. In the prologue Ken says:

Of the 719 boys Biggs sent, not one was rejected by the RAF. Over 50% trained as officers. Several attained the rank of squadron leader and 10 won the Distinguished Flying Cross.

In mid-October 1938 Biggs' Boy Alexander Effa was headed for Liverpool on the *Laconia*. He had worked as a longshoreman with "a salary perhaps as good as anything in Victoria at the time . . ." but wanted to do something more interesting with his life. Biggs supplied the opportunity. Effa served in France, even enjoying two week's leave in Paris, before the Nazi occupation. He escaped through the port of Boulogne, and in England trained as a bomb disposal expert. This dangerous job took him to the airfields of Croydon, Biggin Hill, Tangmere, Ford and others. He claimed the job was "not as frightening as it sounds!"

A group of Biggs' Boys on their way to join the RAF aboard the *Duchess of Bedford* surrounding the ship's captain, W.A. Betts .
Credit: Ken Stofer

Because of these volunteers (and others who joined the RAF without Biggs' assistance) it is estimated that about 900 Canadians had enrolled directly into the RAF before September 1939 and therefore were serving in Britain even before contingents of the Canadian Army arrived.[5] Many of these were in the 242 Fighter Squadron, "with its Moose Head badge and *'Toujours prêt'* (Always Ready) motto".[6]

Albert Prince, son of a Canadian army veteran of World War I, was born in Montreal. About four years before the war his family moved to Britain where he joined the RAF. He became the first of some 10,000 Canadian aircrew to die while serving with Bomber Command, when the Blenheim Bomber he was piloting was shot down during a raid on Wilhelmshaven, Germany on September 4, 1939. He died six days before Canada entered the war.[7]

The majority of Canadian airmen who volunteered for the RCAF after Canada declared war, form the second category. They wore Canadian shoulder flashes and were paid by Canada at RCAF rates, but were under the command of the RAF. They were very unhappy about this arrangement, and several times there were moves to change it, but it remained in place.

Ninety-four Canadians in the RAF, including Biggs' Boy John Latta, fought in the Battle of Britain.

In the very early part of the war Canadian airmen reported to RAF Uxbridge, Middlesex, but in 1942 when Canadian Pilot/Officer (P/O) Murray Peden sailed to England on the *Cavina*, an ex-Fyffe's banana boat, he disembarked at Avonmouth, near Bristol. From there he took the train to Bournemouth, Hampshire, site of No. 3 Personnel Receiving Centre, RCAF.[8] The remainder of his draft arrived in Scotland on the *Queen Elizabeth* before making their way to Bournemouth.

Bournemouth was subject to sudden visits from German Focke-Wulfs that machine-gunned the seafront. After Peden left, a hotel was bombed killing service personnel including a number of Canadians.

Canadian Airman Jack Anderson's journey from Canada was different again:

On July 15, 1942 we took the train to Halifax harbour, and a mixed bag of about thirty Air Force personnel boarded the *Winnipeg II*, a small ship carrying some cargo, the Air Force contingent, and a group of missionaries returning to England from China. We sailed at dusk, part of a large convoy. Thirteen days later we docked in Liverpool and boarded a train for Bournemouth. August in Bournemouth . . . how delightful! The Radar Officers were moved into the Cottonwood Hotel with a view of the English Channel. We could see the German raiders coming in for high-level daytime reconnaissance. First items of business included the issuing of tin helmets, revolvers, ammunition and the necessary webbing. The first major adjustment was the blackout. We had no idea how intense it could be on a moonless night. Unfortunately the beaches were 'off limits' due to barbed wire, barricades and mines. Newly arrived Canadians had a period of leave and I decided to explore. With a rented bicycle I passed through villages with such exotic names as Bere Regis, Turner's Puddle, Tolpuddle and Puddletown, and recall the sheer delight of tea and scones at a table beside a thatched cottage. [9]

Two years later Jack married Scotswoman Doris Winton. He described her as a "stunning young lady". They made their home in London, Ontario.

In 1941 a group of RCAF radar mechanics arrived in Yorkshire to attend the Leeds Technical Institute. Two of them were billeted near the home of Margaret Joan Watts (later Margaret Joan Small) who came to Langley, British Columbia:

> The landlady invited my friend and I to tea to meet two of these fellows, because she 'didn't know what to do with them' - as if they were visitors from Mars! We arrived, rather reluctantly at 4 p.m. My first meeting with my future husband (Dave Small) was to find him coming down the stairs with his trousers over his arm. Not exactly a romantic beginning! After the Canadians left Dave was supposed to come to Leeds on leave but didn't appear. In those days, people could be here today and gone without a trace tomorrow. However, it transpired that he had been shipped off to India and Burma via South Africa. Although he wrote several letters, none got through and I had no address to write to. After three years I did receive a letter and I guess that sealed my fate.

Ian Andrew Cairns of Elrose, Saskatchewan flew as a navigator in a Lancaster that was part of 5 Group's elite Pathfinder Force. He survived his full tour of thirty combat operations and, appropriately, his war bride, Nancy (Briggs) Cairns, flew to Canada in a converted Lancaster bomber.

The British Commonwealth Air Training Plan (BCATP), Canada's major contribution to the Allied war effort, graduated nearly a quarter of a million airmen from 231 sites across the country.[10] Many of the BCATP airfields became Canada's major and smaller civil airports after the war; some have remained as RCAF bases. Thousands of airmen from Canada and Britain trained here, as well as men from Australia, New Zealand, Norway, France, Czechoslovakia, Poland, Holland and Belgium. Among the thousands who participated there were bound to be a few who later made names for themselves. After the war Robert Coote starred on Broadway as Colonel Pickering in *My Fair Lady*; the British-Canadian author Arthur Hailey wrote CBC dramas, books, and Hollywood movies; and Richard Burton, whose air force career became "better known for what he did on leave" than what he did in a plane.[11] His post war career was divided between Hollywood and his two tempestuous marriages with Elizabeth Taylor.

Norwegians in the Air Training Plan had a distinct history. The exiled Norwegian government arranged with Canada to train Norwegian personnel at a base on Toronto Island that quickly became "Little Norway". As the numbers of trainees increased the city fathers probably became nervous about the situation, for "Little Norway" was relocated near Gravenshurst.[12] Among the trainees was Viggo Ullman whose daughter Liv is the well-known actress.

No doubt the isolation of British bomber and fighter stations partially accounted for the low figure (18%) of Canadian airmen who married while overseas.

By September 10, 1939 Canada was at war with Germany. In 1939, unlike 1914, a declaration of war had to pass through Parliament. Militia units were among the first to volunteer. Norman McCaulay left a younger brother to run the family business in La Ronge, Saskatchewan and with three others walked the 250 miles to the nearest recruiting centre in Saskatoon. He was assured that he would eventually be called. While waiting he worked for M & C Aviation as a mechanic.

The record number of young Canadian men who rushed to serve their country was attributed to the widespread unemployment of the time, but military historian Terry Copp, of Wilfred Laurier University, states that 80% of the early volunteers *left* employment to enlist.[13] David Bercuson speaks eloquently of these men:

> It does not matter to me why each one went – for adventure, out of boredom, for three square meals a day, to save democracy, to stop Hitler. What matters is that they did go and that, when they got to where the shooting was, they gave everything they had to give.[14]

The first contingent of Canadian soldiers, 7,500 strong, every shoulder proudly displaying the scarlet patch of Canada's First Division below the word "CANADA", arrived in Scotland on December 17, 1939. The "CANADA" patch, indicative of overseas service, had been sewn on en route. The regiments represented would soon become well-known to the British public and included the Royal Canadian Regiment, the Princess Patricia's Canadian Light Infantry, the Hastings and Prince Edward Regiment (irreverently known as the "Hasty P's" or, even more irreverently, the "Hasty Pees"), the Loyal Edmonton Regiment, the Seaforth Highlanders and the West Nova Scotia Regiment. As the huge troopships moved slowly along the Clyde, Scottish civilians waved in welcome. The Canadians arrived on shore, according to an onlooker, "cheering wildly and waving their rifles above their heads".

For security only the official welcoming party was on the dock, headed by Britain's Secretary of State for the Dominions, Anthony Eden, and Vincent Massey, High Commissioner for Canada. The men stood to attention as the King's welcome message was read. Then they stood easy, and smoked and talked as the light faded.

General A.G.L. McNaughton, in charge of these first arrivals put it succinctly: 'We've come here to do a job, then go home'.
Ben Malkin [15]

On the train south to Aldershot the men experienced the Blackout. They had been warned not to be amused by the small English trains, but it must have been hard to resist a few wisecracks. One new arrival, somewhat older than the rest, is reputed to have said as he boarded: "I've always wanted one of these for my children to play with!" When the Guard blew his high-pitched whistle it was in sharp contrast to the plaintive sound heard on Canadian trains, one that had been known to attract female moose in the mating season. However it didn't take long for the Canadians to be impressed by the speed, efficiency and frequency of the trains under the British system. Next day Winston Churchill, First Sea Lord, announced to the world the arrival of the Canadians.

After their reception along the Clyde the Canadians found Aldershot cold and depressing. The people of this military town had seen soldiers of every nationality so that a few more, even labelled "CANADA", were not likely to cause a stir. However, not every Aldershot resident was unmoved. Patricia (Jepp) Smith of Surrey, British Columbia reported:

> Apparently 330,000 Canadians passed through the barracks in Aldershot between 1939 and 1945, so I guess it was inevitable that I should meet one of these outgoing, fun-loving young men. My parents went to Evening Service and were impressed to see a Canadian soldier share his prayer book with an old lady. They arrived home with this Canadian Scottish soldier (Reginald William Smith) in tow. Not for one moment did my father think he would lose one of his daughters to this man.

The old Aldershot barracks were damp, and the winter of 1939-40 severe. Many Canadians fell ill. In their attempts to keep warm they "liberated" any wooden items that were not nailed down. The memory of the flag-waving Scots had convinced them that Scotland was, in all respects, a much friendlier place. Small wonder that for some time Canadians took their leaves there. But attempts were being made to bring Canadians and English together. A Canadian headline declared:

BRITONS URGED TO INVITE NEWLY ARRIVED CANADIANS INTO THEIR HOMES [16]

Before long the visitors realised that behind their traditional reserve, the English could be as friendly and welcoming as their northern neighbors.

A few of them reacted oddly to having Canadians in their midst. One old dear, on hearing that Canadians were billeted nearby, had all her house locks changed. What exactly she thought this achieved was unclear. A woman who fancied her position in society pronounced all Canadians rough and uncouth, and invited two Polish airmen instead. Rough some might be – I remember a pair of very large Canadian army boots pounding the pedals of my mother's delicate rosewood piano – but the owner of the boots was grateful for my parents' hospitality, thanking them politely when it came time to leave. Above all it was certainly very comforting to know that in the absence of our British troops the Canadians were standing guard.

The arrival in the late summer of 1940 of the Second Division paralleled the First Division's experience as far as Aldershot. Among others, these regiments were in the new draft: the Royal Regiment of Canada, the Calgary Highlanders, the Essex Scottish, the Black Watch, the Régiment de Maisonneuve, the Toronto Scottish Regiment, the South Saskatchewan Regiment, the Queen's Own Cameron Highlanders and the Royal Hamilton Light Infantry (the Rileys).

MEMBERS OF CANADIAN SECOND DIVISION ARRIVE IN BRITAIN

Eager soldiers crowded the ship's rail gathering first impressions of, to many, a strange land. They marveled at rows of houses all apparently modelled after the same pattern — miniature fields covering high hills — craft of all kinds riding at anchor . . . to many it was a return to a native land and a home-coming. Down a rope ladder the troops filed into the tender to crowd on deck for a last look at the mammoth liner that had been a cozy home for a few days . . . (on) the wharf khaki-clad figures on guard served as a reminder that the country was at war . . .

The train gathered speed; factories heavy with smoke flashed by. It was the banks of the Clyde and for miles huge silver Barrage Balloons rode steadily in the sky, wire cables scarcely visible — just to tangle up Jerry, someone said. Cities gave way to towns — then to villages. No names of towns at the stations — no road signs, then sundown and a blackout (and no 'maybe' about it). Tea and lunch (on the Prairies "lunch" denotes a light snack at any time of the day or night) were handed out at York by serious, but warm-hearted civilians. The train sped on into the darkness and weary troops adjusted themselves on the floor — anywhere for a much needed sleep. [17]

Men of the Calgary Highlanders had been seasick on the *Pasteur*, despite good weather and smooth sailing. They were prairie boys with no experience of sea travel, but they soon became acclimatized. Their farewell dinner on board was rudely interrupted by klaxon horns ordering all ranks to lifeboat stations. The men watched with anxious interest as escorting vessels dropped depth-charges, destroying one U-boat and damaging two others.[18]

The Second Division experienced the friendly Scottish welcome and for a time also spent their leaves north of the border. The greatest difference was that while the First Division's arrival coincided with the quiet months of the Phoney War, the men wearing the Second Div.'s royal blue patch were not to know a semi-peaceful England. France had fallen to the Germans, the rescue of the British Expeditionary Force from Dunkirk had taken place, Winston Churchill was Prime Minister, and Hitler was planning to try his invasion tactics on southern England.

The two trains carrying the Calgary Highlanders arrived at North Farnborough station early next morning. The battalion marched four miles to their new home at Guillemont Barracks, Cove (north of Aldershot), a camp of huts built in 1938. Set in the edge of a woodland, the buildings were camouflaged in green and brown with concrete air raid shelters between them. Buckets of sand and water stood inside the entrances to deal with fire bombs.[19] At 11 a.m. the air raid siren sounded. According to Bill they didn't go to the shelters because they were flooded. Anyway, with the optimism of the inexperienced they wanted to see what might happen. Apparently nothing did, but two days later:

Air raid warnings sounded at intervals throughout the day and the men were able to see squadron after squadron of German bombers pass overhead on their way to London. At 11 pm the sirens went again . . . a member of the divisional staff telephoned the code word. 'Cromwell'. A frantic search of (the) cipher book failed to reveal its meaning, and even divisional headquarters could not enlighten the anxious Calgary Highlanders.

The solution was found when some new orders arrived. "Cromwell" was the code word for "Invasion imminent." [20] Church bells rang the alarm in the southern counties, however the code word and the bells were premature. There certainly were landing craft packed into the ports of northern France. Churchill had announced as much in the House of Commons.

Few Canadians realise that if Hitler had successfully invaded Britain "he would have deported every male between the ages of 16 and 45 to work camps on the continent" [21] at a time when the largest number of males in Britain in that age group were Canadian! Canada's First and Second Army Division would have disappeared into occupied Europe with poor hopes of survival. However, the determined attacks of the Luftwaffe were successfully beaten off by "The Few", and without air supremacy Goering dare not advise Hitler to invade. Eventually the invasion plan was dropped, and Hitler turned his attention to Russia.

The shared experience of the invasion threat brought Canadians and British together as perhaps nothing else could:

> Many invitations for Christmas were received by the Calgary Highlanders from local inhabitants, especially from those in the village of Yately (Hampshire). [22]

Those who remained on duty were not forgotten by their NCOs:

> Christmas 1940, the first Christmas away from home for many, was made more bearable and less nostalgic by an excellent Christmas dinner served by the sergeants. [23]

One incident shows how things had changed. On a bitterly cold night in 1943, the Calgarians returned from a exhausting route march at about 2 am. They limped the last few miles through Aldwick village, the regimental piper playing full blast. Next morning there were a few complaints but most remarks were of the "rather them than me" variety. It had been a different story in Aldershot back in November 1941 when the Fort Garry Horse arrived. They marched from the station to their billets to the loud accompaniment of the regimental trumpeters. It was midnight and the locals took a very dim view of the disturbance. [24]

The first Army casualties had occurred on July 6, 1940 when men of the Second Army Workshop, Royal Canadian Ordnance Corps were machine-gunned and bombed by a lone German plane while they were constructing air raid shelters at Salamanca Barracks, Aldershot. Three men were killed and 29 wounded. [25]

In August 1941 the third of the eventual five Canadian Divisions arrived in Britain.

Homesickness was as widespread among these men as it would be after the war among the women some of them chose as war brides. Rose (Pate) Robinson, of Winnipeg, Manitoba recalls:

> Grant showed me pictures of his family and was very homesick. Like most Canadian soldiers he was frustrated that they were being referred to as 'the Home Guard', from being in England so long.

The letters written by Sapper Walter Ottewell to his hometown newspaper in Wiarton, Ontario, and lovingly preserved by his daughter, speak of a soldier's thoughts of home in simple but eloquent terms:

24 January, 1942

I suppose you will be wondering how I am getting along; how I like England. England isn't as good as our country. I don't think there is any place like our fair Canada . . . I have been up to Glasgow, Scotland, twice. They are the finest people I have ever met. They can't do enough for you . . . Every Canadian soldier who has been in Scotland tells how well he is used. We kind of get fed up on it at times and long to get back to Canada again. I have met some of the Canadian soldiers who were in the Dunkirk battle. Everything over here is rationed. I don't think any person over here is starving . . . I guess you will want to know what kind of a trip we had coming over. You don't know the minute a torpedo is going to bore into the ship. We didn't have any mishaps like that happen. The sea was rough; some said they saw it rougher. I wouldn't want to see it any worse . . . the dishes fell off the shelves. There were about 4,500 troops on board.

18 March, 1942

As I was looking through the paper and reading about the different people it made me think I was back home again. The people here are working on the land. They farm different than we do. Before this war started I don't believe they did any farming at all, they bought all their stuff. They could buy it cheaper than they could grow it. I believe they are ploughing up a lot of the pasture . . . they are working on the land here now. I don't suppose they will be started at home by this time. I suppose there will be some snow around yet. I have seen by the paper where you had a real cold winter. They don't get much snow over here, but we get it in rain.

Sapper Walter E. Ottewell, Royal Canadian Engineers.

Credit: Valerie Bowden, daughter of Annie and Walter Ottewell

Spr. Ottewell's dreams of returning to his "fair Canada" were not to be. He died on November 19, 1944 from head injuries received in a bicycle accident on his way to work at Camp Bordon. This happened just

a year after he and Annie Fisher of Linford-Bordon, Hampshire, had been married. His wife received a Silver Cross (presented to widows and mothers of servicemen who die on active service) from Canada. The *Wiarton Echo* that had printed Walter's letters reported Walter's death and details of his Memorial Service in the local Church. Annie Ottewell was delivered of a daughter, Valerie, after the death of her husband. She raised Valerie alone, receiving a widow's pension from Canada until she died in 1988. She did not remarry.[26]

Army training continued long after Canadians arrived in Britain. There were endless schemes and exercises that took them up and down the country. These probably gave rise to the phrase, "The highly mobile Canadian soldier". They marched up Mount Snowden and were told to find their way back to base using only their wits, as they were allowed no money. (Bill, my husband-to-be, found his way down Mount Snowden and coaxed a friendly police sergeant into letting his platoon sleep in the station cells overnight!) At Battle Schools Canadian soldiers scaled alarmingly tall obstacles, and swung across waterways on ropes (Bill, in full kit, fell in the Basingstoke Canal when someone made him laugh). In the name of realism they crawled through shallow trenches strewn with animal entrails from local slaughter-houses, while live bullets flew on a fixed trajectory just above their heads.

Two members of the Royal Canadian Regiment's Motor Platoon who were regular customers in our shop bragged that when they were on army exercises they "broke down" at the first country pub, staying there in comfort until it was time to return to base; exploits that filled my father with an uncomfortable mixture of shock and admiration.

Canadians in Britain continued to suffer casualties in air raids and in accidents on the blacked-out roads. Newly arrived Canadian nurses were in London's Café de Paris when it received a direct hit. They tended casualties, many of them fellow Canadians.

On August 19, 1942 five thousand Second Division Canadians went into action. Along with a small group of British commandos under the leadership of Lord Lovat, a few American Rangers, and with Royal Navy crews manning the landing barges and other craft, they embarked on the infamous Dieppe raid. This early combined operation resulted in shocking casualties, and in the years to come Dieppe would be the subject of much bitter debate. After a bloodbath like Dieppe the hunt is always on for a scapegoat, and it seems that Lord Louis Mountbatten was the easiest target. He was blamed for reviving an action that had been cancelled, with resulting loss of security, although it could not have taken place without the consent of others in the highest places. This is one part of the war for which I can recall no amusing anecdotes. Fred Clarke, 414 Squadron RCAF, was shot down during the raid. He ditched in the Channel, but was back at his squadron the following morning, bandages and all. In November 1942 he married Helen Hope of Newcastle-on-Tyne who came to Calgary, Alberta after the war.

Peggy (Bartholomew) Price of Port Alberni, British Columbia, was living in Sussex in 1942:

Tom's regiment (14th Calgary Tanks) was sent over to be part of the Dieppe raid. About one third of the Regiment never returned. This was such a very sad time. My sister and I watched as the tanks and crew members straggled back to Seaford. Finally we saw 'our' two tanks coming, and knew the boys were safe.

Sadly Celia Phillips husband, Don, of the Black Watch of Canada, was killed at Dieppe, just five months after their marriage. She visited Canada for a while and then returned to the UK.[27] Dieppe was a widow-maker in towns across Canada and among British war brides.

Bill Grant, Royal Hamilton Light Infantry, was in Capt. Denis Whitaker's platoon:

My platoon's first task was to blow a gap through the thickly coiled roll of concertina wire (on the beach) . . . It was about seven feet deep . . . Private Bill Grant bravely crawled up to the wire and pushed the (Bangalore) torpedo in place. Suddenly George Naylor yelled, 'Bill's been hit!' He was dead, shot in the head. (Bill had been in the regiment since 1926 and had married an English girl just a few weeks before Dieppe).[28]

Part of Calgary Highlanders' Mortar Platoon prior to Dieppe raid.
Officer commanding: Lt. F. J. Reynolds (front right). Bill Lyster circled.

Tanks "BERT" and "BILL", were coincidentally on Landing Craft 6 with Bert Pittaway and Bill Lyster. The tanks remained on the Dieppe beach.
Credits: Calgary Highlanders' Archives, ECP Armées DAT 2126 L44, Bundesarchiv 362/2207/37

On the fourth anniversary of the outbreak of war Canadians were on the move again, this time units of the First Division were involved in the invasion of Sicily and the subsequent hard fighting in Italy.

Molly (Gerrard) Schafer, of Dawson Creek, British Columbia, recalls:

> When I met my future husband he had just got back from Italy. He was in the First Special Service Division that Hitler called 'The Devil's Brigade'.

In the aftermath of the successful D-Day landings some stone-hearted Englishwoman (always believed to be Lady Astor) described the men in Italy as "D-Day Dodgers". (The irony was that many survivors of the Italian campaign went on to fight in Normandy.) The Canadian, British, French and US troops who fought the terrible battles in Italy's towns and inhospitable mountains were initially stung by this crass comment, but soon made it their own. They even sang about it to the tune of "Lili Marlene". I recall one verse:

> Forgotten by the many, remembered by the few
> We had our armistice when an armistice was new.
> One million Germans gave up to us
> We finished our war without much fuss,
> For we're the D-Day Dodgers out here in Italy.

- and part of another -

> Dearest Lady Astor you think you're mighty hot
> Standing on the platform talking tommyrot . . .

There are many others, some unprintable!

By late 1941 the entire Canadian Army had been concentrated in Sussex and, except for those fighting in Italy, remained there until D-Day:

> The Corps front in Sussex extended from the Hampshire border on the right to Fairlight Church (a couple of miles east of Hastings) on the left. [29]

This accounts for the high ratio of Sussex women among the war brides. In July 1942 the regiments included the Cameron Highlanders, the South Saskatchewan Regiment, the Black Watch of Canada, le Régiment de Maisonneuvre, the Calgary Highlanders, the Royal Hamilton Light Infantry, the Royal Regiment of Canada, and the Essex Scottish. [30]

FIRST NATIONS CANADIANS

The contribution made by First Nations Canadians must be acknowledged. For many, just joining up brought a double culture shock. On top of the adjustment to life in the armed services, these men had to adapt to a way of life often quite different from their own, and adapt they did. They also brought with them skills that were invaluable in a fighting force. An officer in the Loyal Edmonton Regiment spoke for many others of his time in Italy:

> First Nations men in our regiment were outstanding. If I needed top-notch marksmen, scouts or snipers they were the ones I relied on. [31]

First Nations soldiers served in many distinguished regiments, including:

Argyll and Sutherland Highlanders
Black Watch of Canada
Calgary Highlanders
Canadian Scottish Regiment
Essex Scottish
Fort Garry Horse
Hastings and Prince Edward Regiment
Loyal Edmonton Regiment
North Nova Scotia Highlanders
Princess Patricia's Canadian Light Infantry
Queen's Own Cameron Highlanders
Régiment de Maisonneuve
Regina Rifles
Royal Canadian Regiment
Royal Hamilton Light Infantry
Royal Regiment of Canada
Royal Winnipeg Rifles
Seaforth Highlanders
Stormont, Dundas and Glengarry Highlanders

They were also in the RCAF and the RCNVR. Some were commissioned.

A number of First Nations men married while in Britain. It is a sad fact that many brides could not adjust to the double culture shock when they arrived in Canada, and decided to return home. But by no means was every marriage a failure. Early in 2004 I read the story Anne Rosemarie Paudash had written of her early life in Ontario. [32] Her opening words, "A few years ago I left my home in a little place called Bognor Regis in Sussex, England . . . " started me on a hunt to track her down, and eventually I corresponded with Terry Musgrave, Anne's daughter by her first marriage to an Englishman. I was sorry to learn that Anne had died some years previously; I'd been looking forward to reminiscing with her about our hometown.

Anne married George Regnal Paudash, a sergeant with the Stormont, Dundas and Glengarry Highlanders, who landed with his regiment on D-Day and fought in Northwest Europe. Anne became Number 69 of the Rice Lake Indian Band of Ontario, and was subject to the terms of the Indian Act. She mused that if her situation had disadvantages, it also had advantages. She could not legally be served a drink, but as a

Band member she received free medical, dental and hospital care, and did not have to pay income tax. Anne came to the Hiawatha Reserve on the north shore of the beautiful Rice Lake, situated a few kilometers south of Peterborough. Like so many other halves of successful war bride marriages, Anne had a good sense of humour that shines through her article. Life was not easy. As in so many rural houses of the time the Paudash home, which had been willed to George by an uncle, lacked electricity and running water. George was away all day working at the Canadian General Electric plant in Peterborough.

Eventually, with ten children in the family, washday began early in the morning and was only finished as the older ones began coming home from school. Anne's hobby was knitting and one of Terry's treasured memories is of hearing the click of many knitting needles as her mother, family and close friends shared an afternoon cup of tea. Anne contributed knitted items to United Church bazaars on the Reserve. Ironically, Terry Musgrave is among the overseas-born children of war brides with citizenship problems.

Another good English/First Nation marriage is recalled with affection by the Hon. Minister of Justice, and Attorney General for the Province of New Brunswick, T.J. Burke (see Chapter 19, The Next Generation).

THE ROYAL CANADIAN NAVY

Despite the fact that when the war broke out the RCN had a force of only 2,000 men, it grew to be the Allies' third largest navy, and made a major contribution to the Battle of the Atlantic and the eventual outcome of the war. Much like the RCAF, men of the RCN were virtually merged with their British counterparts. The large Royal Navy base HMS *Ferret*, in Londonderry, Northern Ireland was well-known to many Canadians, but HMS *Niobe*, located at a former asylum, in Greenock, Scotland, was the official RCN Headquarters for most of the war. Members of the RCN, like all sailors, served months at sea, spending a limited time ashore in Britain, so it is not surprising that the Canadian Navy made only 2% of the overseas marriages.

PARCELS FROM HOME

Throughout the long years that the men in this chapter were away from Canada they were not forgotten by the good people back home. Thousands upon thousands of packages made their way eastward across the Atlantic containing anything from a chicken* to hand-knitted khaki, navy or air-force blue socks and scarves, soft-cover books, peanut butter, maple syrup, chocolate bars and cigarettes. For the many thousands who were incarcerated in prisoner-of-war camps food parcels could mean the difference between life and death. D. Kathleen (Hare) Palfrey, a World War I war bride living in Wetaskiwin, Alberta was highly commended in 1945 for her tireless work in this regard. The generous flow of parcels became even greater as Canadian/British marriages took place and were followed by Canadian/British babies. Parcels from Canadian in-laws brought items unobtainable in Britain, and were a joy to new mothers.

WWI war bride, D. Kathleen (Hare) Palfrey was a tireless volunteer. She supervised parcels packed for troops and POWs. She also welcomed and assisted WWII war brides.
Credit: author's collection

*The chicken was sent to Bill Lyster in good faith by his grandmother, who lived a short distance from Camp Shilo, Manitoba, where in 1940 his regiment was in training. Mail was fast and reliable but even the Canadian Post Office was foiled when the mailman discovered that Bill's regiment had gone overseas. The parcel did not catch up with him for a number of weeks. The state of the chicken by then does not bear thinking about.

CANADIAN RED CROSS
PRISONER OF WAR
FOOD PARCEL
FOR DISTRIBUTION THROUGH
INTERNATIONAL RED CROSS COMMITTEE

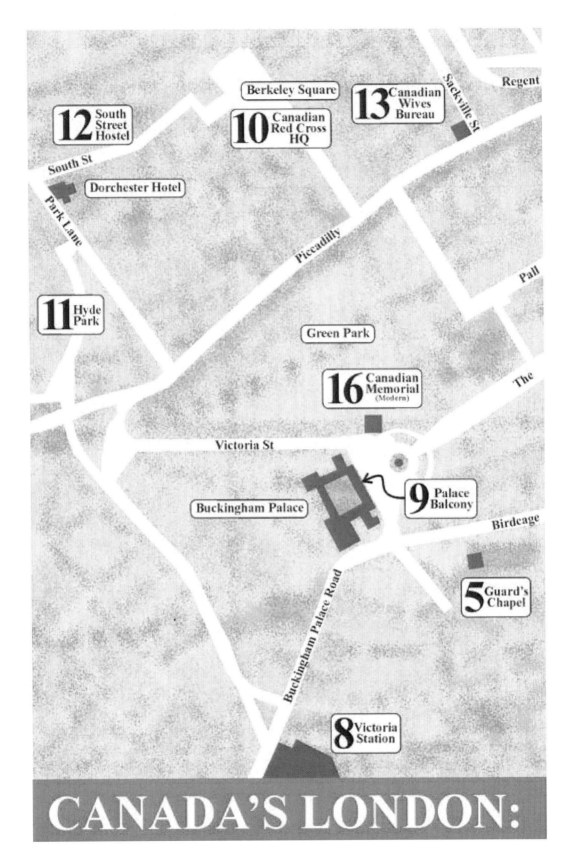

CANADA'S LONDON:

46

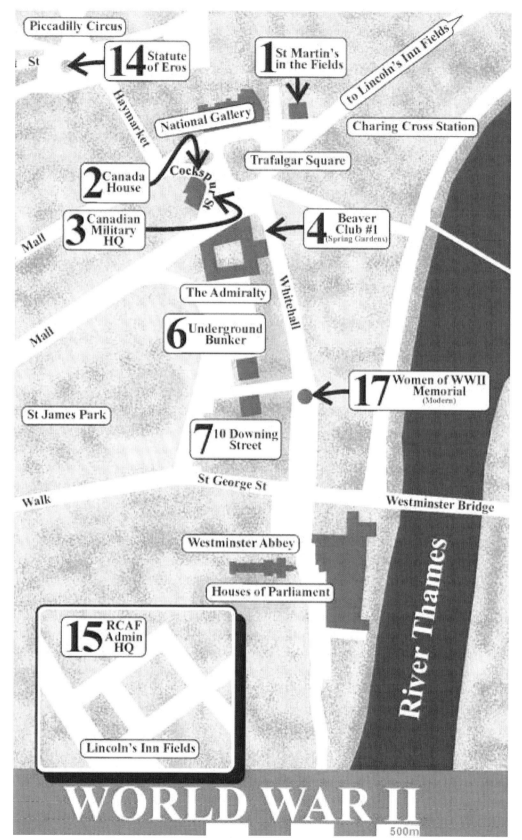

Piccadilly Circus

St

14 Statute of Eros

Haymarket

National Gallery

1 St Martin's in the Fields

to Lincoln's Inn Fields

Charing Cross Station

Cockspur St

2 Canada House

Trafalgar Square

3 Canadian Military HQ

4 Beaver Club #1 (Spring Gardens)

Mall

The Admiralty

Whitehall

Mall

6 Underground Bunker

St James Park

17 Women of WWII Memorial (Modern)

7 10 Downing Street

St George St

Walk

Westminster Bridge

Westminster Abbey

Houses of Parliament

River Thames

15 RCAF Admin HQ

Lincoln's Inn Fields

WORLD WAR II

500m

47

CANADA'S LONDON
World War II (and other London landmarks)

1 St. Martin's in the Fields Church. In a church with an "ever open door" policy, the crypt was always available with meals and warm corners for itinerants, and shelter for passers-by caught in an air-raid. The author remembers being down there one wartime Christmas and being greeted with mince pies, Christmas cake and red and green decorations.

2 Canada House, 1 Cockspur Street.

3 Canadian Military Headquarters (Sun Life Building), 2, 3 and 4 Cockspur St. One floor of the Sun Life Building was occupied at first but eventually most of the building was taken over. **The Royal Bank of Canada** has been on the main floor of the Sun Life Building since 1928. The Bank lost its windows many times in the Blitz, and eventually had to make do with plywood replacements.[33]

4 Beaver Club (No.1) Spring Gardens opened January 1940. Despite being five storeys high it had no sleeping accommodation, but boasted "the world's finest dance floor". It had a canteen that specialized in Canadian dishes, an information bureau, reading rooms where current Canadian newspapers were on hand, and "plenty of heat". (Other Beaver Clubs followed in nearby locations.)

5 The Guard's Chapel, Wellington Barracks, Birdcage Walk. On June 18, 1944 it was hit by a flying bomb during the morning service, killing 121 (including some Canadians and civilians) and seriously wounding many others. The candles on the altar remained alight.[34]

6 Churchill's underground bunker.

7 10 Downing Street, better known as "Number 10", is the traditional London home and office of British Prime Ministers.

8 Victoria Station, the London terminus of the (then) Southern Railway, was familiar to the many thousands of Canadians billeted in Surrey and Sussex. (The entire Canadian Army was stationed in Sussex, 1942 to 1944.)

9 Buckingham Palace balcony where on Victory in Europe (V-E) Day, May 8, 1945 the Royal Family and Winston Churchill waved to the cheering throngs below.

10 Canadian Red Cross Headquarters on the north side of Berkeley Square (former quarters of Brigadier Critchley's Greyhound Racing Association). Early in 1944 the Headquarters was moved to Burlington Gardens.[35]

Canadian Red Cross Escort Staff Hostel at 80 Brook St., home of Red Cross personnel in charge of escorting war brides to Canada (not shown on map).

Canadian Red Cross Corps House, 18-20 Queen's Gate Terrace, Knightsbridge (not shown on map).[36] Number 16 was later added to the complex.

11 Hyde Park which covered many acres was a bustle of activity all through the war.

12 South Street War Bride Hostel was located behind the Dorchester Hotel in the former London home of Lord Abercrombie. Twelve thousand wives and their children were accommodated here overnight before entraining for their various ports of departure.[37] The hostel closed September 1946. Photo is on first page of Chapter 9.

<u>Other Hostels:</u> (not on map)

Brook Street War Bride Hostel at 80 Brook Street slept up to 50 war brides and their children overnight in reclaimed air raid shelter bunks. This appears to be the hostel reserved or continental wives whose paperwork was more complicated than that of British wives. It was here that Dutch war brides and their children were lodged in December 1946 after the *Letitia* was involved in a collision.[38]

The Chesman War Bride Hostel was in Fleet Street. [39]

The Mostyn War Bride Hostel at 4 Bryanston Street was originally the London house of Lady Black, a lady-in-waiting at the court of George II. By World War II it was a hotel that received extensive bomb damage, a fact often noted by war brides who passed through here. Leah Halsall, serving with the Canadian Red Cross escort services, reported there were 700 beds here available for war brides stopping over before leaving for a port of embarkation. Today an extensively remodelled Mostyn is again a hotel. Some of the original architecture survives, including ornate Adam ceilings in the restaurant and conference rooms.[40]

The Onslow Court War Bride Hostel at Onslow Gardens, Kensington.[41]

13   The Canadian Wives Bureau (CWB) Sackville House, corner of Sackville Street and Piccadilly. CWB offices were on an upper floor. War brides and their children came here for paper work and the medical examinations that were mandatory before leaving Britain. Other offices in the building were occupied by staff of Canada's Department of Citizenship and Immigration. The CWB originally had offices above Galleries Lafayette, the smart department store at 188-195 Regent Street, which they quickly outgrew. Some staff remained there after the move to Sackville House.

14   The Statue of Eros Piccadilly Circus. Throughout the war the Eros site was clad in boards that in peacetime had protected the God of Love from over-enthusiastic revelers on New Year's Eve. Wartime observers did not realize that Eros had been evacuated to a safer place in the country.

15   RCAF Administrative HQ 20 Lincoln's Inn Fields. During closing ceremonies of this HQ in 1946, a nearby section of sidewalk was named Canada Walk.

Two modern memorials:

16   The 100,000 Canadians who died in two World Wars are remembered in the **Canadian Memorial**, which stands in Green Park within sight of Buckingham Palace. The late Pierre Gianche chose Manitoba marble for his design, the top of which is angled to allow water to run over randomly carved maple leaves. The Memorial is oriented so that it is in a direct line between Buckingham Palace and Halifax, Nova Scotia, where so many Canadians embarked for Europe in both wars. It was dedicated in 1994 by HM Queen Elizabeth II, and the Queen Mother in a moving ceremony attended by many other members of the Royal Family.

17   The 22 foot-high bronze **Women's War Memorial** designed by sculptor John Mills, was unveiled by HM Queen Elizabeth on July 9, 2005. It stands in Whitehall near the Cenotaph and commemorates the seven million women who served in the WRNS, ATS, WAAF, Nursing Services, Women's Land Army, National Fire Service, Civil Defence, WVS, munition and other factories, canteens etc. War brides served in all these categories.

Canadian and other London sites not shown on map:

The Air Officers League Club run by the Masseys.

British Columbia House on Lower Regent St. had a Service Canteen in the basement.

The Canadian Broadcasting Corporation had an office in a basement at 200 Regent Street, an annex of the Peter Jones store. This was augmented by a mobile recording vehicle designed by CBC Montreal and nicknamed Big Betsy. A more compact version of Big Betsy was taken to Europe after D-Day.[42]

Canadian Records Office (Canadian Pay Office) Bromyard Ave., Acton.[43] (War bride Ethel Millar, of Woodstock, Ontario lived in Acton and worked at the Records Office until she left for Canada in 1946.)

The Canadian Soldier's Club, Gower Street run by the Canadian Legion had sleeping accommodation for several hundred servicemen.[44]

Four **Maple Leaf Clubs** were financed by the Canadian Red Cross for their personnel and to provide meals and lodging for Canadians on leave.

    #1 was near Victoria Station.[45]

    #2 Cromwell Road was for servicemen of different ranks.[46]

    #3 (no information)

    #4 was a Red Cross Officer's Club.[47]

The Ontario Services Club opened in Piccadilly September 1944. It was a day club with lounge, cafeteria, library and information desk, and justified its short existence when it served nearly a thousand Chrismas dinners in December 1944. It closed at the end of February 1946.[48]

Repatriation Office, (for servicemen) Charles II Street.[49]

Waterloo Station, just south of the Thames, was well-known to newly arrived RCAF personnel who entrained here for the Reception Centre, Bournemouth, Hampshire, where they received further training before being posted to fighter and bomber stations.

Note: **The Royal Canadian Navy** had no permanent headquarters in London.

St. Martin's
in the Fields

Women's War
Memorial, Whitehall

Canadian Wives' Bureau

RCAF Administrative HQ, 20 Lincoln's
Inn Fields. Note boarded windows.
Credit: Jeff Jeffries

Bomb crater behind Canada House and
Canadian Military HQ, 1940.
Credit: Department of National Defence
DHH Kardex file 112.3PI (D1432)

The Canadian Memorial, Green Park,
across from Buckingham Palace. In
memory of Canadian servicemen who
died in two world wars.
Credit: E. Jane Lyster

Sgt. Douglas T. McKinley (right) who
married Winifred Morteal.
Trafalgar Square, c 1945.
Credit: author's collection

People are more likely to fall in love when they're in danger. Wartime romances are legendary ... danger is an aphrodisiac.

Diane Ackerman, *A Natural History of Love*

I met my husband-to-be, Michael, at ten minutes to three, June 15th, 1945.

Beatrice (Burrows) Thompson, Erinsville, Ontario

... and as I got to know him I was fascinated with his talk of wheat, horses, snow and hot sun, not your everyday Bolton topics.

Bernadette (Morris) Surgeson, Cornwall, Ontario

Bert Pittaway and Pamela Munn, Southwick, Sussex, c 1942.
Credits: author's collection

Bert and Pam Pittaway, "Trail's End", Qualicum Beach, c 1980.

Chapter 4: Paths Cross

On blind dates, at dance halls, skating rinks, while waiting for buses or in a line outside a cinema . . . paths did indeed cross.

Florence (Hayzen) Phillips of Burnaby, British Columbia, met Percy Phillips when he came to England to play ice-hockey:

My story begins in 1938. I met my future husband at Forest Gate roller-skating rink. This chap with a funny accent came up and introduced himself as 'Scoop' – I thought 'that's an odd name'. Apparently his mother had taken the nickname from a newspaper cartoon character. Scoop enlisted in the Canadian Army in London.

Marion "Wendy" (Oliffe) Kirkpatrick of Parksville, British Columbia left school at fourteen because her father was ill:

I was needed to look after the sub-Post Office in my parents' grocery store. The Thames area had become an evacuated zone, but my Post Office work was considered to be a reserved occupation. The (British) Royal Artillery (RA) had set up a Heavy Anti-Aircraft gun site by Hadleigh Castle. In 1942 the RAs moved out and a Canadian Heavy AA Unit moved in. Our boys were warning our mothers to keep their daughters locked up. 'You can't trust the Canadians, you know.' When some of the advance party popped into the local dance hall we girls decided they looked pretty harmless. I fell for one of the lads and in March 1943 we were married.

Rosina (Simpson) Husband of Midway, British Columbia was also cautioned about the newcomers:

My mother was warning me to be very careful of these fellows from overseas as many of them were married with families in Canada.

Sheila Anketel-Jones wrote from East Sussex, England:

England was chock-a-block with young men from other countries . . . we proceeded to have the most marvellous time, despite the continuation of air raids . . . it was all so very chaste. In the light of today's morals, quite unbelievable.

Iris (Turner) Page, Qualicum Beach, British Columbia spoke of completing her WRNS technical training, adding, "the best part came next":

I met a navy helicopter pilot, Lt. Len Page from Lennoxville, Quebec. He had just arrived with the only helicopter unit in the Royal Navy – three machines, Sikorsky YR4s.

Bernadette (Morris) Surgeson, now of Cornwall, Ontario, met Norman Surgeson and was "rendered speechless" ("Not a common condition for me", she says):

There stood a young man of 19, a little over six feet tall. He was wearing a smart RCAF uniform with buttons, belt buckle and boots all shining. When he spoke the accent was very Canadian mid-western, and as I got to know him I was fascinated with his talk of wheat, horses, snow and hot sun, not your everyday Bolton topics.

The Tower Ballroom, Blackpool, The Hammersmith Palais in West London, the Palais de Dance, Aldershot (where the last dance was always *Who's Taking you Home Tonight?*),[1] the Regent, Brighton and the Pavilion Bognor Regis were all bright and cheerful places to get away from the war for a few hours. The Covent Garden Opera House in London's West End had been converted into a ballroom for the duration by building a dance floor over the seats of the historic theatre. The huge revolving stage held not one but two dance bands, back to back, one of them being the famous Ivy Benson and her All-Girl Orchestra. Halfway through the evening the stage revolved, retiring the first band and presenting the second. Airman Jeff Jeffries and Norma Freeman were two who met here, but their story was interrupted and did not continue until the 1980s, so is in a later chapter.

When Anne (Bourke) Risley of Halifax, Nova Scotia met her Canadian husband she was still mourning her fiancé who had been killed in the fall of France, May 1940:

All the local girls had been rounded up to attend a dance for Canadian officers at a country house near Guildford, Surrey, called Braeboeuf Manor. I came face to face with Robert in a Paul Jones – a rather embarrassing dance intended to mix up partners. We seemed to hit it off and he drove me home afterwards. This dance was to be a weekly affair, and I decided to go back the next week. Rather to my disappointment he was not there. The night he did appear again was a very 'noisy' one with a lot of bangs and searchlights, and my mother did not want me to go. But I was twenty years old, so I went. He was there but to my horror had grown a moustache which looked horrid. He drove me home again and told me how to get in touch with him. Very boldly I did phone Robert and arranged a bridge game, why I don't know as I had only played once in my life. We started going to tea dances in Aldershot and out to dinner at the Talbot Inn, near Guildford. One night as we were driving along the Hog's Back (an elevated land form in Surrey) we saw a great red glow in the sky. It was London burning after one of the worst air raids of the war. When he proposed we were on our way home from the Talbot where we had to get under a table because of the enemy action.

Idina (Kennedy) Kirby, Kelowna, British Columbia met her husband at a Women's Institute dance:

We met again next evening and because I was late getting home (10:00 pm, when the curfew was 9:00) I was CB'd (confined to barracks) for a week. I believe my Dad knew of the Canadian soldier in the village and he was making sure we didn't meet again. However 'love will out', and we continued to see each other from 1943 to 1946 when we finally got permission from my parents and were married. My father said, 'You'll be sorry, my girl, you know they only have outside toilets that are not very nice.' My reply was, 'Oh, Dad, don't be silly!'

For Kathleen (Sadler) Chapman of St. Thomas Ontario, romance began at Brighton's Regent Dance Hall:

I met Gilbert immediately after my engagement to an RAF man was broken. I looked up from a conversation to see this Canadian sapper staring at me across the room. I looked away haughtily as we did not speak to Canadians! Presently he asked me to dance. Our steps matched. I went home with friends but he was there the next week, and the next . . .

Margaret (Earl) Kilner, of Nanaimo, British Columbia met Frank Kilner at a New Year's Eve dance at the Pavilion, Bognor Regis. This is the dance hall where Bill and I had our first date. He called for me with an army truck, a 15 cwt (cwt = hundredweight = 112 pounds) job with a canvas cover, and helped me over the backboard, which was no great problem. Our Navy transports were exactly the same, so I was used to negotiating the climb in a slim-fitting uniform skirt with as much modesty as a girl could muster. The Calgary Highlanders already on board made room for me and then some joker rapped on the window behind the driver and we took off at speed. Bill was left standing in the road, fuming. I told my fellow passengers they were poor sports, but they just laughed at the joke they had played on their CSM. When we arrived at The Pavilion Sergeant Bert Pittaway was looking for Bill. "R.B. Bennett is here", he said. I didn't have a clue who R.B. Bennett might be. (He was not only Honorary Colonel of the Regiment, but also a former Prime Minister of Canada.) He was to present Bill and Bert with Mentioned in Dispatches certificates for their actions on the Dieppe raid the previous August. They had manned a "pom pom" gun on their landing craft and shot down an enemy fighter. Bill finally arrived, having run most of the way, and the presentation took place.

Sonja Henie, the Norwegian, medal-winning ice skater, had stirred English girls' interest in skating through her Hollywood movies, and many romances began at a rink. Brenda (Clapham) Carriere of Vancouver, British Columbia, met her husband this way:

I was a good skater and could dance on ice with a partner. This Canadian air force officer, complete with his wings and DFC (Distinguished Flying Cross) was madly rushing around on his hockey skates. He had the gall to come over and ask me to dance. It is almost impossible to dance on hockey skates, but around we went. I was terribly impressed with his charming French accent. It was a romantic courtship, made all the more poignant because we could not see each other often. Sometimes when he was flying his Spitfire he would 'beat up' our house. It was dangerous, and he came down so low that I could run out into the garden and wave. The neighbours were furious, but I was terribly impressed.

Jean (Wilks) Elmer of Delta, British Columbia, had roller skates strapped to her feet when she met Roy in June 1944:

He was stationed at the Re-Pat Depot near Warrington, Cheshire, when we met at the Birch Park Roller Rink. I was a member of a group of girls that went there every Tuesday night. That night I was the only one to turn up. Roy bumped into me and had been flirting ever since. Finally he skated over and asked: 'Did you come here to skate?' When I nodded he said, 'Well, let's skate!' There were no other dates after that, just Roy.

Dr. Lynn Angus, daughter of the late Doreen (Flaherty) Angus of Orillia, Ontario, wrote of her mother:

In 1943 she joined ENSA (Entertainment National Service Association) to train as a motion picture projectionist. Before reporting for duty she stayed in London at the Russell Hotel for a short vacation. At about 5:00 pm on the Saturday she was awaiting the arrival of a family friend when she was approached by a young Lieutenant in the Canadian 7th Tank Regiment. As an excuse to meet this beautiful young lady, and although he was wearing a watch, he asked if she knew the time. Doreen said that from the first she knew Arthur was the man she would marry. When it was apparent the family friend was a no-show Arthur asked Doreen to join him for dinner. They went dancing at the Hammersmith Palais and arranged to meet for breakfast next morning. Art was on his way to Aberdeen to meet some relatives and Doreen asked if he would like to accompany her to Leeds to meet her parents. Doreen's mother drove a large lorry for the Department of Defence, and had just returned from the badly bombed Coventry where she served hot meals to the survivors and rescuers. Because Doreen's father was in the wholesale meat business she served a steak dinner to Art. It was his first steak since leaving Canada, three years earlier.

Doreen, who first came to Normetal, Quebec received a warm welcome and made lasting friendships, despite the fact that her schoolgirl French was barely understood.

Winston Douglas Birch was an RCAF pilot with Coastal Command, stationed at Castle Archdale, Co. Fermanagh, Northern Ireland. Here he met his future wife Elizabeth Millen, better known as Libby. Libby was fifteen, and at twenty Win was very concerned about the age difference. Libby wrote from Oshawa, Ontario:

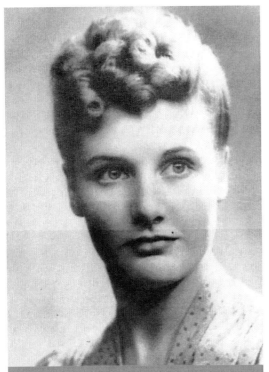

"My sister said she could not hold her head up in respectable society because her fifteen year-old sister was dating a Canadian pilot."
Credit: Elizabeth (Millen) Birch

My sister said she could not hold her head up in respectable society because her fifteen-year-old sister was dating a Canadian pilot. At this point my dad was dying and Win was supportive and extremely kind, and Mum really took to him. We were madly in love, and after Win returned to Canada in May 1945, I cried in my pillow every night. We corresponded for three years and dated freely, but we found that nothing was quite the same. He graduated from university as a mechanical engineer, and I wanted to marry him, that was for sure. Mum was great. In bad financial circumstances herself, she borrowed three hundred pounds from a cousin. It was part of her old-fashioned culture that a bride must have a trousseau. Here I was leaving my family . . . and I think I had that Irish folk memory that when one went to the New World one never returned . . .

Patricia (Collins) McCaskill, of Burnaby, British Columbia had been waiting under the Guildford, Surrey, (England) town clock for her date, when she realised she had been "stood up". As she walked towards her bus stop she noticed that a rather nice-looking Canadian sergeant was shadowing her. She confronted him with, "Are you by any chance following me?":

'Yes, Ma'am, I sure am,' he replied, 'I dearly want to get to know you. I've met my dream girl tonight.' What nonsense, I thought. I walked on towards the bus stop only to see the last bus pull away. I turned and bumped into the Sergeant again. 'Missed your bus, eh?' he said, 'can I walk you home?' He didn't know the Guildford area well so I only let him walk me half-way home as he had to get back to his camp at Witley. We dated after that. I asked if he had a girl-friend or a nice wife in Canada. He hadn't. 'I know for sure I'm going to marry you.' 'That's if I marry you,' I said. 'Oh, you will,' he said. How corny! But it was to be the luckiest day of my life. I liked him more than I cared to admit. He was always well-groomed, a gentleman, happy-go-lucky, considerate. My kind of man.

Mary (Levett) MacDonald of Comox, British Columbia was on leave in Carlisle, her home town. Army convoys had been moving through the city all day, and she was injured while crossing the road in the blackout. She had stepped between a truck and the gun it was pulling. Mary's leave was extended while she recovered and it was then she met Allan MacDonald who was in Carlisle looking up some Scottish relatives.

Although my mother had a full time job at the Aldwick shop she was asked to assist at a Chichester services canteen run by the ladies of the Women's Voluntary Service (WVS). She worked several nights a week dispensing egg and chips when fresh eggs were available. In 1940/41 I sometimes worked there as well while I waited to age sufficiently for the Navy to accept me (I had to be 17 years and three months). The American GIs began arriving 1942. They had studied a booklet while crossing the Atlantic that among other things warned them to stay away from "ladies of the night" who might lead young boys astray and force a quick trip to the MO (Medical Officer). This advice backfired at the canteen when an ultra-respectable WVS worker from one of the county families, feeling sorry for the young lads, invited two of them home for a bath and a proper meal. Instead of smiles of gratitude she was informed they had been warned about "women like you", and they stomped off into the night.

The only time I encountered a Canadian in a canteen was when a soldier stumbled in after the nearest pub closed. He was quite harmless, but a feisty Irish sailor picked a fight with him. By the time the Provost (military police) arrived the Canadian had quietly passed out and the sailor had made himself scarce. The Canadian was hauled away, and I was too shy to put in a good word for him. These canteens were a welcome place for service people who were in-between trains, and the only alternative on a cold night to the ever-present pub. I had never thought of a canteen as a setting for romance, but Catherine (Munro) Mahon of Qualicum Beach, British Columbia met her husband Harold at a WVS canteen in Durnoch, Scotland. Harold was with No. 1 Coy (Company) Canadian Forestry Corps.

Jane (Clark) Atkinson wrote from Nova Scotia:

I worked on the bus that ran to HMCS *Niobe*, Greenock, Scotland, the Canadian dry-land ship that was the Headquarters of the Royal Canadian Navy. I met hundreds of the

Canadian sailors who were billeted there. How could I escape marrying one of them? Don went to sea for five months and we married three weeks after he got back to *Niobe*. My mum nearly had a fit, and my dad's sister told her it was awful letting me go away to Canada!

Inevitably the strange names of English villages would crop up in conversations with Canadians. "What gives," they'd say, "with names like 'Piddletrenthide', 'Puddletown', 'Upper Slaughter' and 'Lower Slaughter'?" When we met again we would have armed ourselves with some Canadian place names. "What gives" we'd say, "with names like 'Spuzzum', 'Skookumchuck', 'Ecum Secum', 'Punkeydoodles Corner' and 'Swastika'?" Slightly crestfallen the Canadians might inform us that some of those were based on Indian names, and that after 1939 the Canadian Government had tried (with little success) to change the name "Swastika" to "Winston".

Mel Hunter, RCAF, and Marguerite Lee, WAAF, were each on leave in the south of England in 1943. They met while picking raspberries.
Credit: Jill (Hunter) Forbes

English Wren, Canadian Glengarry 1943.
Credit: author's collection

War has always been against the marriages it makes.
Patrick White

WEDDINGS OF CANADIANS OVERSEAS CONSIDERED TOO NUMEROUS

The Canadian army overseas has moved to cut down lightning courtships between Canadian soldiers and British girls, and at the same time reduce the proportion of unhappy marriages.
Headline and excerpt, *Hamilton Spectator*, June 9, 1942

How could those who had not shared the war years interpret our mood? Ours was a wartime marriage. There wasn't a thing to recommend its future to a discriminating parent. Eleanor's mother and father, bless them, saw only one logical reason for the union. Their daughter was happy in her first love.
Gray Campbell, *Butter Side Up*

Mr. and Mrs. Cooper, July 25, 1942, South Bersted, Sussex. Kathleen's war work included making wrenches and learning to read the micrometer. She and Arthur went dancing every week at Arundel Castle, Sussex. Kathleen came to Nipawin, Saskatchewan.
Credit: Kathleen (Wilkinson) Cooper

Chapter 5: Wartime Weddings

According to Colonel C.P. Stacey the war bride saga began in January 1940 with a marriage between a Canadian Company Sergeant Major and a British woman at an Aldershot garrison church. Colonel Stacey expressed amazement at the speed of the marriage since the Canadians had only been in England since mid-December 1939. What he didn't realise was the couple had known each other for two years.[1]

The number of marriages increased each year, and by the middle of 1942 had reached a total of 3,500. Canadian authorities found this upsetting, and cited the numbers of similar marriages that had failed in World War I. British servicemen abroad were also upset. The Commanding Officer of a Sussex Regiment wrote to his superior in Britain demanding that "something be done about Canadian marriages" because the morale of his men was being affected. They believed there would be no young women left by the time they got back home.

In 1942 Canadian Newspapers reported new Army regulations that had come into force the previous November. Privates and non-commissioned officers who were planning to marry were now required to pay for the transport of their wives to Canada. (Despite this, the journey continued to be described as "free passage provided by the Canadian government".)

SEQUENCE FROM SERVICEMAN OBTAINING PERMISSION TO MARRY, TO DEPENDENT'S EMBARKATION FOR CANADA*

1. Serviceman applies for permission to marry.[2]
2. Serviceman's fiancée is investigated for good character, usually by regimental chaplain. Alternatively she supplies character references. She has a medical examination and blood tests.
3. If fiancée is deemed eligible serviceman applies for a Permission to Marry form signed by a senior officer. (Church or civil marriages could not be performed without this form.)
4. A three-month waiting (cooling off?) period was required before marriage could take place.
5. The marriage takes place.
6. On return from marriage leave the serviceman submits documentary proof of marriage, which is usually (perhaps not universally) entered in the Regimental War Diary. Serviceman must make arrangements for $200 to be deducted from his pay.[3] ". . . it was now required that a soldier applying for permission to marry declare his current marital status, his ability to maintain a family after discharge, and his consent to a $10 monthly deduction from his pay until the $200 was accumulated. *This would be used to pay for his family's passage to Canada* (author's italics)".[4] Information about the marriage and the deduction goes through channels to the Pay Office and the Canadian Wives Bureau.
7. Monthly Dependents' Allowance is received by war bride, ceasing only when serviceman is demobilized.**

8. Canadian Wives Bureau initiates correspondence with war bride, establishing whether or not she intends to reside in Canada after the war. On receipt of affirmative reply an interview is arranged at CWB offices, Sackville House, Sackville Street, London.

9. Canadian Travel Certificate (in lieu of Passport), printed regulations regarding baggage allowance, instructions re: train to London terminal and liaison with Railway Transport Officer, etc. are all issued by CWB to Dependent.

10. Dependent (and child or children) are cared for overnight at a London hostel and next day escorted by train to port of departure.

* The sequence has been reconstructed from personal experience, from the many interviews with war brides, and from other sources.

* * This regulation sometimes caused hardship if the husband was repatriated ahead of his wife and then demobilized. The Dependents' Allowance ceased on his discharge.

Marriages were also recorded at the Dependents' Allowance Board in Ottawa.

The investigation of fiancées upset many young women and their parents. Mrs. Groom, whose daughter Ethel eventually married Alfred George Hall, wrote to the latter's commanding officer to see if *Alfred* was of good character, even though she found him charming.

The marriages of French-Canadians with British women posed a further problem. Since French-Canadians were almost universally Roman Catholic and British women Protestant, Catholic padres were often outspoken in their objection to overseas marriages. A persistent rumour had it that one even advised: "Sleep with them if you must, but don't marry them."

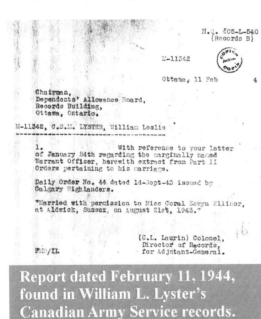

Report dated February 11, 1944, found in William L. Lyster's Canadian Army Service records.

Credit: author's collection

In an early book Ben Wicks spoke of war brides in terms that upset many of them. After intimating that we should have waited for our British boy friends overseas he gave his impression of the young women who were becoming war brides:

. . . thousands of girls followed the boys from camp to camp in the hopes of pursuing a relationship. Concerned at the number of 'camp followers' attending the dances at one American Air Force base in Hertfordshire, the American Red Cross decided to protect their homesick servicemen by making arrangements with the local Women's Voluntary Service. All the girls were hand picked . . . Stories of Canadian and American servicemen being dragged into doorways by sex-starved British girls became part of popular mythology . . . To a great many women who fell under the spell of these North American visitors, the future looked bright indeed, an opportunity to escape from the dismal, shabby, bomb-blasted island of their birth . . .[5]

Ben loses sight of the fact that when the war began and British men went overseas many future war brides were (by the standards of the time) considered too young to date so therefore had nobody to wait for. War brides were insulted by the implication they were "camp followers", or "good time girls", or that they married to escape the "dismal, shabby, bomb-blasted island of their birth . . . " (and by a fellow Brit at that). They strongly objected to the suggestion that their primary reason for marrying was to better their living standards, when they had to deal with saying goodbye to everything they loved: family, home, and country. After Ben came to live in Canada he attended a war bride reunion where he met genuine war brides and he wrote *Promise You'll Take Care of my Daughter*, a much more balanced view.

The disapproval lives on in Britain. My daughter ran into a problem when trying to photograph the old RCAF Headquarters in Lincoln's Inn Fields "for a book my mother is writing on Canada's war brides." The guard interrupted:

Oh them war brides, they chased the Canadians all over England!

Jane attempted to say, "my mother was not like that", but he would neither listen nor let her pass.

War brides were certainly unprepared for shouts of "Go back where you came from" that greeted some of us as we stepped ashore at Halifax, and "Where do you think you are going to live?", a reference to the housing shortage. These attitudes made many of us uncomfortable with the term "war bride" (that it also sounded like "mail-order bride" didn't help one bit). How true are Patrick White's words, "War has always been against the marriages it makes." You wonder how Birks (the Canadian jewellers) managed to sell engagement and wedding rings to servicemen overseas (even offering to take care of the shipping) without losing some of their Canadian customers.[6]

It happened quite frequently in the first half of the twentieth century that a man would meet a young woman and know (or make up his mind immediately) that she was the one he would marry. In the less mobile society of pre-war Britain an outsider must have seemed particularly fascinating. My father came home from World War I, met my mother, and that night told his brother he had met his future wife. Many Canadians seem to have shared his insight.

George Kuhn was brought to the home of Margaret Innes in Bailleston, Scotland by her cousin Jim. Jim later told her that George had said, "I'm going to marry that girl." And he did. Margaret (Innes) Kuhn lives in Medicine Hat, Alberta.

Arthur Fussell went to a supper dance with a friend and saw Nancy Etches waiting on tables, "flitting about like a butterfly, flirting with all the servicemen." "That's the girl I'm going to marry," he said. He was twenty and had been in England for a week. A month later, Arthur and Nancy were engaged. There was a pause while he became a fully-fledged air-gunner and began his tour of operations over Germany:

We wrote to each other every other day and enjoyed a few 48 hour passes together. It was in the blackout, in the doorway of a funeral parlour, where Arthur placed a small ring on my finger. At the time I did not think it was meant to be an engagement ring. I think due to the fact that we never knew if he would return from a bombing raid, or if I would be hurt or killed, we decided to get married.

Nancy came from Bournemouth, Hampshire to Delta, British Columbia.

Some didn't say right away, "That's the girl I'm going to marry," but it must have been uppermost in their minds, judging by the speed of their courtships. Audrey Rosebush had known her Canadian husband for ten days when they were married. An impossible start to a relationship some would say, but years later she was able to look back and say, "I was one of the lucky ones." [7]

Brenda (Burtenshaw) Butt of Foster, Quebec, wrote "I must be the only war bride who met her husband June 11, 1944 and married him July 7, 1944," but of course she was beaten by Audrey Rosebush. The important thing here is not the swiftness of the courtship but the fact that most brides and grooms of the time regarded their marriage vows as lifetime commitments. And of course there was another factor. Mae (Jarrett) McKenzie of Qualicum Beach says it all:

If you believe in love at first sight that is what happened to us!

War made us distressingly aware that we were missing the natural sequence of marriage, home, children, and grandchildren. John Windsor, a twenty-one-year-old officer in the 2nd Armoured Regiment (Strathcona Horse), and graduate of Kingston's Royal Military College, Ontario had not been in England very long when he met his future wife Pam who was in the ATS:

Our original intention was to be married after the war which we felt must soon end, but summer turned into winter and peace seemed further away than ever. If the Allies were prepared to wait I wasn't. [8]

John's war memoir *Blind Date* was the first book published by his friend, Gray Campbell in 1962. The title, chosen by Gray's war bride wife Eleanor, refers to John's war injury which happened after his marriage. It involved surgical removal of both of his eyes.

The British have a well-earned reputation for being reserved, but if they know you well enough, or strongly disapprove of something, they do not mince words. Mavis (Howick) Granger wrote from White Rock, British Columbia:

People would say to my parents, 'How can you let her marry a wild Canadian and go so far from home?' My father said, 'It's her life, she is capable of working and her savings are sufficient to bring her home if she ever needs us'.

Nancy (King) Rioux of Plaster Rock, New Brunswick showed her mother the ring Ivan Rioux had given her:

My mother started crying and predicting all the awful things that could go wrong. When we married my mother's comment was that the only good thing about it was that Ivan was Catholic. And at Christmastime 1943, when he was sent back to Canada with only three days warning, my mother said 'You will never see *him* again!' Three weeks later I got a letter from Canada House to go for a medical, prior to leaving for Canada, and when I saw the look on her face and the tears in her eyes I realized (her anxiety) was because she loved me and feared for me.

Aunts seem to have been particularly disapproving, either in their comments, or by their silence. Joni (Jones) Shuttleworth, who lives in Qualicum Beach, British Columbia was shocked because one of her aunts, on hearing she was marrying a Canadian, never spoke to her again! And Marion (Oliffe) Kirkpatrick (later Donnelly) of Parksville, British Columbia told me:

My father's eldest sister was horrified that my mother would allow one of her daughters to marry a 'Colonial'.

Patricia (Jepp) Smith, of Surrey, British Columbia received advice from several maiden aunts:

They said I should not be so foolish as to marry so young, and to a Canadian! My boss was not pleased that I would be, in her opinion, wasting my hairdressing apprenticeship just when I was beginning to earn good money. One pound a week!

My own aunt put it another way. I overheard:

What on earth would a Canadian see in Eswyn?

But a friend of my father's was more tactful. All he said was:

There won't be any nice girls left by the time our English boys get home.

The charming French-Canadian flier who attempted to ice-dance with Brenda (Clapham) Carriere while wearing hockey skates, was one of the lucky Canadians sent home on leave while the war was on:

When John came back from Canada he did not seem so eager to be married. I thought maybe he had met someone. Later I realised he was really worried about how I would adapt to life in French Canada. He had not realised until he went back how much *he* had changed during his time in England. His family was extremely Catholic and considered marriage to a Protestant a disaster. Our wedding night, spent in London was accompanied by air raid sirens and the noises of Hitler's pilotless robot planes (V1s), and anti-aircraft guns, but we didn't care.

Some Canadians observed the convention of asking the girl's father for permission to marry his daughter. Joyce (Ing) O'Donnell of Vernon, Ontario told me:

> When Joe asked my father's permission for us to be married he agreed, as long as we waited 'til the fighting ceased. We were both very young. Joe celebrated his 18th birthday in England in 1942, and I was three months younger. Joe was wounded in the Normandy campaign and mentioned in dispatches. We were married three months after D-Day.

Hazel (Pausey) Demkin, wrote from Val Caron, Ontario that her husband did all the conventional things:

> When Albert asked my father for my hand in marriage, my father asked what he had in Canada for me. His reply: 'I don't even have a lean-to to keep the rain off her.' Dad said: 'At least you're honest, you have my permission.'

Lloyd Snider was one of three brothers who went overseas and returned with British wives. This was quite a compliment to their English-born mother. Lloyd's wife, Marie-Louise (Newry) Snider wrote from Vancouver, British Columbia:

> Lloyd had applied to his CO for permission to marry, the Canadian padre had come to the house and interviewed me to make sure all was in order and I was not already married and, I gathered, acceptable. Papers completed and nearing the date, we suddenly realized that we hadn't received the permission. Lloyd found that his CO had landed in hospital and the papers were locked in his office safe. Eventually all was sorted out and we were married July 24, 1943.

Bill and I were also married in 1943, the war year writer Elizabeth Bowen termed "the lightless middle of the tunnel". It still did not seem as if we would lose the war, yet no one could predict how long it would take to win it, or what kind of shape we would be in when we did. It was one of the quietest years of the war for air raids, yet Angus Calder writes in *The People's War* that there was hardly a 24-hour period without at least one air raid somewhere in Britain.

Before the wedding my groom and his best man stayed overnight at Mrs. Tooze's guest house in Aldwick village. I'm sure she showed them, as she did every new arrival, the cigarette burn inflicted on a piece of her furniture by an earlier guest, film star Ronald Coleman. Cigarette burn or no, it turned out later that the groom understood that the best man had paid for the accommodation, and the best man understood . . . fortunately my father discovered the omission and made it right.

According to a letter I wrote to my mother-in-law, our wedding day started off with rain, but the sun came out in time for the 11 am ceremony at St. Richard's, my parish church. My mother-in-law, bless her, kept that letter and also the one my mother wrote several days later in which she said:

> Of course we couldn't have things as we would have done in peace time but Bill and Eswyn seemed too thoroughly happy to mind . . . Bill did not know until the previous Wednesday whether he was certain to get leave . . . I think the whole village turned up at the church and if good wishes count for anything they should be among the happiest

couples on earth, for I have had streams of people asking me to pass on their wishes for their happiness . . . both Bill and Eswyn looked radiantly happy; it did one's heart good to see them. One instinctively felt that here was a couple that entered into the true spirit of the vows they were taking . . .

My gown was made of embossed white satin, the last yards on a carefully preserved roll of fabric that my mother charmed away from a Chichester shop where she had been a good pre-war customer. The groom outshone me anyway in his kilt, sporran, knee socks and Skean Dhu (an ornamental dagger in a sheath, worn tucked into the knee sock). There were only eighteen people at the reception, so many friends being in the services or unable to travel. Bill did not have any relatives in attendance of course. His best man was an army friend. Among my family was the aunt who some weeks earlier had wondered what a Canadian could possibly see in Eswyn!

The guests soon split into two groups, the drinkers in one room, the teetotalers in another. My father trotted back and forth bearing his contribution to the feast, a dish of prunes he had marinated in gin. Whenever a guest was brave enough to try one he did the same. Soon even the non-drinkers were aglow, and my father had to be persuaded to lie down for a while.

He was particularly proud of his other contribution to the reception. My mother had baked a traditional if very small fruitcake but only granulated sugar was available for the icing. A family friend volunteered to make what she called American Boiled Icing. This involved beating the sugar with a precious egg white in a bowl over boiling water. I

Wedding party, August 21, 1943, St. Richard's Church, Aldwick, Sussex. From left to right: Stanley Ellinor, Sally Jennings, CSM Bill Lyster, Eswyn Lyster, Coral Ellinor and Sgt. R. L. MacDonald.
Credit: author's collection

forget who donated the egg from their weekly ration. We watched as the friend furiously turned the wheel of the beater and the mixture thickened. Suddenly it turned a light shade of brown and set solid with the beater standing upright in the middle. My mother and the family friend dissolved into tears but my father said, "All is not lost." Somehow he obtained more sugar, but my mother was not pacified. "It's LUMP sugar," she complained. "Leave it to me, dear," he said. He had inherited a mortar and pestle from his father, a dispensing chemist, and for the next few days spent every available minute pounding those sugar lumps into icing sugar, so that the cake received its traditional topping. For the rest of the war my father sweetened his tea with brown chips of American Boiled Icing.

My going-away outfit was a tailored two-piece suit in very fine checks, incorporating many colours. The shoes decided the accessories. They had been the only possibles in the shop, green suede and a size too big, so they were stuffed with tissue paper. My handbag was concocted from strips cut from an old green leather jacket, reversed to the "suede" side, woven together and stitched. My hat was an old one of my mother's steamed over various bowls and other objects into what I fondly imagined was a more flattering shape. We honeymooned in London, enjoying theatre productions that were interrupted by announcements of imminent air raids. We were oh-so-young, and the bombs didn't worry us at all.

These weddings were a triumph of happiness over day-to-day stresses, miseries and tragedies. I think that's why "the whole village" turned up at ours. Something happy was too good to miss. After the honeymoon we both returned to our units and tried not to think of what could happen before the war was over.

Barbara (Bishop) Warner wearing her Mamie Eisenhower wedding outfit.
Credit: Barbara (Bishop) Warner

Rosemary (Jefferies) Bauchman, of Victoria, British Columbia commented:

I found my life was full of immediacies. I didn't give much thought to a future in a new land. Few tempted fate by making plans for the future. The here and now was all we had.

Barbara (Bishop) Warner was one who did not particularly want to be married in her ATS uniform. She heard about the wedding gowns that Mamie Eisenhower, had sent to London specifically for those who would otherwise have to wear a uniform:

I sent my sizes, etc., and everything for my day arrived by special courier, dress, orange blossom headdress, satin shoes, gloves, even a spray of heather on a heart. Everything fitted perfectly and the style was just me! I had asked for no frills. This all had to be returned for the next lucky person, truly a wartime wedding.

68

Many girls did not want to be married in uniform, others were proud to wear one. White gowns often were crafted from parachute silk or loaned by a married friend.

Winifred (Morteal) McKinley of Victoria, British Columbia recalls:

> I borrowed my friend Joan's wedding dress (my going-away clothes were bought on the Black Market for a high price). Joan was my bridesmaid. She borrowed the dress *her* bridesmaid had worn.

In this instance it was lucky that the wearers were the same size. Often the sole criteria for choosing a bridesmaid was: "did she fit an available dress?" One wartime bride had six bridesmaids, each dress quite different from the others having started life at six other weddings.

It was a given that the bridegroom's family would be absent, but occasionally even the bride's relatives could not attend. When WAAF Eileen (Powell) Dallas, who now lives in West Vancouver, British Columbia was married in April 1944 special pre-D-Day restrictions were in place. RAF Station St. David's near Pembroke, Wales, was within a coastal area banned to non-residents, so this meant that Eileen's family could not attend her wedding. Instead RAF and WAAF friends became "family":

> On the day the Cathedral was packed. I was given away by the Squadron Leader and an Air Force friend played the organ.

Margaret (Clarke) Nagy of Ontario said that her husband Alan had no trouble getting permission to be married. But their conflicting religions posed a problem:

> I was not a Roman Catholic and Alan was. The one RC Chaplain would not give us his blessing. Instead we were married at the Whitchurch Registry Office. Our wedding was very ecumenical: Bob, the best man, was Jewish, the bridegroom was Roman Catholic, the bride Church of England and the bridesmaid Chapel! It was Thursday, August 16, 1945, the day Japan surrendered.

Linda Pfeiffer wrote from Waverley, Nova Scotia about her parents:

> My father, Frank Kenwood, joined the air force on his 18th birthday. He met my mother, WAAF Winnifred Woods at Digby, Lincolnshire air base. She was a radio operator and their romance escalated with sweet nothings over the airwaves. Dad piloted a Spitfire, and Mom led him home on occasion. They married in January 1942 and moved into a windmill until Dad was posted to Africa. Before he left my mother was in hospital to have her appendix removed. He said goodbye to her in her hospital bed, and she promised to wait for him. Then he was shipped to Egypt. After being shot down over Africa he was flown across the Mediterranean to Greece, sent by train across Europe, through Yugoslavia and Austria, and spent two years and eight months in a POW camp. Upon his return to England in 1945 he learned my mother was in hospital again. He strode into her ward, located her bed, smiled down at her and said, 'You said you would wait for me but I didn't expect you to wait in the same place I left you . . . ' When they were married Dad wrote in the marriage registry under 'Profession', 'Truck driver'. It wasn't until she landed in Canada that Mom learned that her father-in-law owned one of the largest moving and storage companies in Quebec. This young girl of nineteen had no idea she would end up the wife

of a successful president of his own company, rather than the wife of a long-distance truck driver. My parents attended European business conventions and would be away for five or six weeks every year. They even attended one in Munich, which I know was difficult. It was the first time Dad had been in Germany since he was their guest during the war. Mom didn't join any English Clubs or groups. She assimilated quickly, lost her accent (although she could sure put one on in a hurry when she wanted!) and became totally Canadian.

When Patricia Anne Bourke and Robert Risley were married in Bramley, Surrey in May 1941, she says HQ staff of the Canadian Division "were delighted at the thought of a wedding to alleviate the boredom of life in Aldershot":

I had a wonderful letter from General Odlum congratulating me on my choice of husband! Their wedding gift was a silver tray engraved with all their names, which I treasure, and they organized the entire wedding and paid for it, which pleased my mother as we did not have much money or space. We were piped out of the church under a guard of honour. The reception was at Bramley Grange Hotel, opposite the church, and the telegrams were very funny. My husband made a very good speech ending with a toast to my mother. We honeymooned at Portmerion in Wales, a wonderful place. The weather was good and Noël Coward was staying there. They made their own beer which Robert raved about. It was the most wonderful wedding and could not have been better in peacetime, thanks to the Canadian army.

Anne lives in Halifax, Nova Scotia.

An estimated 200 British war brides joined the Royal Canadian Air Force, WD (Women's Division) many reasoning that they could learn more about Canada and their future neighbors in this way.[9]

Sometimes the road to the wedding was a long and difficult one. Florence (Leggat) Cooper married an Englishman in 1935, and had two children:

My first husband was aggressive, suspicious and jealous, all the wrong ingredients for a good marriage. He was called up and I worked at the Ever Ready Battery Company in Stoke Newington. In 1941 my marriage broke down and after a terrible fight I left, taking the children with me. The first night we slept in the Tube Station. My suitcase was stolen and it took some time to replenish the contents due to rationing. I had to wash and dry my clothes every day for a while. One day at work the baby sitter called. My husband and his mother had taken the children. I did not see them for three years. I then met Canadian Walter Cooper. We had a three-year courtship and I adored him. We wrote scores of letters some of which I have today. I decided to gain my freedom. At the hearing I saw my children but they had been instructed not to speak to me. I was given an ultimatum about the children, and decided this was the way it had to be. I was deeply in love with Walter and I put him first, something I have never regretted. We were married Christmas 1945 and spent Christmas 1946 with my family and our new little son. Walter and I sailed for Canada in February 1947 on the same ship, the *Aquitania*. I did not mind leaving England, too much heartache there for me.

In 1976 "by a miracle" Florence found her two lost children. In 1986, when Walter died, he and Florence had spent forty happy years together.

Catering the reception was always a problem. Joan (Fisher) Reichart of Nelson, British Columbia recalls her reception:

> It was a very modest affair, a few speeches, fewer toasts, and Spam sandwiches. We left on foot for the honeymoon: one night at a small private hotel. When we arrived they weren't expecting us - a slight oversight by the best man! Mine host, a very silent and serious man, obviously didn't think we were married, but eventually found us a room. After escorting us to our accommodation he intoned, with great solemnity, 'The WC is down one floor, but there is a chamber pot behind the screen.' This reduced me to repeated and most unromantic giggles.

A family friend of Jean Wilks drove Roy Elmer to their wedding. Roy told her later that this man actually stopped the car en route so that Roy could "escape" if he wanted:

> Our neighbours had a little cabin on the beach at Prestatyn, Wales and let us honeymoon there, so off we went loaded with a bag of tomatoes, a tin of Spam, dried eggs, bread and a bit of marge (margarine). As my husband used to say, we were as happy as if we were in our right minds. On the train home we noticed the streets were decorated with flags and bunting. Roy said in not too quiet a voice, 'Boy, you'd think the war was over!' The lone gent sitting across from us slowly lowered his paper. 'Where have you two been?' he said. 'On our honeymoon,' says Hubby, grinning from ear to ear. I turned five shades of red. It was VJ Day and we didn't even know it.

If the Scottish girl in C.P. Stacy's "famous first marriage" was Canada's first World War II war bride, then Norma (Freeman) Jefferies must surely have been the last, and the last one to come to Canada. She met Norman Jefferies (Jeff), a senior NCO at RCAF Administrative HQ, Lincoln's Inn Fields, when her older sisters took her dancing at Covent Garden. Unlike other war brides there was to be a very long delay between meeting and marriage. Norma required her mother's consent to be married, but Mrs. Freeman was adamantly opposed to the match. Jeff made many unsuccessful attempts to change her mind, but eventually he and Norma parted. That was 1943.

Norma went on to a successful career with a merchant bank, but she never forgot Jeff and never married. Jeff married a Canadian girl serving in the RCAF (WD) who was stationed at the Lincoln's Inn Fields office. They returned to Canada, raised a family and Jeff pursued a career with the RCAF. Four days after their 40th wedding anniversary Jeff's wife died and he was inconsolable.

Jeff's family knew of Norma, his wartime love, and when he was slow to come out of his depression they suggested he try to get in touch with her. He thought the suggestion ludicrous. He pictured Norma married, with a family; hearing from him would be an embarrassment. Eventually at a friend's urging he placed a call to the house where he had last seen her. Norma happened to be there and, shaken by the call, she said "No, not you! I still carry your picture in my wallet," and they talked for twenty minutes. Jeff learned she had never married. He promised to phone next day but when he did Norma's phone was off the hook and remained so. Jeff then wrote a very long letter saying all the things he would have said on the phone. When Norma received the letter she replaced the phone.

Many calls and letters later Jeff flew to England where he and Norma were married on March 12, 1986. Norma flew to Canada with Jeff at her side. No seasickness, no tears of homesickness, just the happy completion of something that seemed intended to be. How do I know? Norma and Jeff live in Qualicum Beach just a short distance from my home.

With marriage the die was cast. No turning back now, except for a quirky few who had never intended to move to Canada in the first place, and some inexperienced girls who, when push came to shove, found they could not leave their homes. Those who had been in the services or had attended boarding schools had the edge. For us, leaving one home and finding another among strangers would not be quite so difficult.

Ethel and John Tryon, April 26, 1944, with a Land Army Guard of Honour outside St. John's Church, Blackpool (see page 27).
Credit: Ethel (Cunliffe) Tryon

Rodney and Nora Williams, April 7, 1945, Norton, Durham.
Credit: Nora (Booth) Williams

Anyone who lived in the Park (Windsor Great Park) was able to be christened at the Royal Chapel . . . I had my son christened at the dear little Chapel.

Florence (Hayzen) Phillips

The alternative to a home birth and a midwife, if you could afford it, was a private nursing home, and it was a standing joke that to get a bed you had to book ten months in advance.

the author

Linda Anderson, the daughter of Doris (Winton) and Jack Anderson, wore a very special gown for her Ottawa christening.

the author

Coral Ellinor and grandson Terry, Bognor Regis, Sussex, 1944.
Credit: author's collection

74

Chapter 6: Curity® Diapers and Johnson's® Baby Powder

Approximately 21,500 children were born to British war brides before they left for Canada. The best calculations suggest that 20,997 of them made the journey to Canada. These children had suffered many traumatizing events, sometimes coming into the world to the sound of sirens and exploding bombs. Pamela (Munn) Pittaway of Southwick, Sussex and Gwendoline (Harms) Keele, Thornton Heath, Surrey were two of many war brides who gave birth during heavy air raids.

Much has been written of British civilians who could "take it", but little about the cumulative effect on them of nearly six years of war. It is generally agreed that by 1945 sleep deprivation was affecting most British civilians. The Flying Bombs (V1s) were particularly bad. They flew just above the rooftops, putt-putting along until their fuel ran out, then they crashed to earth. At night, every time you put your head back on the pillow you imagined you could hear yet another one approaching.

Babies are said to pick up on the anxieties of their mothers, but we must have been raising a particularly stable group of babies. They slept well, smiled a lot, and seemed as bonny as those born in happier times, but undoubtedly some did suffer long-term effects.

A benevolent government issued bottled orange juice (or vitamin-rich rose hip syrup) for our infants as well as an extra milk ration, and they thrived on that good old British standby, cod liver oil.

There seemed to be no shortage of formula when Terry was born in 1944. It must have been one of the food items for which we could thank Canada and the United States. The thousands of parcels sent by generous Canadian grandparents-to-be brought us baby cereal, Johnson's Baby Powder and lengths of white flannelette.

Linda, the overseas-born daughter of Doris (Winton) Anderson, wore a very special gown for her Ottawa christening. It was sewn by her grandmother from parachute fabric brought to Canada by Linda's father Jack. While serving with the RCAF in Peschici, Italy Jack headed a mission to rescue a downed American flier. To show his gratitude the airman presented Jack with the parachute that had saved his life.

Hospital births were unusual in Britain, especially in wartime when beds were reserved for casualties and the critically ill. It had long been the custom to have home births supervised by a registered midwife. The alternative to a home birth, if you could afford it, was a private nursing home, and it was a standing joke that these beds were so scarce you had to book them ten months in advance. I know of one case in Sussex where a war bride's child was delivered by the Medical Officer of a well-known Canadian regiment.

Hospitals were often targets for German bombs. The maternity ward in one of these was rebuilt with donations from Canada. When Queen Elizabeth visited the ward she spoke to a war bride mother about her North American trip with the King in 1939 saying, "You will love Canada. It is a wonderful country."

Wartime babies were prepared for in "make-do-and-mend" fashion. Laundry baskets were made into cradles, baby spoons and rattles recycled from previous generations. The

Canadian Red Cross supplied Canadian-made layettes if they were needed. We loved the Curity diapers from Canada, but couldn't quite see how they would replace the bulky terry cloth squares we used at the time. Baby powder was diverted for our own use, talcum powder being one more casualty of war. Our excuse was that British babies were not used to it. Most of us stoutly ignored our mother's advice to cover a large English penny with sticking plaster and secure it over the baby's navel with a tight belly binder. We said it was "old-fashioned" while our mothers said it prevented protruding belly buttons. They were disturbed, as mothers always are, by the ideas of the next generation. When we suggested that belly-binding was a probable cause of digestive problems our mothers countered with "What do you think Gripe Water is for?"

The son of Florence (Hayzen) Phillips, was baptized in a special place:

> One of my best friends lived in Windsor Great Park where her husband was a gamekeeper. When I was expecting my first son she asked me to stay with her. Anyone that lived in the Park could be christened at the Royal Chapel. My son, Raymond, arrived in March 1944 so I had him christened at the dear little Chapel.

Joan (Palfrey) Montgomery, Edmonton, Alberta and Rosina (Simpson) Husband had special accommodation for the 1944 births of their babies. Joan was escorted to a large private estate near Tunbridge Wells:

> It had been converted to a military facility solely for the benefit of servicemen's families, supposedly away from the buzz-bombs. We had excellent attention and stayed for three weeks before being released for home.

Rosina's experience was similar:

> Our daughter was born in Wellesley Castle in Derbyshire. A month before the babies were due they figured we should get away from the Buzz Bombs and rockets in London, so we were taken to the Castle.

Olive (Rayson) Cochrane, who also had her baby at a country Manor House, kept a diary for 1944. The book is small, the entries necessarily brief. In January Olive is working at ICI (Imperial Chemical Industries) in the daytime and fire-watching two nights a week. On the 19th she pays duty on five pairs of silk stockings, a gift from her father-in-law in Canada. On the 20th she records two heavy air raids, then for a time the raids are background to other events.

Olive and her husband, Lloyd, exchange daily letters. In March Olive's doctor confirms she is pregnant. The raids and the fire-watching continue and by May she has some minor problems connected with pregnancy. Iron pills are prescribed.

Olive (Rayson) Cochrane in 1944. She came to Canada in 1946.
Credit: Michelle Rusk

EXCERPTS FROM OLIVE'S DIARY

June 6 DAWN, INVASION STARTED, KING SPOKE. Going well. Letter to Lloyd.

On June 16, and for seventeen consecutive days, the entries read: 'Buzz Bomb raids, 'or 'Very bad raids'. Pregnancy, the wartime diet, Lloyd's as yet unconfirmed participation in the Invasion, & the new terror weapons, result in stress problems.

June 26 Toothache . . . First night sleep in shelter.

On July 1 Olive has an abscessed tooth removed, and the consumption of a 'new laid egg' warrants an entry.

July 2   Lloyd in France.
July 4   No letter. Nearly lost baby.
July 5   No letter. (none until the 18th)
July 7   Still in danger of losing baby. In bed.

By July 12 Olive is on a rest holiday in Wales.

July 18 Letter from Lloyd.
July 29 Finchley now evacuation area.
Aug 1   Bad raids.

Aug 5   Rotten pain. (Still in Wales.)
Aug 9   Home at 2 pm.
Aug 11 Saw doctor. I'm OK.

On the 12th Olive saw the film *This Happy Breed* at the local Odeon.

Aug 14 (and for the next seven days) Raids.
Sep 14 Paid £13 for trunk and case (for her journey to Canada).
Sep 18 Two French cards in German envelope from Lloyd who is in Belgium.
Oct 6   Car convoy to Oxford. At Manor House. (Olive has been evacuated for
        the delivery of her baby.)
Oct 13 (a Friday) Fed up.
Oct 25 Pains again.

The next two days Olive reports 'High blood pressure'. After more days of pain
Olive goes into a three-day labour.

Nov 2   Paul born 3:30 pm. Egg.

On November 19 Olive dresses for the first time. By December 11 she is home and taking Paul, now 9 lbs, to the baby clinic. November 10 and 12 "bad raids". Lloyd's letters are arriving in clumps. Mail, although recognized as essential to military and civilian morale, had to take its turn in the organized confusion of post-D-Day Channel shipping. Correspondents numbered envelopes so the letters could be read in sequence. For the rest of the month Olive is busy with Paul. There are no entries for Christmas week. Presumably Olive, Paul and his grandmother spent a quiet Christmas together.

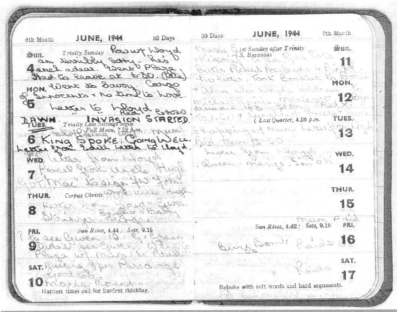

Olive Cochrane's diary with entry for D-Day.
Credit: Olive's daughter, Michelle Rusk

78

War brides and children wait.
(Large maple leaf pin courtesy of Mary Rand)
Credit: Basil Fox

. . . everybody knew that something was up, but nobody said a word.
    Patricia Risley

Early this morning the Allies began the assault on Hitler's European fortress.
    BBC Radio, June 6, 1944

Soldiers, Sailors and Airmen of the Allied Expeditionary Forces: You are about to embark upon the Great Crusade towards which we have striven these many months. The eyes of the world are upon you. The hopes and prayers of liberty-loving people everywhere march with you. . . . Good luck! And let us all beseech the blessing of Almighty God upon this great and noble undertaking.
    General Dwight D. Eisenhower, June 6, 1944 [1]

A Canadian soldier inspects a captured V2 rocket.
Credit: Pictorial History of the Canadians at War (1947)

Chapter 7: On to Victory:
D-Day and Ever Present Dangers

In April 1944, a strip ten-miles deep along the coast of England, from the Thames Estuary to Lands End, was declared out of bounds to anyone but residents and the military. Those attempting to come into the area without written permission were turned back by the police. This was the first indication that something big was about to happen.

Hitler had one of his most capable commanders, Field Marshal Erwin Rommel, in charge of German forces in northern France. On June 3, persuaded by the extremely poor weather conditions that there was no possibility of an Allied attack, Rommel decided to drive to Berlin (by a quirk of fate his wife's fiftieth birthday was June 6). He took with him a birthday gift, said to have been a pair of French shoes.

Patricia (Bourke) Risley, of Halifax, Nova Scotia remembers the utmost secrecy surrounding the preparations for the invasion. She lived in Surrey:

> Convoy after convoy of military vehicles rumbled past the house and everybody knew that something was up, but nobody said a word. We didn't speculate or even voice our thoughts out loud.

D-Day, the opening of Operation Overlord, the invasion of German-occupied Europe, was about to take place. For several days in early June massed invasion craft hugged the coast of southern England. Delayed by gales and rough seas the Allied troops on the ships coped with the miseries of seasickness. At least the bad weather kept German reconnaissance planes away. Waiting Americans had time to remember the wisecrack that had greeted their arrival in England in 1942, "They're overpaid, over-sexed and over here!" and were now cheered by the answer that one among them dreamed up. "The British are underpaid, under-sexed and under Eisenhower!"

General Dwight D. Eisenhower had been appointed supreme commander of the Allied Expeditionary Force in charge of every man aboard the tossing boats. He was sequestered with his staff at his headquarters in Southwick House, near Portsmouth. Known to the Allied world as "Ike", he agonized over committing these men to a Channel crossing in such foul weather. The alternative was to miss the last suitable tides for months to come and the decision was his alone. Eisenhower reluctantly cancelled the landings for June 5. Later that night his thoughts turned to the possibility of defeat. He pencilled a note to read, just in case:

> Our landings in the Cherbourg – Harvre (sic) area have failed to gain a satisfactory foothold and I have withdrawn the troops. My decision to attack at this time and place was based upon the best information available. The troops, the air (sic) and the Navy did all that Bravery and devotion to duty could do. If any blame or fault attaches to the attempt it is mine alone.[2]

The evidence of Eisenhower's fatigue and strain is in the omissions (the "Le" in Le Harvre, etc.). A few hours later word came that the weather would clear for a short period on June 6. Ike gave the word. Operation Overlord was "on" for the 6th. (The pencilled note remained, forgotten, in Eisenhower's pocket and was not discovered until several days later.)

In the very early morning hours of June 6 residents of southern England were awakened by the constant drone of aircraft flying low and flying south. When I pulled aside my bedroom blackout curtains I saw that each plane towed several gliders. The operation we had hoped for, yet deeply dreaded, had begun. No Dieppe raid this, but an invasion in strength designed to get a permanent foothold in Normandy and go forward from there. Next morning the BBC announced:

> Under the command of General Eisenhower, Allied naval forces supported by strong air forces began landing Allied armies this morning on the northern coast of France.

By nightfall it was evident that the Allies were in France to stay. To the British Ike was the hero of the decade, the man who could bring together the prima donna personalities of the generals who served under him. (With the possible exception of the French General de Gaulle, that is.)

On D-Day Betty (Barber) Fouchard, WAAF, was on duty at Biggin Hill:

> I saw that the table in the Ops room showed the English Channel full of ships heading for France and our fighters above them for protection.

In Berlin Rommel had been chagrined to learn of the invasion and hurried back to France. There's no doubt that his actions added to Hitler's distrust and led to Rommel's eventual downfall.

Sheila Anketel-Jones wrote of D-Day:

> Suddenly everything changed. We had been aware it was coming, were aware of the tremendous build-up of personnel and equipment, and we had watched as the road convoys passed, continuously, for several days. They waved to us and we waved back, only too aware that many of them would not be coming back. Now the streets were deserted and for the next days we listened to the wireless (radio) and the only topic of conversation was 'the landings'. The war had moved into Europe and we could all go to bed and know that we could stay there all night.

Sheila's relief that at last we "could go to bed and stay there all night" was short-lived. Soon after D-Day the first of Hitler's promised "secret weapons" exploded in Southern England.

Molly (Gerrard) Schafer of Dawson Creek, British Columbia remembers the summer, fall and winter of 1944:

> One night we went to a show in Forest Hill. When we came out it looked like the whole of London was alight. We sheltered until the early hours and then walked home. A Doodle Bug had fallen in our back yard and a fire bomb had come down our chimney into the fireplace. Our house and lots of houses around were badly damaged. We had a big plum tree and it was blown sky high, boughs were on roofs in the next street.

At Biggin Hill, Betty (Barber) Fouchard was beneath the flight path of Flying Bombs as they headed for London:

They were launched from France and Holland and we had several crash near us. Enough to shake us up - lots of broken glass, but no injuries.

V1 TERROR WEAPON
(also called Flying Bomb, Buzz Bomb or Doodle-Bug)

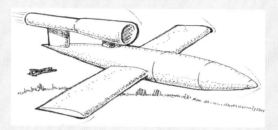

From June 13, 1944 to March 1945, 9,300 V1 pilot-less planes (or large bombs with wings) fell on Southern England. They were launched from German bases in occupied France and Holland. The V1 was powered by a small amount of inferior fuel that caused the distinct and nerve-wracking "motor cycle in bad need of a tune-up" effect. The engine was programmed to cut out when it reached its target (London). However many fell on Kent, Surrey and Sussex. If you happened to be underneath one of the fixed trajectories (which unfortunately Aldwick was) V1s came overhead at intervals, day and night, in good weather and bad. The unfortunate people on the ground lost sleep, concentration and eventually much of the optimism they had clung to for so long. The sputtering sound gave the impression the fuel was about to be exhausted even if it wasn't. Putting your head on the pillow at night produced muffled sounds that were ignored in less hazardous times, but during the ordeal you *had* to raise your head to determine whether another bomb was on its way.

The "V" in V1 and V2 is from "Vergeltungswaffe" for "vengeance weapon".

Rosemary (Jeffries) Bauchman was a WAAF Sergeant in 1944. Not long after her honeymoon she had some bad news:

I received a card from a hospital in Ashford, Kent, baldly stating that my husband was there with head injuries. My commanding officer made enquiries and we learned that Perry had been injured in an aircraft accident. I was given a 48-hour pass and went by train through bomb-ravaged London. The train inexplicably stopped between stations, we heard a deafening explosion and we then moved slowly forward. We halted again and again as workers frantically cleared debris from the track. The driver had seen the flying bomb and stopped. One of those close calls. Perry couldn't recall the details of his crash. One moment he had been flying, the next he found himself in hospital. It appeared he had crashed on landing and bashed his head on the gunsight. How two fingers got crushed he never knew.

Olive (Risley) May from Ilford, Essex met her future husband George not long after D-Day at her sister Lily's Dorking, Surrey home. On the night of June 24, just after Olive returned to Essex, a direct hit from a Flying Bomb demolished Lily's 300-year-old house. Three people managed to crawl from the wreckage but Olive's eldest sister Lily, 30, her sister-in-law Irene, 28 and little Royston, Olive's 18-month-old nephew, were all killed. Her sister Joan, who emigrated to Canada in the 1950s, suffered a painful back injury. When I spoke to Joan recently she recalled that terrible night as if it was last week.

V2 TERROR WEAPON

The V2 rocket was the world's first operational ballistic missile. No warning could be given of its approach because it travelled faster than the speed of sound. One rocket could vaporize buildings at the point of impact and demolish 40 or 50 more. Between September 8, 1944 and March 27, 1945, 1054 V2s fell on British soil, mostly on London.[3] At first these horrors were dubbed "Flying Gas Mains", because they were mistaken for violent gas explosions caused by regular bombs. By the time Londoners realised that they were dealing with a new terror weapon they had been through too much for too long and no nicknames were forthcoming.

The last V2 fell on London's Tottenham Court Road and suddenly it was late April 1945, and we knew that in a matter of days the war would be over.

On April 23, 1945 Bill Lyster, by now promoted to Captain, was riding in a small armoured car with his driver, Leonard Pepper, through the Reichwold Forest in Germany. They were returning from the Calgary Highlanders' battalion HQ to the front line when they were ambushed by German snipers hiding in a ditch. Years later Bill described the events to historian David Bercuson:

> I went to get my Sten gun up and it had fallen out of my hand. I looked at Pepper and he was out cold. All I had was a pistol on my right hand side that I couldn't get my hand on. I took off out of that carrier and landed on two Germans. That's all I remember.[4]

The noise attracted fellow Calgary Highlanders to the scene. They arrived to find Bill delirious, and Leonard Pepper unconscious from what were later determined to be superficial head wounds. Bill was rushed to a forward medical station where a tag was tied to his big toe signifying that he was not expected to survive. The regimental padre,

The Rev. Charles P. Bishop, arrived and stayed all night beside Bill's stretcher. Next morning the tag was removed. Bill always credited Charles with saving his life.

I received one of those dreaded telegrams with the line "regret to inform you . . ." followed by Bill's name and "sustained gunshot wounds to left chest and right shoulder, presently in hospital". My father and I, knowing that wartime telegrams were sometimes garbled, concentrated on the word "presently", giving it the English meaning of "some time in the future". The war was just about over by the time Bill was evacuated to the Canadian Military Hospital, Horsham, Sussex. When we visited him he was lucid and cheerful, but running a high fever and it was obvious he had been seriously wounded.

Although Bill's injuries affected the rest of his life, he lived until December, 1996.

Bill Lyster aboard the hospital ship, *El Nil*, taking him home to Canada, 1945.
Credit: author's collection

My Bonnie lies over the ocean, my Bonnie lies over the sea . . .
>   Telegram sent by Jack Anderson, repatriated RCAF pilot to his MLA protesting the delay in his wife's arrival in Canada

Once the open sea is reached we forget how we clung to the pilot in the storm.
>   Harold Nicholson, on Churchill being voted out of office

I could hardly accept His Majesty's offer of the Garter when his people have given me the Order of the Boot.
>   Winston Churchill, on turning down the Order of the Garter

Civilians and Allied troops of many nations celebrate VE Day, Piccadilly Circus, May 8, 1945.
Credit: Terry Lyster

Chapter 8: The War in Europe Ends:
The Men Go Home, War Brides Wait

At the beginning of May I went to a movie with another war bride, Kay May, who had been widowed some months before. The movie stopped, the lights went up, and the Manager came on stage to announce that Germany had surrendered. I turned excitedly to Kay but she was staring straight ahead. "Sam will never come home now," was all that she said.

We endured a brief "Phoney Peace" while we waited for the official VE Day, (Victory in Europe Day) to be announced. Casualties were being reported until the last minute. Unlike the 1918 Armistice that could be so fully celebrated, there was still the war with Japan to be fought. We were deeply grateful but also deeply apprehensive.

   With foresight, King George VI had ordered the Buckingham Palace balcony to be repaired and reinforced. It had suffered some air raid damage but, on May 8, 1945, the official VE Day, there was no danger that Winston Churchill and the Royal Family might topple into the cheering crowds below. A family story from 1918 tells how my Grandmother Stuart, a seamstress, sat up all night finishing the outfit she wore to join in the London celebrations. In 1945 I was unable to follow her example of travelling to central London, but my cousins Jane and John Green were among the crowds outside Buckingham Palace with their Uncle Tommy, so family tradition was upheld:

> We danced in a conga line in Piccadilly Circus, then made our way through Admiralty Arch to Buckingham Palace. It was the atmosphere, even to a sixteen-year-old, that was beyond description - one of deliverance from Churchill's 'abyss' I suppose. My memories of London that day exclude Uncle Tommy and John, but they were there. VE Day was an unplanned explosion of rejoicing, men of the Empire's forces marching and bands playing. [1]

Bill was moved to the Canadian Military Hospital at Marston Green, Birmingham so I went there by train carrying Terry, a folding stroller and a heavy suitcase, only two of which could be moved at one time. At the hospital I encountered true ravages of war: men with single or double amputations, men blind or paralysed, some traumatized but without visible wounds. Bill returned to Canada on the hospital ship *El Nil* in July 1945.

   The immense task of repatriating servicemen to Canada began even before VE Day. As they arrived in England from Northwest Europe and elsewhere they reported to repatriation centres to await

Long-service chevrons worn near wrist.
Bottom is white for enlistment in 1939.
Red chevrons for each further year.
Credit: author's collection

passage. Those who had been away from Canada the longest had priority and those who volunteered to fight in Japan were given even greater precedence, and promised leave in Canada before embarking for the Far East. A few volunteers gambled that they would be first home, and the war with Japan would end before they could be shipped out, which of course is what happened. Most of the 82,474 Canadians were content to wait their turn. Despite overcrowding the ships with troops, the repatriation lasted until the end of January 1946. As we had been warned would happen, war brides waited. Janet (Petrie) Etches wrote of this period in her life:

> It was time for Jim to return to Canada and get a house for us. We had been living in England, and as I returned to Scotland I recalled over and over what he had confessed the night before. When we met he'd said his father was a World War I Lt-Colonel, his mother a teacher and he had a share in a business, all fabrication. I was now pregnant. I had made a commitment 'for better or for worse', I couldn't go back on that, neither did I want to. With God's help I went forward. Jim wrote that he had a house on Sea Island, British Columbia, obtained through the Veteran's Land Act. The lot measured an acre, and my father, used to much smaller pieces of land, said 'What on earth are you going to do with an acre?'

Whatever doubts Janet had about her naive young husband, he quickly matured once he was in civilian life.

Lily "Joni" Shuttleworth also found this transitional period extremely difficult:

> My mother became seriously ill and died the same morning that my husband left to rejoin his unit, prior to returning to Canada. He was refused an extension of leave. I will never forget Friday the 13th of July, 1945. I was devastated, and not feeling well. I had just discovered I was pregnant.

In Britain the promised post-war election was at hand. Churchill, realist that he was, mused "I have nothing to offer them now . . . " yet he dearly wanted a hand in shaping the post-war world. It was not to be. Returning British servicemen and women voted not so much against Churchill as against the old ruling classes he represented. The Labour Party came into power with a stinging majority. When Clementine Churchill, who wanted him to retire from politics, said that it was perhaps a blessing in disguise, Churchill replied that the blessing was certainly very effectively disguised.[2] I listened to the election results over the radio feeling strangely detached. Bill was in a military hospital in Canada and my thoughts were literally thousands of miles away. Churchill would serve his country again, but not until after war brides were settled in Canada. There were two more horrors to be endured. In August 1945 the atomic bombing of Hiroshima and Nagasaki caused Japan to surrender. It was difficult to accept that peace had to be bought at this horrendous price. But while I was struggling with my uninformed view, the late John Stroud of Ontario knew only too well what the atomic bombs meant to himself and thousands like him. He had landed with the Royal Rifles of Canada in Hong Kong in November, 1941 and all too soon was enduring the miseries of the Niigata POW camp. No war bride or light-hearted flirtations for Stroud or his fellow prisoners. For four long years they dealt with basic survival, and John's arithmetic was entirely different from mine. If Hiroshima had been clouded over, Niigata, where he was imprisoned, would have been the alternate target. If Japan had been invaded the Japanese were ordered to kill all prisoners-of-war. A land war in Japan would have caused multiple thousands of Allied and Japanese casualties. John estimated that however awful the two bombings were, the alternative would have been much worse.[3] John Stroud weighed 182 lb. when he was captured, 62 lb. when he was freed.[4]

I was at the Canadian Wives Bureau on the morning of VJ Day (Victory in Japan Day) finalizing my voyage to Canada. Afterwards, I walked to Victoria Station, aware that everyone else was going in the opposite direction, drawn to Buckingham Palace. Once again I missed out on the family tradition, but my mother was caring for Terry and anxious that I get home. When I did I "celebrated" by washing diapers!

A few war brides had been given passage during 1945, usually for pressing compassionate reasons. The rest waited impatiently as did GI brides. British newspapers shelved their often hostile attitude to all things American to publicize the "plight" of waiting American wives. Canadian war brides were stung that no column space was given to us when our situations were exactly the same. When rumours flew that the British-owned *Queen Mary I*, that had operated from New York throughout the war, would be available for GI brides, Canadian war brides marched on the Canadian Wives Bureau to protest. One who was part of the protest was Faith (Harley) McKinnon who came to Spring Valley, Prince Edward Island:

The author and son Terry outside Ellinor's Newsagency, Aldwick, Spring 1945. Victory flags and lack of stock in window tell all.
Credit: author's collection

I joined with other war brides and travelled to the Canadian Wives Bureau to see what was going on. They listened to my story of living in a two bedroom flat with my parents and three brothers coming out of the Services and I soon got my sailing orders.

When dedicated GI Bride and Canadian sailings are compared they began at about the same time: GI brides on January 26, 1946,[5] Canadian brides ten days later.

PARTING WORDS:
    Mother: "Write often."
    Father: "Chin up, keep smiling, and write often."
    Eighty-four-year-old friend of the family: "Eswyn will never see a grand piano!"
    The mother of one of my friends, who spent a few years in Winnipeg: "There's absolutely nothing west of Winnipeg."
    Young friend: "Send some nylons."
    Very young friend: "Will you be anywhere near Hollywood?"
        the author

    After starting to complete the forms Stevie had brought for me my sister and I burst into tears and Stevie destroyed them.
    Dorothy (Searle) Stephenson, Okotoks, Alberta

    I honestly cannot remember after all these years whether I fully understood the enormity of what I was doing. I only know that Grant was the person I wanted to marry. He never promised me a rose garden, just a warm family and a steady job to go back to.
    Nancy (Bennett) Sutherland, Milton, Ontario

Doorway to Canada: Sackville House, just around the corner from Piccadilly. The Canadian Wives Bureau was on an upper floor.
Credit: E. Jane Lyster

Chapter 9: Leaving Home

Saying goodbye when moving far away is difficult at any time, but in wartime the farewells were exceedingly stressful. Security demanded that only the war bride's parents be informed of the departure. Other relatives and friends had to be advised after the travellers had arrived on Canada's eastern shore. Crossing the Atlantic to live in the New World was almost equivalent to going to the moon. Jean Spear's experience was typical:

> The memory of my confused emotions so long ago still engulfs me. To hug a beloved grandfather and other family members without saying goodbye was heartbreaking . . . but worse was to come. My parents knew I was leaving and my father insisted on coming to Waterloo Station where he walked a few steps behind me. A woman in Red Cross uniform approached, called me by name and asked me to follow her. I took advantage of her back to turn and blow a kiss to my father. He stood and waved, a picture forever etched in my memory.

Even women who left after VE Day remember the shock of hearing from the Canadian Wives Bureau that they should be ready to leave within the next few days. Perhaps a month's notice would have been easier to deal with, but with so many dependents to be moved that just wasn't possible.

THE CANADIAN WIVES BUREAU

The Bureau was located at Sackville House, 40 Sackville Street, London, England. It was in existence from August 1944 until December 1947. In charge of the Civilian Repatriation Section (movement of the dependents of Canadian servicemen to Canada) was 34-year-old Major Victor Gill. He was assisted by ten officers, 12 stenographers and 35 clerks. In January 1945 the office was so busy that it was quite usual for the entire staff to work late, and often all day Sunday. A contemporary account noted that Major Gill had touches of grey around his temples. The report goes on to illustrate one of many possible reasons for the grey hair:

> It is decided that 800 wives, their children and their personal effects can be moved on such-and-such a date. Major Gill makes his plans accordingly. And then, perhaps three days before sailing, the ship is needed elsewhere to move troops and war supplies. A small ship is assigned to the Britain to Canada run and Major Gill's passenger quota drops from 800 to 400. Four hundred wives are then notified they will have to wait a while. And then perhaps next day the plans are changed again.

During this period pregnancy gave wives top priority, followed by "husbands discharged in Canada, and husbands hospitalized in Canada." Wives requiring medical treatment only available in Canada also had some priority. [1]

When notice did arrive there was a flurry of activity. There was a second-hand steamer trunk and a suitcase to pack and, if coupons allowed, a warm coat to buy. (If they could afford it mothers insisted on the latter even for a daughter travelling in August.) All traces of former ownership were removed from the trunk and the war bride's name and Canadian address applied in aluminum paint, usually by her father, (only he would call it "al-u-<u>mini</u>-um" paint). Why this was the paint of choice is unknown. Perhaps it was something usually found in most father's tool kits. Janet Etches, had a trunk with this kind of lettering:

> The wardrobe trunk that travelled so far with me now graces my son's home in San Francisco, my name on it in silver paint.

A few waspish relatives and acquaintances confronted the departing bride with: "Leaving the sinking ship, eh?", for Britain was showing no signs of a swift recovery from wartime restrictions. Others made inane remarks like the one about my never seeing a grand piano. As I didn't play even a regular piano this seemed pointless. My mother didn't argue. For all she knew there *were* no grand pianos in Canada. Relatives and friends often waxed emotional about the separation, thinking they would never see us again. In most cases saying goodbye to your mother and father, was the hardest of all.

We were instructed to look for a Canadian Railway Transport Officer at the London terminal. Probably not all of them were like the very young one I identified outside Victoria Station. He was wearing a brand new uniform as if he had been newly commissioned. His clipboard had a list of the war brides he was responsible for delivering to the hostel. I thought of him when I read Sheila Jane (Beatty) Davidson's story:

> I arrived at Paddington to find the truck waiting for our luggage and the bus to take us to the overnight hostel. While having my name checked off a list by a harried young officer, a very 'tarty-looking' girl swept up on a uniformed arm. Polish, if my memory is correct. 'My name is Mrs. Whatever,' she told that young man, 'and you can tell my 'usband 'e's 'ad it!' and she swept off again.

The South Street Hostel, Mayfair, remembered for its marble staircase, a hazard for exploring toddlers.
Credit: E. Jane Lyster

The map in Chapter 3 gives some details of the London hostels where war brides gathered before going to the port of departure. If the war bride lived in the south it seemed logical that she would leave from Southampton; if in the north from Liverpool or a Scottish port, but this was seldom the case. With stringent wartime restrictions still in mind ("Is your journey really necessary?"), we felt it was terribly extravagant to send us on unnecessarily long railway journeys. Of course the governing factor was the location of the port where our ship was waiting, and the necessity of gathering us at a central point for last minute checks on our health, documents, etc. It was not clear to us at the time, but authorities were following the system used so successfully to repatriate our husbands. In retrospect the monumental task was handled extremely well.

Not every overseas wife of a Canadian settled in Canada. Of the 48,000+ marriages just over 44,000 wives came to Canada. The reported 10% marriage failure seems to stem from this discrepancy, but there were other reasons behind it. Sometimes a divorce *was* pending. Sometimes when push came to shove a young wife changed her mind about leaving everything she knew, but there were many instances where the husband decided to make his home in his wife's country. Five hundred couples settled in the vicinity of Brighton, Sussex, [2] and Stacey records that "the best figures available" indicate that up to December 1946 the number of Canadians discharged in the United Kingdom was 5,818.[3] (Some of this number may not have had war brides of course.) Sometimes the delay was caused when a widowed mother became ill. In those days of few social services a war bride, may have stayed for months or years caring for her mother.

Mary (Martin) Aikenbrack of Eastbourne, Sussex was a special case. She had lost her sight in a bombing attack after her engagement to George Aikenbrack of Napanee, Ontario. They were married and she came to Canada, but found the adjustment too difficult. She and her husband planned to return to England in February 1947.

The Canadian Wives Bureau maintained lists of brides who, despite having applied for passage, did not follow up on arrangements. Reasons ranged from the benign "husband has decided to join wife in Europe" or "wife has already proceeded to Canada" to sad and seamy notations like: "husband does not appear interested", "suicide", "in jail" and "bigamous marriage". It is not known how many women came to Canada and then left because of impossible situations or insidious homesickness. Shipping records did not list any east-bound passengers as "returning war brides". A report in the December 13 issue of the Toronto *Globe and Mail* refers to a letter written by Senator W. Rupert Davies, publisher of the Kingston, Ontario *Whig-Standard*, to the British *Liverpool Post*. In it Senator Davies protested a headline in the Liverpool newspaper reporting the arrival of the liner *Cavina*: HEARTBREAK SHIP HERE ONCE MORE; BRIDES AGAIN BACK FROM CANADA. Davies protested that it gave an inaccurate picture of living conditions in Canada, and suggested the paper might "try to find out something about the thousands of English girls . . . who have found happiness and contentment."

My research reveals many war brides who experienced trying circumstances but stayed and handled their lives as best they could. A large number reported marriages with "ups and downs", but said they did not regret their choices. In addition there were some lucky souls who indeed seemed to live "happily ever after". Almost without exception and whatever their circumstances, those who stayed expressed gratitude that fate had brought them to this country.

In reading government reports of wives who, having applied to go to Canada, either indicated that they had changed their minds or did not reply to the Department's letters of enquiry, you get a sense of the frustration the Canadian Wives Bureau staff must have felt. They had done their part, the wheels had been set in motion, and yet they could not close these cases. There were of course many reasons for the wife's behaviour, she could have learned her husband did not want her in Canada, she could have been ill, or the couple, as noted above, may have decided to settle in the wife's country. I wonder how many of the reluctant travellers realised that several thousand Canadians were being held in Britain to complete the repatriation of war brides because some cases could not be resolved. Many on staff had been away from home for years and were anxious to get back to Canada.

Because of the Canadian Army's long stay in Britain, marriages there were spread over seven years or more. Marriages and engagements in continental Europe were concentrated in the relatively short period between Liberation and the repatriation of Canada's servicemen. These marriages and those with many nationalities other than British are the subject of Part II.

Department of Mines and Resources

IMMIGRATION BRANCH

Calgary, May 31, 1945

IN YOUR REPLY REFER TO
NO. 14881

INSPECTOR-IN-CHARGE

Dear Madam:

We have received an application dealing with the proposed admission to Canada of your daughter-in-law, Mrs. Coral Eswyn Lyster, who would be accompanied by her child, born July 13, 1944.

Will you please advise whether you are prepared to offer your relatives a home and if so please advise as to your financial and general circumstances, housing accommodation available, and the number of your dependents at home. You should also secure a letter of recommendation from your Local Municipal Official and this letter may be forwarded with your reply or sent direct to this office by the official concerned. Please advise as to the present address of your daughter-in-law.

A stamped addressed envelope is enclosed for your reply.

Encl.

Yours truly,

Jno. D. McIlhargey

Mrs. J. L. Lyster,
EMPRESS, Alta.

John D. McIlhargey,
Travelling Investigating Officer

Part II:

War Brides from Northwest Europe, the Rest of the World

... and Newfoundland

I didn't know as much about Canada as the Americans of today do, and that isn't saying much.

> Dutch war bride Martina (Brink) Tassell

The Dionne Quintuplets were well known in Holland as they often appeared in advertisements. When he heard I was engaged to a Canadian a friend said, 'Don't have quintuplets!'

> Jannicje "Nan" (Jansen) Casey

Under Dutch law, women who married Canadians lost their Dutch citizenship, and there were cases where over-zealous municipal officials had deprived these women of their ration coupons, thus causing nutritional problems.

> Kaufman and Horn, *A Liberation Album*, p 163, (quoting an unidentified Canadian officer attached to the Canadian Wives Bureau in The Hague)

I no like it heer.

> anonymous Dutch war bride

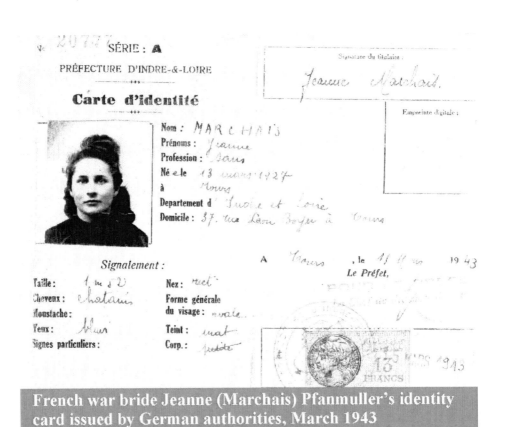

French war bride Jeanne (Marchais) Pfanmuller's identity card issued by German authorities, March 1943
Credit: Jeanne Pfanmuller

Chapter 10: Brides from Holland, Belgium and France

The invasion we dreaded in Britain never came, but in April 1940 Norway and Denmark were attacked and occupied by German forces. In the early hours of May 10 Nazi troops smashed their way into Holland, Belgium and Luxembourg, aided by the bombers of the Luftwuffe, and giving the world a new word: "blitzkrieg". Dutch citizens awoke that May morning to the sounds of battle, some to the sight of paratroopers in their back gardens. One Dutch businessman phoned his office and was answered in German.[1]

Rotterdam suffered a devastating bombing attack that first morning. Sophia Pauw (married name Sherwood), who become a Dutch war bride, remembers the great pall of smoke that hung over the city. In Britain we did not witness our fathers and brothers being dragged away to labour camps, nor our neighbours being executed in the street outside our homes. We may have been deprived of many things but never actually starved or froze to death as Dutch citizens did that last frigid winter of 1944-45.

Canada strongly discouraged marriages between their servicemen and young women in continental Europe, but as always Canadians did not feel obliged to obey directives they did not agree with. Many had family roots in the very towns they were liberating.

HOLLAND

A negotiated cease-fire took place on May 3, 1945 allowing Operation Manna, in which 6680 tons of food were dropped to the starving Dutch populace by pilots of the Canadian and US air forces. This life-saving measure has never been forgotten by the Dutch people.

Understandably emotions ran high when Holland was liberated by Canadian troops. War bride/writer Olga Rains has said of that time:

> It was a mad, crazy summer, that summer of '45. A newly liberated Netherlands was busy celebrating, temporarily putting aside the tensions and grief of the long war years.

Anticipating that the Canadian-British marriage phenomenon was about to be repeated in Europe, if on a much smaller scale, Canadian authorities issued special instructions that are quoted by C. P. Stacey:

> Canadian Routine Order No 788 stated that the general policy was to 'dissuade members of the Canadian Army from a marriage in foreign lands,' but it was no more effective than the efforts in Britain. [2]

A telegram from the Canadian Embassy in Brussels is quoted in a letter from the Department of External Affairs Canada to the Director of Immigration, Department of Mines and Resources addresses this point:

TELEGRAM No. 3395, January 8, 1945:

Marriage of foreign girls by our servicemen.

Considerable number of marriages of our men with Belgian girls taking place or planned. These girls acquire British nationality by a marriage and require new Belgian identity papers. Also understand services now studying regulations to be applied to such marriages and presume arrangements for transportation of Continent wives to Canada, similar to case of British wives, will eventually be applied. Anticipate demand for travel documents for these wives. Please advise if issuing of such travel documents in Belgium is to be responsibility of this embassy and procedure recommended. Belgian authorities, in any case, will require confirmation of post-marriage nationalities for wives' new Belgian identity cards. Husband's birth certificate and his nationality would appear necessary as Army documentation apparently based solely on soldiers (sic) statement.[3]

These Belgian marriages required that a branch of the Canadian Wives Bureau be opened in Brussels as well as The Hague, Holland and Paris, France.

In the aftermath of war commodities had a higher value than currency. When Herbert Gates, of the Perth Regiment, married Wilhelmina Brand in Leeuwarden, Holland he paid for the wedding rings and the photographer with 1100 cigarettes, and settled the hotel bill with cigarettes and chocolate.

Jannicje Cornelia Jansen, better known as Nan, came from Zeist, Holland where she had married Frank Casey of the Saskatoon Light Infantry. They moved to a mining camp on the mountain above the town of Hedley, British Columbia:

> The Nickel Plate Mine was a gold mine. There were about forty families living up there. We had a two-bedroom house and there was a bunkhouse for the unmarried men. There was a cookhouse where all the cooks were Chinese, a nice school, a rink, a large hall for dances, a library, a bowling alley and once a week a movie. For groceries we went down to Hedley or sent a letter and the order came up on the skip. Not everybody had a car. We had a 1929 Chevrolet. It was quite a trip to go up and down the hill. Chains were necessary. Most cars overheated and had to be cooled down with creek water, or in winter with snow. The doctor came once a week. We were very happy together, and more so when our first child was born. He was a Spina Bifida baby, and of course nothing could be done for him at that time. We took him to Vancouver several times, but to no avail. We just loved him and looked after him, and I think it made our marriage even stronger. Of course we lost him when he was three years old. By that time we had two more boys, and we ended up with six children. It was hard to get electrical appliances and I did not get a washing machine until 1948. We had snow from October until halfway May. No dryer, of course. Summers were beautiful there, all wild flowers. We also had bears. We got a larger house after we had our second boy. The houses were very cheap, we paid $8, and water and electricity were free. We lived at the mine site until 1952.

The Nickel Plate Mine closed before the end of the 20th century. The small town of Hedley, where Nan used to buy her groceries, has a museum which displays mine artifacts. In recent years the Upper Similkameen Indian Band has developed the mine site under the name Mascot Mine Tours. Visitors are taken to the top of the mountain where over 500 wooden steps lead down to the level where Nan and her family lived.

Martina (Brink) Tassell came from Groningen, Holland, where she was married in 1945. Her destination was Little Pond, Prince Edward Island. She recalled the shock of invasion:

I remember getting up one morning and finding my mother and our neighbour crying in the kitchen. War had been declared and the following four-year nightmare I won't go into. An English plane shot down near our place had no pilot, at least the Germans couldn't find one. My girl friend and I made dresses from this pilot's parachute. After the war I learned my father and his cronies had smuggled the pilot back to England. Groningen was one of the last places to be liberated. We lived along the main road to Delft from where the remnants of the German army hoped to escape to Bremen. They walked in rags, or with stolen horses and farm wagons that were a far cry from the trucks and tanks in which they had arrived.

In the last days of heavy fighting before their town was liberated the Brinks took refuge with many of their neighbours in the basement of a factory:

No privacy, little fresh air and open toilet buckets. Not exactly Buckingham Palace, but we were safe. One morning my brother sneaked out and came back yelling, 'The Allies are coming, they are Canadians!' A company of soldiers was marching our way, their leader continually checking both sides of the road. I loftily told my brother, 'Those are not Canadians, stupid, those are white people!' Please remember that our teachers were not allowed to teach us anything about the Allies, so all I knew was that in Canada there were Indians and a few courageous European settlers here and there. I didn't know as much about Canada as the Americans of today do, and that isn't saying much. We were all dumbstruck, couldn't believe that we were free again. We started singing, 'Now thank we all our God . . .' with our choked up throats and tearing eyes. Men were asking the soldiers for weapons so they could help fight, women and girls were hugging and kissing the soldiers. Their leader asked us to please allow the men to do their jobs as there were still Germans about. Next morning the lady across the river ran out waving a sheet which she swore a Canadian had rested on, and she was never going to wash it again. More than likely it was a German sniper as the Canadians had no time for rest, but she was happy so let her dream. Every third or fourth house sported signs saying: 'This family speaks English (and/or French) all Canadians welcome.' The all clear sounded and the church bell started ringing. That bell had been sunk in the river to hide it from the Germans all these years. I called to a neighbour, 'What is it?' 'My good girl, peace has been declared. We've got peace!' I met and married my first husband in the glorious, crazy-with-joy days of 1945 after our liberation, when Canadians were only slightly below the angels, and in Holland they still are, that at least hasn't changed.

The late Antonia Maria (Zom) Schiller flew to Winnipeg in 1947 via KLM airline with her Dutch-born son, Joseph. Her youngest son, Mark Schiller, wrote to me in July 2007. He said his uncle (Antonia's brother) produced an underground newspaper. Distribution was always a problem:

My Mom and her friend used to put the papers in the baskets on their bikes, cover them with clothing or food, then get through the German check points by flirting with the young German soldiers. If my Oma and Opa (Grandmother and Grandfather) had ever found out what she was doing that would be the end. If the Germans had found out I would not be writing this. I have a feeling she did not do it often. I am very proud of her.

Often future husbands were repatriated before a marriage could take place. If both parties solemnly declared that marriage was their intention, the European fiancée was allowed to travel to Canada to be married, but her passage was delayed until every married war bride had been processed. Once in Canada the fiancée was required to marry before a stated deadline or be deported to Holland. In addition to the usual documents required for marriage with a Canadian, Commanding Officers in Holland were instructed to obtain a certificate of the woman's political reliability. (Some Dutch women had fraternized with German troops during the occupation.) This regulation particularly irked Josta Visschers whose political integrity had qualified her for a sensitive

Tom and Josta Tryon
Credit: Josta Tryon

postwar government position overseas. Josta was born in Deventer, Holland. She and her family had a terrifying war experience. The German SS arrived early one morning and ordered them into the street. They were charged with signalling to the enemy and were lined up to be shot. Salvation arrived in the form of an officer in the regular German army who knew Josta's father well, vouched for the family's integrity, and insisted they be released. The source of the charge was a faulty house light that flickered whenever V1s were launched nearby, but looked as if the Visschers' were signalling to Allied planes. Josta says the officer might not have been so friendly had he known that during the whole terrible episode a downed Allied airman was concealed beneath the Visschers' floorboards, or that on occasion Josta delivered messages for the Underground.

Josta had met Tom Tryon in 1945 and corresponded with him after he was repatriated. She dated other men, but would always see Tom's face and know there was nobody else for her. Tom returned to Deventer and asked her to marry him. Josta came to Parksville, British Columbia in May 1949. A month later she and Tom were married in the old log church of St. Anne's. Forty-five pioneer farmers had built the church in 1894 using oxen to haul the logs. Josta must have wondered how a church built in 1894 could possibly be considered old when back in Deventer there were two churches dating from the 13th century!

THE DUTCH-CANADIAN CONNECTION

There are many reasons for the special relationship between Holland and Canada. When the Dutch royal family fled to England after the Nazi occupation of their country Queen Wilhelmina's daughter and heir, Princess Juliana, was sent on to Ottawa, Ontario, where she remained in exile with her children until 1945.

While in Ottawa Princess Juliana gave birth to her third daughter, Princess Margriet. The rooms occupied by the Princess in the maternity wing of Ottawa's Civic Hospital were declared to be Dutch territory, so that the new baby's succession to the Dutch throne would not be compromised. The Princess was christened at St. Andrew's Church, Ottawa, with her grandmother, Queen Wilhelmina, and Prime Minister Mckenzie King in attendance.

Canadians were in the forefront of the final liberation of Holland in May 1945.

In the fall of 1945 Princess Juliana presented the City of Ottawa with 100,000 tulip bulbs in recognition of the safe haven she and other members of the Royal Family found there. They also expressed her country's gratitude for the part Canadian forces played in the liberation. Ottawa's annual Tulip Festival is a continuing reminder of this special relationship.

Following Queen Wilhelmina's abdication in Septermber 1948, Juliana succeeded to the throne. She was Queen of the Netherlands until January 1980 when she abdicated and was succeeded by her daughter Beatrix. Juliana died in March 2004.

Dutch men who survived the war must have viewed the Dutch/Canadian marriages with sadness, even anger. The war had stripped them of their health and their money. They had little to offer a young woman. A Dutch journalist commented "Dutch men were beaten militarily in 1940, sexually in 1945." [4]

Dutch war brides were brought to England on the *Lady Rodney* and the *Lady Nelson*.[5] Olga Rains went to England from Rotterdam on the *Lady Rodney*, and landed at Tilbury, a port on the Thames in the East End of London. Dutch war brides were trail-blazers for the 110,000 immigrants who came to Canada from Holland in the post-war period, sometimes sponsored by war brides.[6]

Nearly two thousand Canadian-Dutch marriages are recorded in CWB files, but Kaufman believes this figure is low, because it does not include the unknown number of marriages that took place after escorted passages ended.[7]

BELGIUM

As in France and Holland, the people of Belgium had to endure the post-D-Day fighting in their towns and villages as the Allies drove the occupying army back towards Germany. The city of Antwerp was recaptured, but the port, the largest in Northwest Europe, remained in German control. They had orders to destroy the docks rather than let them fall into Allied hands. Meanwhile every conceivable item required by the combined American, British and Canadian armies, from food and gasoline to ammunition and replacement troops had to be trucked from the distant Normandy ports. The task of clearing the approaches to the city of Antwerp, along the banks of the Scheldt Estuary, was assigned to the 2nd and 3rd Canadian Infantry Divisions. This was accomplished at the cost of many lives, and Antwerp was captured, more or less intact.

Marie-José Debbaut, who was born in Antwerp, married Canadian Howard Henry in March 1946, in Niklaas, Belgium and came to Vancouver, British Columbia. Marie-José became a close friend of French war bride Germaine Robertson, and is the "aunt" mentioned in Germaine's story below. She was one of 649 Belgian war brides who settled in Canada.

FRANCE

When I was about twelve I remember thinking, "I can't wait to be thirty, and to dress like a Frenchwoman!" All those years ago France had a reputation for producing elegant young women who at thirty were in their prime and were examples of quiet sophistication. They were renowned for concocting a stunning wardrobe out of one black dress and half a dozen scarves. Many years have passed since they were thirty, but French war brides still have that natural elegance. The two I have interviewed were slim, and well dressed. I met Jeanne (Marchais) Pfannmuller, from Tours, France, at the 2003 Calgary Reunion hosted by Jeanne's Edmonton branch of the Alberta War Brides Association. Although the busy Secretary of the Association she chatted with me without any signs of "let's get this over quickly." My tape recorder did not capture the interview so we corresponded. Jeanne wrote:

One speaks of 'war brides', 'war victims', 'war widows'. One could also speak of 'war children' and 'war survivors'. It appears that my whole destiny was forged by the war. The period before the war was not a carefree time for the French. Adults knew of the menace on their eastern frontier, and the gullibility of the English and French diplomats. I was twelve when the War broke out. All conversations were punctuated with 'before the War' speaking of better times, or 'after the War' when we would undertake various projects. Life came to a standstill. Buildings were no longer heated. During class, one afternoon a week, we knitted items for the soldiers in the front line. That first winter I was devastated when I lost my school friend, Eleonore Kelin. She was arrested by the French authorities and sent to a prison camp with her family. They apparently were Germans, suspected of being spies. Later I came to believe they were German Jews who had escaped and settled in France before the war. When spring came, Tours having many bridges on the Loire river, a military air base nearby and an explosives factory, was the target for air raids. Enemy troops began their push through northern France. The French, at great risk of being gunned down along the roads, deserted their villages and towns. A long string of families loaded with all they could carry, crossed our city on their way south. They were hurting, tired, hungry, and thirsty. Some heartless residents *sold* them water. My mother would have liked to be evacuated with the rest of her office but my grandparents refused to leave their home 'for the enemy to enjoy'. The enemy was on the north side of our river. Bridges were destroyed, the water mains broken. The city was had been burning for three days when a thunderstorm put the fires out.

102

After France fell to the Nazis it was divided into the northern, occupied zone and the southern so-called "free zone", headed by Marshal Philippe Pétain. An obscure French General, Charles de Gaulle, escaped to England, where he claimed to represent the legitimacy and continuity of France, and declared himself head of the "Free French in exile". Jeanne was staying with family friends in the countryside, eighty kilometres south of Tours, where she often spent her summer holidays, and consequently found herself in the "free zone":

My mother began a long process of application with the Kommandantur, to obtain the documents for my return. At a specific hour and day in late October she and I were to be at our respective ends of a bridge. My mother handed a paper to the sentry who then crossed the bridge and handed the paper to another German sentry. I kissed my friend goodbye and walked across the bridge to my mother. I was fifteen. We were the defeated, the occupied. The 'Resistance' sabotaged the telephone lines, derailed trains, but the reprisals were so harsh on the whole population that they went underground. I lost another good school friend. The Gestapo knocked on her door in the middle of the night and Elisabeth Rosenthal and her family disappeared. For several months they had been wearing the compulsory yellow star ordained by the Nazis.

Although Tours was a long way from Normandy, on June 6, 1944 air raid sirens sent residents running for shelter, six or seven times:

We did not know a historical event was taking place on the beaches of Normandy. Then the word 'liberation' plunged us into some kind of ecstasy, yet I felt sad. For so long the French had felt abandoned by their former allies. The only news we had was of German victories. We could not hear BBC broadcasts because of interference on the airwaves. My grandfather was the only person I knew who believed the Americans would come to our rescue, but he did not live to see it happen.

Jeanne's grandmother received letters through the Red Cross from her sister in Canada, telling her that Jeanne's second cousin Max, who did not speak French, was in France with a Canadian unit. Jeanne was asked to correspond with him since she had been studying English:

My style was elementary. I signed my letters 'your little cousin', the literal translation for 'second cousin'. The war in Europe ended, the sirens blew for the last time, the church bells pealed and Max arrived at our house. When I opened the door he was expecting a little girl. He came back many times after that and soon convinced me that it was inconceivable for him to return to Canada without me as his wife.

When I met Germaine (Baillieul) Robertson (or as she would have written it: "Germaine Emma Robertson-Baillieul") she was living in Qualicum Beach. She pointed out the loss of the "e" in the spelling of her birthplace, Bailliul, that was in her maiden name. She didn't say so, but the two names must indicate a lengthy connection. The town was not well-placed for civilians, either in the First World War or the Second, being on the route north to Dunkirk and west to Ypres.

Ninety-eight percent of the town had been destroyed by shells and bombs in July 1917. After the Armistice it was painstakingly restored. Germaine met her husband in the early summer of 1945. She was walking with some girl friends when they were accosted by several drunken Canadians. John "Jack" Robertson, a Quartermaster stationed at nearby Péteren, came along and sent the soldiers packing. He was soon visiting Germaine's home, endearing himself to her family with gifts of coffee (a rare treat after the wartime roasted grain substitute). Germaine's journey to Vancouver Island was epic:

> I left for Paris October 30, 1946, went to Brussels and joined several Belgian war brides. An Army truck took us to Rotterdam where a few Dutch girls were added. Then by open boat to England, and train to London where we stayed five days. I met a Belgian girl who has been an 'aunt' to my children ever since.

After an uncomfortable voyage to Halifax on the *Lady Rodney* came the long train trip to Vancouver. Germaine crossed to Nanaimo, Vancouver Island, on the Canadian Pacific ferry, another two and a half hours. There she was met by her father-in-law in a big Plymouth car. The Island Highway was under construction and they became bogged down in the mud. After being pulled free Germaine says she saw nothing but trees all the way to Fanny Bay. It was late, dark, and Germaine was exhausted. The whole family had gathered for a turkey dinner prepared by Jack's mother. Germaine's brother-in-law played his accordion, even the local schoolteacher was there. Germaine was mesmerized by the huge portions of salad, turkey and vegetables everyone piled on their plates. In France, even before wartime privations, portions were small and served as separate courses (hence the slim French figures I so admired).

Mrs. Robertson, Senior, ran the Fanny Bay Post Office, so next day when Audrey Sawchuk came to collect her mail Germaine met her first Vancouver Island war bride.

When asked what she liked to drink with her meals Germaine's answer shocked her mother-in-law, but she was bound she would have her customary beer so she stopped at the local liquor store. She immediately realised she had strayed into strictly masculine territory. Germaine silenced a couple of burly loggers who whistled at her with a cool Gallic stare.

The community was small and without electricity. I asked if she was lonely, especially with Jack still overseas. "You have at times the blues", she said. There was no phone in her Bailliul home, so she could not call her parents.

In later years Germaine developed Parkinson's Disease. Whenever I attended Vancouver Island war bride reunions, or even the one in Calgary, when Qualicum Beach was mentioned someone would ask with affection about Germaine. Sadly she died at the Nanaimo Regional General Hospital, February 7, 2004. Jack died four years later. Jeanne and Germaine were just two of the 100 or so war brides who came to Canada from France.

A war bride, who was a latecomer and not French at all, managed to thoroughly confuse an Immigration officer at Dorval Airport, Quebec in September 1949. She had flown from Scotland on a Trans-Canada Airlines Northstar Skyliner (prop plane) with a stopover at Reykjavik, Iceland. Yes her name was Agnes McMorrin (French) Megaw, she assured the Canadian official in her strong Scottish accent, but she was not French, and yes her husband's name was Samuel English Megaw, but he was Canadian!

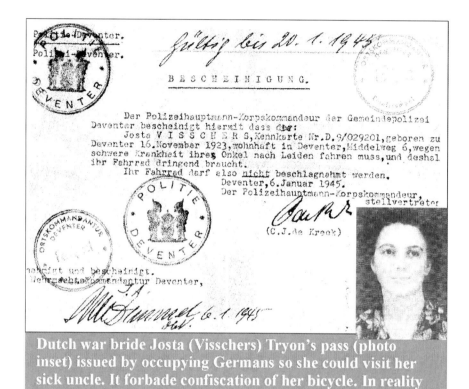

Dutch war bride Josta (Visschers) Tryon's pass (photo inset) issued by occupying Germans so she could visit her sick uncle. It forbade confiscation of her bicycle. In reality she was delivering documents for the Dutch underground.

Credit: Josta (Visschers) Tryon

I met people from all walks of life, like having Moose Stew in Billy Stork's cabin, and eating it from a silver spoon with his family crest on it.

Ellinor (Thun) Ueland, Norwegian war bride

In Germany, as elsewhere, Canadians found young women they wanted to marry, but Canadian authorities were inflexible. No marriages were permitted on German soil. Fiancées, of whatever nationality, had to wait until every wife had been processed and then travel to Canada at their own expense and be married there. German fiancées appear to have been left to the very last.

the author

One country that is never mentioned in contemporary newspaper clippings, CWB records, other war bride books, or anywhere else so far as I can discover, is so obvious that it is easily overlooked.

the author

German war brides aboard the *Beaverbrae*, July 1948.
Credit: Gertrude (Neuner) Lowe

Chapter 11: Brides from the Rest of the World

ITALY

One of the reasons Melynda Jarratt chose "The War Brides of New Brunswick" as her thesis project is because she had grown up in Bathurst with Anna (Perugine) Lavigne, an Italian war bride, as a close neighbour. She admired the way Anna adjusted to a life in Canada that was very different from the one she had left.

In Avellino, Italy, Anna's father was a surgeon. The family maintained an elegant town apartment as well as a farm in the country. Avellino was occupied by the 6th German Armoured Panzer Division after which Americans of the US 509th Parachute Battalion were dropped into the town. To escape the fighting Anna's mother hurried her family to the farm. They witnessed from their mountainside vantage point the first bombing of Avellino.

After the liberation Anna met Canadian Aurele Lavigne. They were married in June 1946. Anna arrived in Halifax on the *Lady Rodney*. She was met by Aurele who took her the rest of the way to Bathurst. Anna was not able to speak English fluently, but Aurele's Acadian family did their best to converse, and Anna was welcomed with open arms. For the first few years the Lavignes and their growing family lived in the fishing community of Shippigan, New Brunswick. Anna coped successfully with problems of language, culture, and homesickness, creating a rewarding life for herself and her family. Today she says:

> I consider myself very lucky in finding Aurele. He is such a good man.

Anna was one of only 26 Italian war brides. (Anna's story courtesy Melynda Jarratt.)

DENMARK

Included on one of the CWB lists is the name of one of the seven Danish war brides. She is Karen, wife of Sergeant I. Bonde. She advised the Bureau that her husband had decided to settle with her in Denmark, and was already on his way there.

HUNGARY

CWB records show three Hungarian children, without any mention of a mother or mothers. However two sisters, described in a Canadian newspaper as Hungarian, arrived in Canada in 1946. They were: Elizabeth Girouard, travelling with her daughter, Sylvia, and Mrs. Don Brisenden. A war bride (who crossed on the *Britannic*) mentions travelling on the Canadian train with a Hungarian war bride "who had been in Britain during the war".[1]

I met Canada's only known Norwegian war bride at a writers' function in Vancouver. Ellinor (Thun) Ueland was on holiday in Britain when war broke out and trapped her there. She was born in Holmsbo, Norway, and fully expected that the next time she boarded a ship it would take her back to her native country. Instead, in November 1944, following her marriage to Canadian Gilbert Ueland, she was aboard the *Andes* with a few other war brides, headed for Halifax and a very different life in the backwoods of British Columbia. Typical of post D-Day crossings the ship had wounded troops on board who were destined for Canadian hospitals. One night when a submarine was detected nearby, passengers were ordered to their lifeboat stations. Frightened mothers tried to comfort their babies. Ellinor, having no children, helped with the wounded troops, many of whom were blind. They sang hymns to keep up their spirits until the danger passed. Meanwhile the ship tossed, in Ellinor's words, "like a nutshell!"

Ellinor (Thun) Ueland, Canada's only known Norwegian war bride, wearing her native costume.
Credit: Ellinor (Thun) Ueland

Ellinor's husband worked for the BC Forest Service in the remote community of Elko, near Roosville in northern British Columbia, a hamlet named for a Mr. Roos, a ballet dancer who had come from England to study traditional native dances. Ellinor told me:

I met people from all walks of life, like having Moose Stew in Billy Stork's cabin and eating it from a silver spoon engraved with his family coat of arms! This was at the time of our present Queen's wedding. Billy had an invitation . . . ever so elegant it was. Who was Billy Stork? Royalty? I did not know. It was rumoured he was fifth in line for the throne!

LUXEMBOURG

A Luxembourg national, Marguerite, is listed in CWB records among those unable or unwilling to proceed to Canada. She had married Canadian Captain G. Rochereau de la Sasliere. This seems to be the only record of a Luxembourg war bride.

The CWB records list only six German war brides. These would be German nationals who were in Britain when war broke out. They married in Britain and travelled to Canada by the same route as British dependents.

When Charles Rosekat, from Kitchener, Ontario met his bride-to-be, Helga, he was attached to the British Army occupation forces in Germany. He obtained permission for Helga to join him in England where they were married on January 27, 1947. Helga arrived in Canada in March 1947 where a newspaper headline described her as "the first German war bride to enter Canada." If Charles Rosekat had been serving with a Canadian unit he would have found it much more difficult to marry. Order Number 1067, dated April, 1945, addressed to all nations connected with the Occupation, reads:

> Germany will not be occupied for the purpose of liberation but as a defeated enemy. In the conduct of your occupation and administration you should be firm and aloof. You will strongly discourage fraternization with the German officials and population.[2]

Apparently the British interpretation of the Order allowed some leeway in how it was carried out, but while Canadian and American authorities followed it to the letter their troops did not. Many Canadians and Americans were of German descent and had a natural affinity with the young women they met in post-war Germany. Others sympathized when they realised how terribly German civilians had suffered in the war. In Germany as elsewhere Canadians found young women they wanted to marry. While no marriages were permitted on German soil engagements could not be forbidden. Fiancées, of whatever nationality, had to wait until every wife had been processed and then travel to Canada at their own expense and be married there. German fiancées were placed at the very end of the list. It was not until April 1948 that the first group of thirty German fiancées reached Quebec on the SS *Beaverbrae*.[3] (Shukert and Scibetta writing of GI Brides in *War Brides of World War II*, list 86 German GI war brides who participated in their study, suggesting the total German brides to be quite large.)

A Hamilton newspaper speculated that Gisel Cudney, wife of (US born) Sgt. Bert Cudney, who came to Brantford, Ontario in February 1948, was the "first German war bride to arrive in Canada". The marriage was in Germany in December 1947. Presumably the marriage regulations had been relaxed by that time.[4]

Gertrude (Neuner) Lowe of Sudbury, Ontario, was living in Zahlbach, Germany when she met her future husband:

> I wanted to attend university but was drafted into the *Arbeitdienst* (National Service) where all young people had to work a year for the state. I worked half the year on farms, and the other half in a munitions factory. Just before the war ended I was allowed to return to my home. On April 6, 1945 American troops of General Patton's 3rd Army occupied our village and since I was fluent in English and had no political affiliations whatsoever I was asked to be an interpreter. In September I was asked to go to Bad Kissengen. There I met Staff Sergeant Samuel Nelson Lowe. He was 11 years older than I, big, strong, handsome, good-natured and educated. At first my father was not too happy at the idea of me keeping company with an American. He had recently returned from an American prisoner-of-war

camp where he and his comrades were treated badly. However since Samuel was a Canadian who had been in the USA when the Japanese attacked Pearl Harbour, and had joined up there, and my father could speak enough English to sustain a conversation, they got along well. The British were more lenient with their soldiers in regard to marrying German girls and we hoped Canada would follow suit, but we miscalculated. It only did so, under great pressure, in 1948.

Gertrude's group left Bremerhaven on the *Beaverbrae* July 8, 1948, sailing through the newly-opened St. Lawrence Seaway and docking at Quebec City on July 19. Gertrude and Samuel were married at Copper Cliff United Church, Copper Cliff, Ontario in August 1948. Gertrude believes there were two further sailings of German fiancées in May and September 1948 bringing the total to about 100. Her attempts to contact some of these brides to arrange a 40-year reunion were thwarted because she knew only their maiden names.

During the Allied occupation of Germany Ursula Nordt-Greiser was not allowed to correspond with her relatives in the United States. When Gustav Arndt of the First Canadian Postal Corps learned of this he offered assistance. He was born in Saskatchewan into a family from a German community in the Ukraine. He was fluent in German and also spoke Russian and Ukrainian. Ursula describes him as a good, kind man, and says her family liked him, but her fellow Germans looked down on her when she was in the company of her Allied soldier. This did not bother Ursula unduly, since as a refugee she was already treated by the West Germans as if she didn't belong there. Ursula came to Canada on the same sailing as Gertrude Lowe, and they have been friends ever since. She reports that on the European leg of the journey they were billeted in a former concentration camp in Hannover-Muhlenberg for ten weeks. There were no tables or chairs and the beds were straw-filled sacks (a bit reminiscent of my WRNS palliasse) set on wooden slats. The staff, knowing the young women's destination, were hostile. Ursula says that when the group boarded the *Beaverbrae* they could hardly believe the clean, pleasant accommodations, the wonderful meals and the entertainment, film showings and dances. She says it allowed them to remember happier times in their lives, and the smoothly operated ship restored their sense of order and security.

EGYPT

It would be nice to know more about "Flo O'Neil", the Egyptian war bride Sheila (Lemon) Percival met in London, but I've not been able to trace her.

AUSTRALIA

There are 24 Australian war brides in the CWB records, and C.P. Stacey certainly gives details of Canadian servicemen in Australia. [5] The Australian war brides I've located were all living in Britain when they met their Canadian husbands. Australian Mollie Gillen is discussed in Chapter 17.

SOUTH AFRICA

Three brides discovered in my research were born in South Africa, but only one was still living there when war was declared. Sheila (Lemon) Percival, of Red Deer, Alberta, was born in Naauwpoort. She joined the South African Woman's Air Force in Pretoria in 1940, served in North Africa, and was almost immediately evacuated from Cairo when Rommel's army advanced:

> We were evacuated to Aswan. When I got back to Cairo I met a Spitfire pilot, Tom Percival, who was with RCAF No 17, City of Windsor Squadron (the only Canadian squadron to serve in the Middle East). When it was rumoured that he was to be transferred to India we were, with some difficulty, married by a British padre in the chapel of Cairo Cathedral, on July 1, 1944. It proved to be a costly wedding as most of the squadron was on leave in honour of Dominion Day! My discharge from the SAWAF was effective the day we boarded a troopship at Suez that September bound for Glasgow. Tom was not going to India, but being repatriated to Canada. On arrival in London Tom and I were separated. I was housed with a Canadian nurse and an Egyptian war bride, Flo O'Neill, in a boarding house in Kensington. The nurse, Norma Nicholson, ran into an officer she had known in Canada, and he intervened to get us transport to Canada.
>
> After 4-5 weeks we were glad to be on our way as London was having nightly raids. When we reached Glasgow all three husbands were on the same ship, the *Ile de France* (the same ship that had transported me to Port Said in 1942 . . . there was nothing recognizable from the luxury liner I had known then).
>
> We were not permitted to be with our husbands. I ended up in the ship's hospital with chronic seasickness, being in the early stages of pregnancy. When we arrived in Halifax Tom went to an RCAF station and I went on by rail to Ottawa. I was met by a WWI war bride. She was truly an angel, and I received loving care in her home.

When Sheila was strong enough she continued her train journey to Edmonton. Tom's family met her and took her to their home:

> A short time later there was a visitor at the door, a Red Cross representative who presented me with a corsage and profuse apologies for missing me at the station. She said she had been looking for a 'black' war bride from Africa.

JAMAICA

Neil Hysert served in Jamaica with the Argyll and Sutherland Highlanders of Canada. His Jamaican war bride came to Canada on the *Aquitania* and settled in Hamilton, Ontario. Private Robert E. Topping, in the same regiment, welcomed his wife Gloria and their son Robert when they arrived in Hamilton in April 1945. Jack Barkwell, with the Irish Fusiliers, met his future wife, Eileen, in Jamaica. Born in England, she had moved to Jamaica with her family. She came to Canada from a home with servants to live in primitive conditions in an Ontario village, but had no complaints:

> . . . pioneers had a dreadful time, but we had some hardships too, compared to the way the present generation lives. I would not change with them; they don't know they are living. Our appreciation of what we achieved far outweighs theirs . . .[6]

CHILE

In 1939 Elizabeth Alexandra Riddell was attached to the British Embassy in Santiago, Chile, as a secretary. When war broke out she volunteered for service with British forces. Through the British National Service Committee, Valparaiso she was sent to England where she enlisted in the WAAF. While in England she married William Rankin Wheeler, RCAF. Elizabeth Wheeler was repatriated to Chile by British authorities in February 1946, and by January 1947 had arrived in Canada. [7]

SINGAPORE

CSM (Company Sergeant Major) George Suzuki and CSM George Obokata, two Japanese-Canadian soldiers, serving in the Canadian Intelligence Corps, brought their war bride wives to Canada from Singapore. All four arrived in Canada in April 1947, having travelled across the Indian Ocean, through the Suez Canal and the Mediterranean to England and then on to Toronto. Both Suzuki and Obokata had worked as interrogators of Japanese POWs and civilians in Singapore. They had enjoyed spending their free evenings at the movies, purchasing their tickets from their future wives, who alternated at manning the theatre box office.[8]

RUSSIA, BERMUDA, INDIA, etc.

Other home countries of women who married Canadian servicemen are listed in files and correspondence of the CWB and Immigration Records. "Marriages have taken place in British Guiana, Russia, Bermuda, Trinidad, India and the Middle East."

The US is a country not mentioned anywhere as a source country for Canadian war brides. The unknown number of American women who married Canadians training in the US, or serving with the US forces, most certainly qualify as war brides, just as Shukert and Scibetta include Canadian women who married GIs in their count.[9] The Americans have been overlooked precisely because they didn't arrive in this country on war bride ships with all the attendant publicity. Yvonne G. (MacDonald) Brown was born in New York, USA. She attended Barnard College (Columbia University) in New York city. She and her Canadian husband of 58 years, Lieutenant Clifford Francis Brown, RNVR, lived in Calgary, Alberta.[10]

"On May 10, 1948, I received notification to report to the Canadian Emigration Camp in Hannover-Muhlenberg. My excitement was replaced by shock when I arrived at the camp, which had been a former concentration camp. As soon as the staff, which consisted primarily of displaced persons, realized we were war brides, we were treated with less friendliness than were the other emigrants. We were horrified to see what would become our home for ten weeks was dirty and it took us hours to clean it."
Credit: Ursula Renate (Nordt-Greiser) Arndt

Sweet Creatures, did you truly understand
The pleasant life you'd live in Newfound-land,
You would with teares desire to be brought thither:
I wish you, when you goe, faire wind, faire weather.
      (extract) Robert Hayman, poet, c 1575-1629 [1]

Winds of fifty, sixty and even seventy knots were commonplace . . . 'Glitter storms,' which I had known by the less lyrical name of 'freezing rain,' were frequent and as enchanting as a Christmas window.
      Claire Mowat, *The Outport People* [2]

You cup your ear to the paneled mahogany door,
hear Lorne clear his throat and ask
for your hand in marriage,
strain to hear your father say,
'Mary may lose her sight.'
Lorne's voice is clear:
'Then I'll do the seeing for both of us.'
      Dianne Hicks Morrow, *Newfoundland War Bride*, fourth stanza [3]

When Newfoundlanders speak of Confederation they refer to 1949 not 1867.
      the author

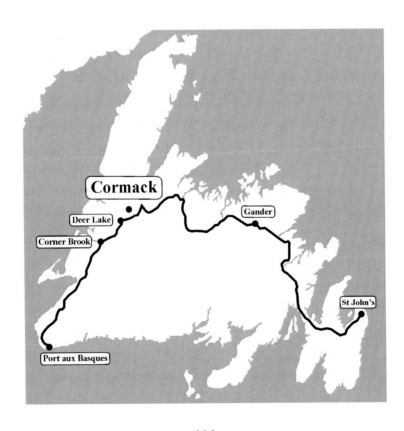

Chapter 12: Newfoundland: A Special Case

Why "a special case?" When Newfoundland's war brides (mainly from Scotland and other parts of Britain) arrived post-World War II the Island was not part of Canada and would not be until 1949 when it became Canada's tenth province. Before that it had been a British colony dating back to the fifteenth century.

ABOUT NEWFOUNDLAND

In 1497, under the name "Newfoundland", Newfoundland and Labrador were claimed for England by the explorer, John Cabot. Newfoundland has long been described as England's oldest colony, although its status has undergone changes from time to time. For a short time it even had Dominion status.

Its position as the part of North America closest to Europe assured its connection with two important developments of the modern world, communications and aviation. By 1866 the Atlantic Telegraph Cable between Heart's Content, Newfoundland and Cork, Ireland was in operation. Fifty-three years later Alcock and Brown left Lester's Field, near St. John's, on the first ever successful non-stop flight to Europe. Although Lindbergh's solo flight did not originate in Newfoundland the rooftops of St. John's were his last sight before heading out to the Atlantic.

Gander, Newfoundland and Goose Bay, Labrador airports were of vital importance in World War II, and in post-war commercial aviation until the development of jet aircraft which were able to take a shorter route over the North Pole.

In 1939 Britain called for recruits from Newfoundland. Its Governor, painfully aware of the catastrophic 710 casualties that befell the 790-member Newfoundland Regiment in the Battle of the Somme twenty-three years earlier, insisted that his troops serve only in artillery regiments that were deemed to have fewer casualties. Many Island men served in Scotland with the various Newfoundland Forestry Corps units. Others crossed to Canada and joined the three Canadian services. It is estimated that 800 war brides came to Newfoundland.[4]

The island's main industries have always been cod fishing in the frigid and dangerous waters of the Grand Banks; and later, logging and mining. The products, whether cod or paper pulp, were exported. In the 20th century Newfoundland's trees provided the raw material for the London *Times* (the proper newspaper for the proper English gentleman), and other British newspapers owned by Alfred Harmsworth, Lord Northcliffe.[5]

The islanders' diet was drastically limited by what could be grown on the rocky terrain (in a climate where one month a year, July, is usually frost-free), or caught in the surrounding waters. Cod, fresh or salted, was the staple foodstuff, and the main ingredient in the traditional "fish and brewis" (pronounced "bruise"). Brewis is very dry bread broken in pieces (was it originally the hard tack known as ship's biscuit?). When war bride Elsie (Edney) Snow first encountered "fish and brewis" she thought bad fish was being cooked!

Those who deplore the nature of the traditional seal hunt might want to read *This Marvellous Terrible Place, Images of Newfoundland and Labrador,* especially Lloyd Rideout's memories of "Jack", an orphaned seal pup he tried to save, and his view of a hunt that for many years was the means of his children's survival.

A total of 2337 Newfoundlanders served in Britain with the Royal Navy and Royal Air Force, and in Artillery Regiments. Of these 72 lost their lives.[6] Newfoundland Overseas Forestry Units were stationed in Scotland, felling trees to replace the lumber no longer arriving from Canada because food and war supplies had priority on Atlantic shipping. These Foresters were in a civilian organization whose members signed an engagement for a stated period or for the duration of the war.[7]

Newfoundland war brides can be divided into three categories:

- British, French, Dutch, Australian and German women who married men serving with Newfoundland Artillery units in Britain attached to the (British) Army, in the Royal Navy, or the RAF; or in Newfoundland Overseas Forestry Corps, etc. Note that some couples remained in the wife's country after the war.[8]

- The wives of Newfoundland men who crossed to Canada and served in Canadian units overseas. These wives were moved to Newfoundland by the Canadian government after travelling to Halifax on Canadian war bride sailings.

- Newfoundland women who married Canadians stationed on the Island. They moved to Canada post-war to be with their husbands.

An example of the last category is Lulu Taylor. She was born in St. John's, Newfoundland, married a Canadian serving in Newfoundland and came to Sydney, Nova Scotia as the wife of Joseph Louis March.

Not every war bride stayed in Newfoundland:

> Of the 800 war brides . . . it is commonly claimed that up to one-quarter of that number returned to their homeland. According to verbal accounts, many of them had been overwhelmed by the isolation, the lack of employment and proper housing, (and) the poor prospects for the future . . .[9]

Returning to the homeland does not necessarily signify marriage breakup. Maida (Wilson) Fudge, for instance, returned to England with her husband and children when she required specialized surgery that was unavailable in Newfoundland. The family eventually returned to North America, this time settling in Canada. When I met her she was living in Qualicum Beach. Maida introduced herself as "a back-door Canadian war bride", meaning she did not become a *Canadian* war bride until Newfoundland joined Confederation.

Maida was in the WAAF so early that the service still had its World War I name: the Women's Royal Air Force (WRAF), which was changed to the Women's Auxiliary Air

Force (WAAF). She served at RAF Station Yeadon, Yorkshire, quickly achieving the rank of Sergeant:

> Early in 1940 I met this airman, Walter Fudge, who spoke somewhat differently. He had joined the RAF in Scotland where he had been with a unit of volunteers from Newfoundland. We were both at RAF Station Digby, Lincolnshire, and when he was to be posted away from Britain we were married at St. Stephen's Church, Leeds. We were back in less than a week, then away Walter went for two years.

Maida had a rough crossing to Halifax on the *Scythia* in April 1945 with her small son, Malcolm. They arrived dressed for an English Spring:

> My trunk had been lost before it even reached the *Scythia*, so a ladies' association member took us shopping for warm jackets and boots. Very kind they were in this new and different world.

Now warmly dressed they crossed by ferry to Newfoundland and arrived at Walter's home in Grand Falls in time to celebrate VE Day.

Elsie (Edney) Snow of Gloverton, Newfoundland, served as a switchboard operator with the National Fire Service at Havant, Hampshire, a small town, but a busy railway junction (where I regularly changed trains when I had leave from HM Signal School). Elsie wrote of her wartime experiences:

> Because, just across the bridge on Hayling Island, beacons were lit when there were ships in Portsmouth Harbour, we got our share of air raids. I think the doodle bugs (V1s) were the worst. You could see them and you didn't know when they were going to drop. One came down on our warehouse, killing two Home Guards as well as six civilians and a number of cattle. The farmers had their fields 'ploughed up' repeatedly. Winston Snow, RN, was stationed on Hayling Island. He had been taken prisoner in North Africa, and was involved in the only prisoner of war (POW) exchange of the war, being one of 800 exchanged for Italian Navy internees held in Saudi Arabia. We met during the last year of the war and were married at St. Peter's, Hayling Island. Winston was repatriated to Newfoundland on the aircraft carrier HMS *Trumpeter*.

Elsie arrived at Pier 21 on the *Scythia* in March 1946, and to her delight Winston was waiting on the Halifax dock to escort her the rest of the way. Like Maida Fudge they crossed from North Sydney, Nova Scotia to Port-aux-Basques, their ferry being the SS *Kyle*:

> The gulf was full of ice and I saw seals on the ice pans. At Millerton Junction it was dark and we were met by Winston's folks, his father carrying a lantern to light the way. There were no bakeries. Everyone made their own bread, cakes and cookies.

In England bread came from a bakery, and cakes and cookies were a rare luxury because of shortage of ingredients.

What must a young war bride have thought when she came across some of Newfoundland's place names? Names like Cupid, Heart's Content, Heart's Desire, and

Heart's Delight? Little Heart's Ease, Little Seldom, Come-by-Chance, Bare Need, Witless Bay, Joe Batt's Arm, Indian Tickle, and Tickle Harbour? Tickle, far from being a frivolous activity, is the Newfie word for a treacherous current or any hazardous areas that are difficult to navigate. I still think some early cartographer had a sense of humour, or why Tickle Me? The place names are occasionally French, and an interesting bit of Franglais is the local corruption of Bay D'Espoir, meaning "Bay of Hope", into "Bay of Despair". According to Memorial University, some of the more colourful place names almost certainly originated from the names of early sailing ships.

In the 1940s Elizabethan-English words, often traced to west country English settlers, survived in Newfoundland's outports (remote coastal settlements). A gale-force wind was "a blow", a stupid person "a chucklehead", a tin cup "a bannikin", and a kind of seaweed "dulse", a Gaelic word still well understood in parts of Ireland, and one that the Oxford English Dictionary traces back to 1547. Many a war bride must have heard the phrase "come from away", referring to a newcomer to the area.

After Confederation the first Premier, Joey Smallwood, legislated resettlement of many of the outport people into more accessible areas where education and health care could be more easily provided, but the change meant that a lot of the old words and the old ways disappeared.

As for the weather, poet Robert Hayman's words quoted above ("faire wind, faire weather"), seem designed to persuade prospective settlers they would be coming to another England. This could be because the poet was also Governor of the Avalon Peninsula colony and interested in encouraging settlement. A modern travel agent's advice is more realistic:

> . . . when visiting Newfoundland waterproofing is advisable throughout the year.

The war changed Newfoundland profoundly. War planes built in Canada and the US were flown from Newfoundland to Britain by pilots of Ferry Command, an incredible feat when you realize that previously only pioneer aviators like Charles Lindbergh had flown across. When the war ended, the British Government made it possible for wives to travel on the same ship as their husbands directly from Britain to St. John's. However at least 500 Newfoundland brides came with wives of Canadians on the *Scythia,* that docked in Halifax on March 26, 1946. Elsie (Edney) Snow, above, was on board. She was in the first category, on·her way to Newfoundland.[10]

The late Yvonne (Nethersole) Wiseman, who had been a Volunteer Aid Detachment (VAD) nurse in a military hospital in Penshurst, Kent, landed in Halifax. She took the overnight ferry to Port aux Basques, where she caught the train known as "The Bullet". This part of her journey took 27 hours, and she still had not reached her destination.

THE NEWFIE BULLET

War brides arriving at Port aux Basques, travelled on by this narrow gauge railway (unless of course their journey ended at Port aux Basques). "Newfie Bullet" was a nickname bestowed on the admittedly slow railway by a GI who was monumentally unimpressed by it. However it was the island's only form of land transportation, there being virtually no road system in place. Railway employees always claimed The Bullet was capable of greater speeds, but Company regulations kept them low. The railway, despite its critics, did yeoman service in moving men and materials throughout the war. The postwar network of roads spelled the end of The Bullet. Passenger services closed in July 1969, and the last freight run was made in December 1988.

In recent years the tracks have been taken up and the 900 km rail bed became the "T" (sic) Railway Provincial Park", a part of the Trans-Canada Trail.

The Bullet is immortalized in a mixed drink made with Newfoundland rum that is retailed under the name Newfoundland Screech (for the sound alleged to have been made when an American serviceman first tasted the stuff). Should you be so bold as to mix 1 oz of Screech with 1 oz of coffee liqueur you have a drink called "Newfie Bullet". If you mix 1 oz of Screech with 1/4 oz Triple Sec or Grand Marnier and 2 oz of cream you have a "Muffled Screech" [11]

Enid (Gates) Stevenson's story is a little different. She was born in Scotland, but in 1932 her family moved to Petries in the Bay of Islands, Newfoundland. There she met David Stevenson whose parents managed the local golf course. Their paths crossed again in wartime England where Enid had moved to train as a nurse:

We were near Catterick Camp, and Canadian and US airforce squadrons were in the area. Eventually we received the overflow from the military hospital, mostly airmen with burns, some of whom went on to the wonderful burn unit in East Grinstead, Sussex. At the time of Dieppe we received a number of survivors, including a father and son. I was on night shift at the time of D-Day, and remember hearing and seeing masses of planes going out early in the morning, and later, scattered ones returning home. David had enlisted in the 166th Newfoundland Field Regiment RA, and so we met again.

In January 1943, Enid and David married. It had to be a quiet wedding as nurses in training at Enid's hospital were not permitted to marry. Two weeks later David's regiment shipped out to North Africa, and then to Sicily and Italy, so for two years they kept in touch by letter. In one, Enid remembers, even the kisses were blacked out by an overzealous censor! After VE Day they returned to Newfoundland where Enid's mother was still living. Enid wrote to me from Cornerbrook, Newfoundland:

We sailed from Southampton on the *Queen Elizabeth I* (to St.John's). I shared a cabin with 12 war brides, all of us pregnant and seasick! What a start to a new life.

Catherine Maclean married James Boland of the #205 Newfoundland Foresters and sailed directly to St John's on the *Drottningholm*:

I was born in a small village on the Isle of Skye called Roag in Dunvegan, then my parents moved to a farm on the mainland. I was living in Inverness when I met my husband. When I told my family about him Mother shook her head. 'What! In Newfoundland the people run around in the woods naked!'

119

Brenda (Burtenshaw) Butt sailed with her husband, Austin, on the *Mauretania*, December 24, 1945:

> The Newfoundland Government of the time had arranged that its returning veterans could elect to travel from England together with their wives and children. This meant a delay in England to await suitable transportation. On the *Mauretania* we wives and children were placed together in civilian accommodation with sentries guarding the corridors to deny entry to everyone else including the husbands - it should be remembered that this was essentially a troopship and there were many thousands of returning veterans on board. To visit with our husbands it was necessary for them to arrive at our corridor entrance and wait for a sentry to escort us out. We could then take a short stroll around the promenade deck. On our return I would be escorted back to my quarters.

Brenda and Austin landed at Halifax and took the ferry from Sydney to Port aux Basques ("a horrendous crossing"):

> The first meeting with my in-laws I'll always remember as a joyous occasion, filled with hugs and kisses.

The last mile of their journey was by horse-drawn sleigh, with lots of blankets. Their eldest son was born in 1947 "in the oldest city in North America, St. John's." Later children were born in England, South Africa, Ontario and Quebec.

CORMACK

In 1946 returning Newfoundland veterans were offered land at Cormack as part of a government Agricultural Resettlement Scheme. Cormack was in a remote forested area at the base of the Northern Peninsula, ten miles from the town of Deer Lake. Applicants were allocated fifty acres of land, ten of which had been cleared. There was a house with two completed rooms, a horse, some pigs, some implements and funds to build a barn. A number of war brides settled at Cormack with their husbands. The work was hard and there was no transportation to distribute farm produce, but the prospects seemed good. By 1948 ninety-six farms were established. Yvonne Wiseman and her husband John moved from Heart's Delight to Cormack in September 1946. Yvonne had been a VAD in Penshurst, Kent. She was completely unused to farming, but wrote in her memoir, *The Story of a War Bride,* "We set out with enthusiasm. We were young, in love and ready to conquer all!" Yvonne describes the un-insulated house, and winters where the temperature dipped to 30° below zero Fahrenheit. One morning she was late making the bed and found ice had formed in the hot water bottle. An August frost ruined their crops. They gave it a good try, but early in 1949 the Wisemans and their children left Cormack to seek their fortunes elsewhere. By this time Yvonne could harness a horse, milk the cow and catch runaway pigs.[12]

Easy road access eventually became a reality, but too late for the Wisemans and many other settlers. Brenda (Burtenshaw) Butt and her husband Austin, and Margaret Roberts and her husband Bruce were two other war brides who shared the Cormack experience.

Newfoundland and Vancouver Island serve as Canada's east and west bookends, so to speak, and have several things in common: memories of bountiful fishing seasons, alas now greatly depleted, a colonial past, regional dishes (cod and brewis in the east, Nanaimo Bars in the west!) and Attitude with a capital "A", though perhaps it's a little more pronounced in our eastern cousins. According to mainland visitors, we both tend to live on a slower "Island Time", and we share occasional half-serious threats to secede. Perhaps it is because of the vast distance between us, but I noticed I was often corrected when pronouncing "New-Found-Land" however often I changed it! In the interests of accuracy I sought guidance from a native. This is the e-mail that set me straight:

Just in case no one gave you the pronunciation yet . . . if you can say 'understand' you can say 'Newfoundland'. Same t'ing . . . 'bye.   Pamela Coleman.

Thank you, Pamela . . . 'New-fund-**land**', right?

HELP
WIN THE WAR
BRITAIN ASKS
NEWFOUNDLAND
TO SEND OVER MORE FIGHTING MEN

One Thousand
NEWFOUNDLAND FISHERMEN AND
SEAMEN ARE NEEDED TO HELP
MAN NEW SHIPS

Two Hundred
MEN ARE REQUIRED TO ENSURE THAT
THE 57TH AND THE 59TH ROYAL
ARTILLERY REGIMENTS ARE KEPT TO
FULL FIGHTING STRENGTH

ROYAL NAVY	ROYAL ARTILLERY
AGE 18 to 35	20 to 35
HEIGHT 5 ft 2 in or over	5 ft 4 in or over
WEIGHT 112 lbs or over	112 lbs or over
CHEST 33 in or over	33 in or over

MUST BE ABLE TO READ AND WRITE

THE CALL IS FOR **MEN**

----- REAL MEN -----

Part III:
On To Canada

Instructions to war brides travelling in wartime:

In the interests of security you should not divulge the name, type or class of ships in which arrangements may be made for your passage, nor should you make any reference either in conversation or correspondence to sailing or arrival dates either before or after your voyage.

Canadian Wives Bureau

. . . bringing the total number of servicemen's dependents to come to Canada between 1942-48 to 43,454 adults and 20,997 children, for a total of 64,451 dependents.[1]

You brave and adventurous women, yours is a story of the human spirit . . . of finding love in the middle of war.

Robbie Shaw, Chair, Pier 21 Society, in 2006, celebrating the 60th anniversary of the *Mauretania II* arrival, 9 February, 1946; the first all-war bride sailing

Mauretania II departs Liverpool February 5, 1946, the first "all war bride" sailing bound for Canada.
Credit: National Archives of Canada / PA-175804

Chapter 13: On Board Ship

Once the Continental and other non-British wives reached London and had been "processed" (their paperwork was more complicated), they joined the stream of British war brides and from then on the journey was a shared experience. Many of these wives did not speak English fluently so that language would be added to the required adjustments. They would rarely hear their own National Anthems again.

British war brides were leaving a unilingual society whose Saxon forebears and Roman, Scandinavian and Norman-French invaders had long ago been absorbed into a recognizable group (even if it was split into horizontal layers by the ever present class system). We were headed for a Canada that would soon be officially bi-lingual and unofficially a multi-lingual society with a multitude of hyphenated Canadians. Times were a-changing, but initially we saw red postal vans labelled "Royal Mail", found many things in the shops labelled "Made in England", calculated in pounds and ounces and feet and inches, and sang "God Save the King" as often as "O, Canada".

War brides left Britain from Southampton, Liverpool, Greenock, Gourock, Glasgow or even Birkenhead, (just across the Mersey from Liverpool). With few exceptions we disembarked at Pier 21 in Halifax, Nova Scotia. A small number landed in New York City and went on by train to Canada. A few flew, either in converted Lancaster Bombers, or with fledgling commercial air lines. These flights were not offered as alternatives to ship and rail so were paid for by the war bride. Some of the 1948 and later arrivals sailed through the St Lawrence Seaway, arriving at Quebec, and unknowingly followed the sea route the pioneers had made in small sailing ships. But in the main war brides had their first glimpse of Canada at Pier 21.

Between January 1942 and the summer of 1944, 1160 brides and 576 children made the wartime crossing to Canada. I remember being given the option to do this, with the comment that there would be a long delay once the European war was over, because of the repatriation of servicemen, but Bill was still in Europe and I didn't want to leave my family before I absolutely had to.

WARTIME SAILINGS

You will appreciate how important it is to get as many dependents moved as possible before the collapse of Germany, and fill all the shipping space while it is available. . . . The majority of these we will be sending forward in the immediate future will be preceding husbands.[2]

Some war brides had reason to make the risky wartime crossing. Their husbands might be in Canada recovering from wounds, or have been posted there as instructors in the ever expanding Air Training Plan. They may have lost family and family homes in the bombing. More than one Canadian husband wondered why the Canadian government thought the Atlantic safe for his dependents, when the British had cancelled the evacuation of their children to North America after the loss of 77 children in the 1940 sinking of the *City of Benares* :

> Out there in the Atlantic they were sinking a lot of Allied shipping. . . . But if the Canadian government in all its wisdom decided to send the war brides over to Canada, then they must have had special knowledge as to protection and everything it entailed. I wondered, but I went along with it. A Canadian soldier was not expected to think.[3]

The earliest record I have of a war bride journey to Canada is found on the "Boat Boards" [4] maintained by the Vancouver Island War Brides Association. Ethel Coulter's name is under the name of her ship, the *Baltrover*, followed by the date of her arrival: September 1941. The Canadian government's decision to offer "free repatriation" to dependents (wives, widows and children) of Canadian personnel who served overseas was announced in January 1942.[5]

These early travellers received instructions from Canada House. Because of the submarine menace they left Britain under tight security, forbidden to discuss the details with anyone but their parents. Trains carrying them to ports in the north or south had the windows blacked out. Station names had been painted out as had names on ships. Rose (Pate) Robinson, Winnipeg, Manitoba who travelled in May 1945, was on one such ship:

> There was no name on our ship but they called it 'the Drunken Duchess'. The voyage took two weeks because of zig-zagging to avoid U-boats.[6] I washed the few undergarments I had (thanks to family and friends' coupons). They were stolen from the line. All I had left was what I was wearing. After that I washed them and pinned them to my bunk each night.

Jean Spear of Ottawa, Ontario was on board the *Pasteur,* December 1944:

> The Atlantic was probably no worse than any other December. If you have the choice avoid it like the plague. It was grey and heaving. Many of the 300 war brides were doing the same. Sonia d'Artois was tall, blond and beautiful. She had parachuted into France and joined the French Resistance, but she was no match for the Atlantic.

The Lyall story illustrates what could happen when husband and wife took it into their own hands to reunite, and why Canadian supervision seemed so rigid. Imagine the chaos if 44,000 couples had tried the same thing! In April 1940, Kathleen Roe of Fleet, Hampshire married Kenneth Lyall of the Royal Canadian Army Medical Corps. Shortly afterwards Kenneth was invalided out of the army and returned to Canada. By March 1941 he was more than anxious to be reunited with his wife. Because of wartime secrecy he could not inform Kathleen of his decision to work his way to Britain on a freighter. Alas Kathleen had finally been given space on a troopship. The British *Daily Sketch* had a field day with the story:

> (Mrs. Lyall) is due in Canada this week and Kenneth is expected in Hampshire today . . . but when Mr. Lisle (sic) misses Mrs. Lisle, and Mrs. Lisle misses Mr. Lisle, doubtless this serial story is TO BE CONTINUED.[7]

126

BANANA BOATS

War brides often report travelling to Canada on a "Fyffe's banana boat". In pre-war England "Fyffe" was synonymous with "banana". Ships of the Elders & Fyffes' fleet arrived regularly at Avonmouth, near Bristol, Gloucestershire carrying millions of bananas. These ships crossed the Atlantic independently and at speed due to the perishable nature of their cargo. After the outbreak of war fourteen out of the fleet of twenty-one ships were sunk by enemy action. In 1940 importation was suspended for the duration. Fyffe ships used in the transportation of war brides include the *Bayano, Cavina,* and *Ariguani.* [8]

Peggy O'Hara's comment on her journey, "Things were definitely not organized when I left for Canada in July 1944," was an understatement. It was midnight, during an air-raid, when she left London's Kensington Station with a small group of wives and children. Twenty-six hours later they arrived at Gourock, Scotland. There had been no milk or food on the train for the children, only water. Once at sea the *Empress of Scotland* turned north to avoid U-boats. Peggy was pregnant and too sick to be frightened. Passengers were told the change of course was just a precaution - her reaction was "Yeah, right!" She arrived in Halifax and things did not improve.

Peggy had to pay for her train tickets and was never reimbursed. She was unfortunate; she must have been on the first sailing after the pre- and post- D-Day ban on civilians leaving the country was lifted. Her journey was made during the changeover in responsibility for war bride travel and there were inevitable glitches.

Canadian authorities made heroic efforts to adapt the ships for women and children, but they were not a good environment. Ships had been overloaded with returning servicemen (three men often shared the same bunk, each having an eight hour occupancy). Despite cleaning and fumigation, dysentery was an ongoing problem.

Evelyn (Weaver) Payne, of Coleman, Alberta, sailed from Birkenhead in November 1945:

> The *Manchester Shipper* was a small freighter built to carry twelve passengers in comfort, and there were seventy-seven of us on board. Gales and mines sent us north. We tied up overnight in the Bay of Fundy and then at St John, New Brunswick, and experienced the 40' tide.

Evelyn arrived at Natal, Alberta at 4:00 am. The temperature was 35°F below zero with lots of snow. Her husband had been released from hospital to meet her.

Bread was one of the few foods not rationed during the war. Godfrey Smith had mixed feelings about Britain's wartime loaf:

It may have been sad stuff, grey, grimy, coarse and bland; but at least you could eat as much of it as you liked . . .[8]

It is well known that the pristine white bread in the ship's dining rooms made a lasting impression on war brides. One war bride watched others at a nearby table crumble pieces into envelopes to send home.

Jane (Clark) Atkinson, was from the port of Gourock, Scotland, but sailed from Liverpool on the *Pasteur,* in April 1944:

> U-boats were following us and the ship stopped twice, but there was no panic. On nice days we sat on deck and munched on dry bread rolls to keep from getting sick. What brave hearts we were! When I look back I feel I was in a trance the whole trip. I had never been to England before and never travelled anywhere alone.

SEASICKNESS

Before World War II the medical profession and the Royal Navy had a strange attitude towards seasickness. "It's all in your head," was the usual diagnosis. But there's a wonderful story, written by John Rhodes Sturdy in *Maclean's* magazine, and quoted in *The Canadians at War, 1939/45,* Volume 2, about Stoker Mahoney who had chronic and disabling seasickness, but kept being sent back to sea, and how a group of RCN medical officers were conned into discovering that seasickness is very real.

Brenda (Clapham) Carriere, wrote from Vancouver, British Columbia about an unexpectedly fast reunion:

> As we walked towards the *Scythia* there was John waving from the top deck. Apart from a General's wife, I was the only one with a husband aboard. We could not share a cabin. I was on A deck and he was on D. There were armed sentries at each end of our deck to protect us from unwelcome advances of the troops but John, in his RCAF officer's uniform was saluted and allowed to pass. John was given permission to eat with us, and was the only man in our ornate dining room. That night the sea became rough that I was wretchedly ill and didn't go near the dining room again. John had to continue eating with six other war brides, three of them quite visibly pregnant. A ship is the most amazing place for rumours: a U-boat had been sighted, wives had been found in the lifeboats with soldiers, Hitler had committed suicide . . . By the time I reached Halifax I was so ill I was bringing up blood. The Army Doctor was reluctant to let me travel further, but said as I was only going to Montreal, I could go.

Gwendolyn (Stratton) Goodey, of Chilliwack, British Columbia left on the *Ile de France* from Gourock with her two sons:

> My mother was very superstitious, and worried because I left home on Friday October 13, 1944. I met the military police under the four-faced clock at Waterloo, as instructed, and they took me to Canada House. After two days I went on to Glasgow by train. There

128

were two other war brides who had one child each. We put blankets on the luggage racks and strapped the children up there for the night. On the ship we had to go up on deck in our life jackets three times because of U-boats. We had the first shipment of wounded from the invasion on board and were told we would not get a lot of help until we got to Halifax. A very nerve-wracking journey. At Halifax the children were looked after while I had a bath, saw a doctor and had a meal. I cried a lot. We docked at night and when I saw all the lights I cried some more and thanked God for my safe journey.

The orange canvas life jackets of the time had thick pieces of cork sewn into pockets. They were bulky, making it very difficult to hold a squirming toddler who was similarly clad.

The late Vera (Nicholson) Dalrymple and her daughter June, now Feswick, were on the same sailing as Gwendolyn. June wrote:

> Mother never mentioned a hostel, and as everything was blacked out she wasn't sure where she went until much later, which turned out to be Scotland. During the voyage the ship's Captain announced: 'Mothers, look after your children. This ship will stop for no one.' I find it very chilling, but understood why the safety of the whole ship could not be put in jeopardy if someone fell overboard.

Soon after June wrote this I heard from another war bride who took her child up on deck for some much-needed fresh air. The ship rolled, the toddler pulled free of her grasp and slid towards the rail. Then the ship rolled again delivering the child back to its frantic mother.

Toddlers fell from bunks, or became dehydrated from seasickness. Children 18 months or older usually recovered from dehydration, but in an infant it could be fatal. The dysentery that had plagued troops in Northwest Europe (where it was known as the Normandy Glide) and even in the crowded conditions of their repatriation sailings, became a problem for babies and toddlers on the war bride voyages.

Aubrey Jeffries, a merchant seaman, was 4th Engineer on the *Lady Nelson* which was operating as a hospital ship under Canadian Army Charter:

> On the ship we had sixteen wards. I think fifty in a ward. We had three operating rooms with six army surgeons and either twenty-four or thirty-six Canadian army nursing sisters. We had literally dozens of male nurses . . . who looked after the wards. Thirteen of the wards were mental wards. We had amputees, burns - air force and tank guys badly burned, . . . – a few guys blind. But mostly guys psychiatric, been damaged forever. We had guys come on couldn't stop cryin'; we had guys couldn't stop babblin'; we had guys come on gone morose, tuned out of life, in the depths of depression, fear or whatever the hell it was. We had a lot of navy guys, an awful lot of sailors. . . . We made I think two voyages when we stopped in Halifax and converted half the ship to carrying war brides. They made a bit better accommodations for them. I think we brought somethin' like 150 brides back first trip. We had a couple of births on board . . . When we got back to Halifax they discharged all the war brides . . . There were some of the war brides who had to return, didn't get off. Either they had been abandoned, they didn't have anybody to go to, or else they didn't like what they saw. I think we took back twenty-four.[10]

War bride Elsie (Nash) Mills, a nurse, speaks of the grief she felt for a young mother whose baby died and was buried at sea during her sailing on the *Britannic*. [11]

In rough weather mothers became desperately ill. Motion sickness could make them incapable of breast-feeding or even caring for their babies. Joan (Palmer) Watson a nurse who came to Lasalle, Quebec, was on the February 22 – March 5, 1946 crossing of the *Mauretania II*:

> I worked in sick bay all the time, and two of our babies died. It was so sad to come off the ship and see the Mums greeting the Dads with such bad news.

Peggy Bell of North Vancouver, British Columbia was halfway to Canada on the *Athlone Castle* when news came that the war in Europe was over. The war brides were served a celebratory glass of port, and then charged 9d (nine "old" pence) each.

Ethel Sherrin travelled on *The Duchess of Bedford* ("The Bouncing Duchess") after VE Day, but the Atlantic was still not safe. Apart from free-floating mines:

> There were still U-boats in the waters so we had to go in convoy flanked by mine-sweepers, three on each side, one fore and one aft, guiding five liners on their way to Canada and the United States. I will never forget the little boats coming out from Halifax to welcome us.

As Ethel says not all German U-boats surrendered when the war ended. There were estimated to be nearly 100 still at large.

Peggy (Fiddimore) O'Hara of Airdrie, Alberta, records a baby dying of pneumonia on the train when she was en route to Montreal. [12]

After Terry and I boarded the *Mauretania* we made it to the dining room the first day or two, then Terry became ill. It was the first time so many, 943 war brides and babies, had been aboard one ship, and we had a rough crossing. The escorting staff must have been overwhelmed for the only help we had was from other war brides, and from our Cabin Steward, Perce. To be Irish about it, if there had been enough nurses and Red Cross volunteers aboard there wouldn't have been room for war brides!

I was a fairly good sailor, but Terry wasn't and required my full attention. In that airless cabin, surrounded by sick brides, I was woozy and lost my appetite. I left when Terry was sleeping, and then only to stagger to the lowest deck and wash clothes by hand in sea water. One afternoon I was called to the purser's office to confirm my railway destination. It was rougher than ever. The carpet rose to hit my feet one second, then fell away at odd angles the next. Grab ropes had been attached to the hand rails to facilitate progress, and large signs forbade access to the open decks. I was issued a train ticket for "Halifax, to Bassano, Alberta", but I knew that Bassano had no line connecting to Empress, my final destination. At my insistence the ticket was changed to "Halifax to Swift Current", where Bill planned to meet us.

That rough voyage on the *Mauretania II* can be likened to an extended air-raid. Instead of listening for the next drone of a bomber, you braced yourself for the next monster wave. The *Mauretania* was completely at the mercy of the Atlantic. Leaning one way it rode up to the giant wave's crest, paused, slowly came upright, tilted so far in the other direction that you were sure it would capsize, then rode down, down, into a watery valley where it righted itself, tackled a few smaller waves, then repeated the performance, over and over and over. As in an air raid there seemed a distinct possibility of sudden death. Until the voyage was over there was not much you could do but hang on to something and endure. Our cabin stewardess was invisible after the first day. Perce had his faults, but he was always there with crackers and hot sweet tea (the universal British panacea for distress or shock), and day or night with warmed bottles of formula. Without him I don't think we'd have survived. We forgave his little shipboard jokes about the "lovely greasy breakfast bacon" awaiting us in the dining room, and his none too accurate accounting when exchanging our pounds for his Canadian dollars. (We'd been warned not to do this, but he offered, and in our condition it was easier than standing in line at the Purser's office.) When it came time to tip Perce we were as generous as finances would allow (we were only allowed to take £10 out of Britain). The invisible stewardess received one farthing (the smallest denomination in the old Pound Sterling currency, worth a quarter of an old penny) in her envelope.

A press clipping, courtesy Melynda Jarratt, gives some details of this *Mauretania II* sailing. Colonel W. E. Sutherland, the Ship's Commandant praised the Red Cross and the Stewardesses (he evidently didn't hear about ours!) for their good work. Noted was the absence of cheering crowds at Halifax, in contrast to the previous arrival of the *Mauretania* bringing the last of the troops home.

M. Joan (Watts) Small, who came to Vancouver, British Columbia remembered the *Mauretania* voyage, with the help of the diary she kept:

We sailed on February 5, with a band on the dock playing 'You'd be far better off in a Home'.

Joan was on a lower deck and counted herself fortunate to get a top bunk near a porthole. She says "Merchant navy types" in the dining room were good at feeding the children. (When I read this I realised that because so many mothers were seasick the support staff were kept busy seeing that the children were fed, and generally looking after them, and I rather regretted the farthing tip for the stewardess.)

After a session carrying GI brides the *Queen Mary* was made available for Canadian war brides. Those who sailed on her were aware of the graffiti that was a legacy of troopship days:

. . . they would carve their initials . . . At the end of the war great pieces of these rails were . . . replaced. They were cut up and sold for souvenirs . . . It was teak, you know, and it was hard to carve too, but they'd spend their time doing that. They weren't deliberately destructive of things, no, not at all.[13]

Ethel (Small) Whitehead, who came to Claresholm, Alberta, was on the *Queen Mary* in June 1946:

I remember thinking how terrible it was that all the beautiful woodwork had initials, etc., carved in it by troops who had sailed in her.

My first reaction was the same, but then I thought of those thousands of men, of how young they were, eighteen and up, sailing into the unknown. The GIs had been drafted, most were not volunteers. The war was a European one that, until Pearl Harbour, they had been told was not their war. As they crowded into the *Queen Mary* they would only be human if it crossed their minds that for many of them it was going to be a one-way journey. Perhaps carving your initials affirmed that for that moment at least, you were here, and you were alive. Pieces of these carved deck rails are preserved in the Cunardia Museum aboard Cunard's new ship the *Queen Victoria*.

Canadian Red Cross escort officer Leah Halsall, aboard *Lady Rodney*, November, 1946.
Credit: Leah Halsall

Doris (Foulkes) Clarkson sailed on the *Letitia* September 30, 1946:

I remember journeying to London and spending the night at a hostel, which had been the peacetime London home of Lord Aberconway. I remember how we girls strolled along Oxford Street for one last time. The following day we travelled by train to Liverpool, but I have few memories of that train journey. We sailed at 11 pm aboard the *Letitia*. On arriving in Halifax we learned that the ship's name had been changed en route to the *Empire Brent*. The enclosed copy of a postcard purchased as we left the ship may be of interest.

It's considered bad luck to change a ship's name. In 1946 the *Letita* had been sold to a British company whose vessels all had names prefixed with "*Empire*".

THE *LETITIA/EMPIRE BRENT* AND THE IRISH CATTLE BOAT

Stories about the *Letitia/Empire Brent* abound. The ship was carrying 300 British and Dutch war brides and 200 Canadian servicemen [14] when it left Liverpool in the early morning of November 19, 1946. Not far along the River Mersey it collided with the *Stormont,* an Irish cattle boat that sank leaving cattle floundering in the water. Some of the women witnessed the scene from the deck, but most slept on, unaware of the accident. The *Empire Brent* returned to the dock, but gale-force winds kept it from docking for another eight hours. Luggage was lost in the confusion, and there was a long wait for a train to London. British war brides were returned to their homes to face a second painful goodbye when the *Empire Brent* was made sea-worthy. Bureaucracy played its part, and these brides were unable to obtain ration books for the time they were back in their British homes. Dutch war brides could not be sent home so were housed at the Chesham Hostel, London where they whiled away the time hand-stitching baby clothes from new diapers, (probably donated from Red Cross gift layettes).

The ship sailed for the second time December 13, arriving in Halifax after a rough trip. Twenty GI Brides were on board, en route to the United States, as well as 23 Canadian VADs returning from service overseas. Rosina (Allen) Saxby, of Cobourg, Ontario remembers that twins were born on this sailing. By strange coincidence the Canadian train carrying some of the *Empire Brent* passengers, was held up for several hours near Rimouski, Quebec while the wreckage of a de-railed cattle train was cleared from the tracks!

The names of war brides known to have been aboard the jinxed sailing include:

Eileen (Orton) Aedy, Sarah (Lynch) Bolin, Cathy Coupal, Mrs. Davies, Catherina (Vermaelsen) Dallaire, and her son Roméo, (the future General), Mabel Flannigan, Joan Harper, Theresa Langrille, Elsa (Bromley) Lintott, Jean (Pithouse) Pinotti, Victorine Prout, Julia Salter, Rosina (Allen) Saxby, Jessie (McTeer) Sinclair, and Christina Tanner. [15]

T.S.S. "EMPIRE BRENT"

T.S.S. "LETITIA"

The *Letitia* collided with a cattle boat while transporting war brides.
Credit: Doris Clarkson

If some countries have too much history, we have too much geography.
    William Lyon MacKenzie King
    (Holland's area totals 13,500 square miles, the UK, 93,629 and Canada, 2,849,674.)

No newcomer to Canada should arrive in November.
    Estella Spergel

Our stop is coming up,
caught in the light
snowflakes fly sideways against the darkness,
and my own reflection stares back at me.

The measured ringing of a bell
announces our arrival.
People are sliding past the window
and there,
under the light,
is a blessedly familiar face.
Arms are helping us down,
my foot crunches into snow
and for the first time,
though England is ten days and seven thousand miles away,
this frozen land
begins to feel like home.

    from "Ten Days and Seven Thousand Miles", Eswyn Lyster,
    first published *Legion* magazine, December 1982

The only known photograph of a War Bride Special train in transit. It accompanied an article by war bride Kathleen Watt in the Islander section of the Victoria *Times Colonist* in 1980. The newspaper archives do not date back that far and all efforts to contact the writer have failed.
Credit: Unkown

Chapter 14: The Canadian Train

As we stepped ashore into post-war Canada we had few profound thoughts. We were tired and grateful that an uncomfortable voyage had ended, especially if we had young children. We were glad they were coming to a better existence than they had experienced in their short lives. Now we were here, so much depended on the love and integrity of one person. If he failed us . . . it did not bear thinking about.

A lot of pressure was on our young husbands. For years their basic needs of clothing, food, income and lodging had been taken care of. Now they must find all these things for themselves and for their families as well. If they spent too much time with their service friends their fathers were quick to say, "When are you going to settle down and get a job?", but the job market was overwhelmed with men looking for work. Barry Broadfoot has a funny, loving story "A Place for the Bride" in his book *The Veteran's Years,* pages 76-82, about one veteran's extraordinary effort to give his war bride a home.

Before we began our journey the Immigration Branch and the Canadian Red Cross had ensured that our "settlement" in Canada was satisfactory. In many cases in-laws had indicated their willingness to take us into their homes.

With us on the trains were Red Cross volunteers, a medical officer, a nurse, and a Movement Control Officer. Some coaches held only Army or Air Force Dependents, some a mix of both, according to our destinations. Local newspapers carried reports of ships' arrivals in Halifax, as well as lists of war brides and children destined for that area. Husbands or in-laws could then work out on which day "war bride special" trains could be expected to arrive.

The Canadian press used journalistic terms of the day. Brides selected for interviews were "vivacious brunettes" or "statuesque blondes", terms that to us were pure Hollywoodese, and today would be politically incorrect. Yet when identifying individual brides the formal "*Mrs.* A. B. Smith" or "*Mrs.* C. D. Brown" was often written. Right there is evidence of the dichotomy that was Canada, part twentieth-century United States, part nineteenth-century Britain.

Patricia Anne (Bourke) Risley's husband met her as she left the *Aquitania* and took her to Halifax's Lord Nelson hotel:

> I was so homesick for England that I criticised everything and everybody and I cried a lot. Why my husband didn't ship me back or strangle me I'll never know. While I could see the smoke stacks of the *Aquitania* I felt better . . . an escape route? . . . but after she was gone I felt really cut off.

Sheila Anketel-Jones was greeted at dockside by "a largish lady in over-the-top pastel-coloured clothes":

> She approached me with outstretched, gloved hand, beaming smile and the questioning word 'Bride?' It was all so out of context with war-torn Britain and the awful ten-day crossing that for a moment I was completely nonplussed . . . then the penny dropped. Of course, '*war* bride'. So I smiled and took the gloved hand. I later discovered she was a bishop's wife doing her bit to make the war brides welcome. I realise we must have presented a sorry collection as we unsteadily came down the gangway. It apparently had

been one of the worst crossings ever. The dockside was one great mass of seething, moving people, troops, brides meeting in-laws, officials . . . Carrying my holed suitcase I made my way as best I could in the direction of the wonderfully deep voice with the Canadian accent calling, 'All aboard! All aboard!' On hearing this I knew for sure I was in North America. On the train a very old man smoking a pipe, and without the least sign of embarrassment, stared at us. 'Where yer going?' he asked. 'To Victoria,' I replied. 'What d'yer wanna go there for – people only go there to die.' My heart sank.

When Terry and I docked at Halifax the city was obscured by heavy swirling snow. Sea, sky and land, all were seagull shades of dull grey and white. We came ashore into Pier 21's drafty customs shed, where our luggage was piled under letters of the alphabet. I carried my sick son in a blankct. The ever-faithful Red Cross hurried us into the warmth of the waiting train. Terry was taken over by a Canadian nurse and although it was morning I was shown to a made-up berth and urged to catch up on lost sleep. Of course I couldn't sleep and instead rested while enjoying the view of the snowy countryside. As we detoured through Maine I watched brightly-clad children throwing snowballs as they returned home from school. At last the windows frosted over and I fell asleep.

Joan (Piller) McLean, who came from Cardiff to Toronto, listened to recorded messages on board the *Queen Mary,* "about the 'Golden West' ", obviously meaning the whole of Canada:

> We docked in Halifax and if you have never seen Halifax in the rain you haven't missed much.

Joan found Toronto life "incredibly dull" after six years in the WAAF and the hectic wartime years, but after a while couldn't imagine living anywhere else.

Nancy (Etches) Fussell arrived on the *Aquitania* in March 1946:

> We were all so relieved to be at last in Canada and to experience the warmth of the Canadian people as they welcomed us to their country. As we walked down the gangplank many of us carrying our beautiful babies (I was carrying Michael) a brass band struck up 'Here Comes the Bride'. We did not feel bride-like after the rough trip.

A war bride who had changed her English notes for dollar bills on the *Letitia* said the Canadian currency didn't look to her like real money, adding "*Now* it would be nice to get $4.04 Cdn. for a pound!"

Daisy (Bohannon) Zerbin of Calgary, Alberta, came on the *Aquitania* in June 1946:

> When we arrived in Halifax a reporter said, 'Is there anyone going to Saskatchewan?' I put my hand up. 'Did your husband tell you he had a gopher ranch?' I said he *could* have one, but if so he never told me. For years I couldn't figure out what the laughing was all about.

(A gopher is a small ground squirrel found on the western prairies and considered by farmers to be a pest.)

The railway journey was made longer because the trains stopped so many times for war brides to alight, and were diverted to sidings to allow scheduled trains to proceed. Also at some main centres we left the train for refreshments while our children were cared for, giving us a much-appreciated break. We made allowances for our trains, but it would come as a shock later on to learn that in wintertime even regularly scheduled trans-continental trains could be hours, sometimes days, overdue because of blizzard conditions and snow slides.

INSTRUCTIONS TO PASSENGERS ON "WAR BRIDE SPECIAL" TRAINS

Dear Fellow Canadians:
We have no PA system so we are taking this means of advising you on matters which we are sure will prove useful to you.

DON'T Send telegrams without first referring the details to a Train Liaison Officer. We appreciate you are anxious to advise your husband, etc. about arrival times, but this is unnecessary as he or they have been told by the Canadian authorities the time and place to meet you. Our experience has shown that wires giving times of arrival have frequently caused confusion and upsets in well laid plans. If you must send a wire, speak to the Train Liaison Officer first.

DON'T Use the occasional stops of the train for shopping purposes. Unfortunately we have found that the girls at stops have gone into the town's shopping areas. You are not familiar with Canadian money or Canadian prices and it is more than just a possibility that you may make a mistake which you will not be able to detect. Shop in your new home town.

DON'T Give money to strangers at stops in order that they may purchase something for you. Speak to the Officers on the train about your needs.

DON'T Over tip. If you don't understand the money value, ask any of the Train Staff.

DON'T Stray too far from the train when it stops when you are permitted to get off. You may be left behind.

DO Be careful at mealtime. Rich foods, lack of exercise and long rail journeys, especially in the summer months cause many minor complaints.

DO Make certain you understand the route letter you secure when you move independently to another train.

DO Try to keep your accommodation area neat and washrooms clean, please.

DO Keep your handbag with you at all times as tickets must be checked at intervals on the trip.

DO Consult the Doctor, Canadian Red Cross (CRX), or VAD nurse if you or your child feel ill.

DO Refer any problems concerning money, transfer of funds etc. you have to the Train Liaison Officer whose only interest is your wellbeing.

DO Send air mail letters to relatives in the U.K. instead of costly cables. Air mail will give seven days service and CRX will supply Air Mail forms.

If you desire to show your appreciation to the CRX or other voluntary organizations for their services, join one of them in your own home town.

Issued by Department of National Defence, Ottawa, Ontario [1]

Marie-Louise (Newry) Snider was on her way to Vancouver, British Columbia:

We had been given our last allowance money on the ship and were dying to buy something without coupons. When we reached Toronto we were told we could go shopping as we would be there a few hours. Sally (a girl from Bromley) and I, along with a horde of others, headed for Eaton's. It was just opening time and I'm sure the commissionaire nearly had a fit when we descended on him. Sally was going to High Prairie, Alberta, and she chose a high heel sandal in hot pink with gold studs (she later told me there were no sidewalks in High Prairie). I bought a lovely red, high wedge shoe. I'm sure Lloyd's mother had a fit when she heard what I had paid for them, but she didn't say a word.

When Jean (Wilks) Elmer's train stopped at Winnipeg she too went shopping:

Two of us decided we needed some fresh fruit. We shot out of the station, turned right, walked for about ten minutes and saw a greengrocers across the street. There was one small problem, no crosswalk, but there was a policeman, bobby's hat and all. So I asked if he would take us across the street. You should have seen the look on his face! He laughed. 'Where're you from?' he roared, as he stopped traffic and beckoned us across. He waited for us and then repeated the performance, still laughing.

Occasionally when a bride stepped down from the train there was nobody to meet her. Members of the Red Cross would not let us go unless they were satisfied we were in good hands. Kay McCaskill, an officer in the RCAF Women's Division, escorted one bride to her new home and detected little warmth in the mother-in-law. She worried about leaving her, but had no alternative. A few years later she read of the young woman's divorce. [2]

The widow who was in my *Mauretania* cabin left our train at a whistle stop late at night somewhere along the north shore of the Great Lakes. Those of us who stayed up to wave her goodbye watched her climb aboard a horse drawn vehicle and immediately move out of the range of the lights of the train. She was to visit for a while with her husband's family and then return to England.

Joan Small was on the same train. Her diary continues from Chapter 12:

On February 12 we travelled through Quebec and Ontario. At Quebec City we were escorted to the station restaurant. As we walked through, many adverse remarks were made. I guess they didn't realise that some of us understood French. Not much of a welcome. On February 13 we were held up at North Bay and arrived at Winnipeg the next day, five hours late. We were at Edmonton on February 15. It seems Dave's aunt had been meeting all the trains that day as she had word that I was passing through. She greeted me with a box of chocolates and some nylons. I did weep that day! We got to Jasper very late, where I was amazed by the sight of full moonlight on the mountains. A trainload of women had started from Halifax and only five of us ended up in Vancouver at 2:00 pm on February 16. My new family met me and took me for a ride around town on the way to Dave's parents' home. I had left home well and strong and arrived at my new home in a poor state. My legs and feet were swollen and I had slept in my shoes for two nights for fear that I wouldn't be able to get them on again if I took them off.

Jane (Beatty) Davidson remembers what she calls an "unhappy" incident at a small station in Quebec:

A few of us got off the train to buy cigarettes and be sociable, only to have a man say, 'Why don't you English bitches go back where you came from?' which sent us all back to the train in tears. I have to say that the Lieutenant in charge, whom we had thought rather wimpish, rushed to our defence and tore such strip off (that man) and the coffee shop full of men that it did our hearts good.

Canadian trains had no provision for infants and toddlers, but the Canadian Red Cross volunteers made us as comfortable as possible. Nobody was able to solve the problem of washing diapers in those minute washroom sinks, a subversive activity anyway because it was frowned upon by the train crew. How to deal with soiled diapers was the greatest problem especially in the hot summer months and before plastic garbage bags had been invented. In desperation some diapers were thrown from the train.

One war bride had a very understanding friend:

At Montreal a friend with whom I had shared lodgings in Training College came on board with a bag of clean diapers and took away the soiled. A friend indeed. She had come to Canada as a war bride six months earlier. Jim travelled to Edmonton to meet me. He asked the porter if he knew where I was. The porter said 'Oh, there's a very nervous lady underneath that bunk with her baby.' 'That'll be them,' said Jim.

Gladys (Bauley) Armstrong of Etobicoke, Ontario remembers the kindness of the Red Cross:

They were not only on the trains but met us at all the major stations and gave us tea, biscuits, fruit, cigarettes and magazines. They were just wonderful. At dusk I found myself sitting in the dining car looking down at the Blue River crashing its way through the canyon, while way above snowcapped mountains were outlined against the darkening sky. Soon the stars appeared, the mountains began to blend with the darkness and I had to pinch myself to make sure I wasn't dreaming. The next morning I was up at five which was fortunate as the train ran out of water for washing which was very hard on the girls as they wanted to look their best for their husbands. We were ready hours before the train pulled into Vancouver. The suspense was awful. Ted met me amongst a seething crowd of husbands, wives and relatives. After a cup of coffee, again supplied by the Red Cross, we were interviewed by a press reporter and then driven to Ted's parents' house by a generous volunteer.

May (Tanner) Collison, of Lively, Ontario, remembers:

On the train one woman managed to get a newspaper and read out from the Lost and Found column: 'Lost, a pair of sneakers.' We all laughed as we didn't know sneakers were running shoes.

Faith (Harley) McKinnon, who now lives in South Surrey, British Columbia was on her way to Spring Valley, Prince Edward Island:

The trip to Canada was the best memory, as things went wrong after getting off the ship. Our daughter Margaret got travel-sick as soon as we left on the train. I had to change trains at Sackville for PEI and I landed, bewildered, on the platform, wondering how I was ever going to find the Red Cross to help. I turned around and there was my husband and his brother with the car.

One war bride was surprised by an unsolicited comment:

When we stopped at Moncton, New Brunswick a group of small boys standing at the station asked if we were refugees, and one commented that I talked 'like one of them girls from Newfoundland'.

On the train Sheila Anketel-Jones saw a girl who had refused to attend life-boat drill unless she could take her baby with her:

She was obviously very poor, both she and the baby in old, dirty clothes, hair unwashed, a baby bottle stuffed in a torn pocket. In a moment of silence she said, 'My Dad told me if I didn't like it I was to write 'im a letter and he would send me the money to come 'ome.' I had sat there feeling terribly sorry for her, but not any more. In fact I envied her with all my heart. Her father had said this to her, mine had said, 'Now, remember, you made your bed and must now lie on it. There is to be no running back if you don't like it.' Looking back from this great distance of fifty years I know he only thought he was saying the right thing, he loved me deeply and was devastated by my leaving, but to me it was as if a great door had closed. I never told a soul until now . . .

Joyce Hibbert quotes an anonymous war bride:

We arrived at the old Bonaventure Station in Montreal. The ropes were up and hundreds of relatives were there waiting to see what they had drawn in the great marriage lottery.[3]

When Kathleen (Galvin) Harris arrived in Windsor, Ontario:

It was the day of Windsor's tornado and all was black, no lights anywhere, but I hardly noticed. It was so like England in the blackout.

The movement of so many women and children was a gigantic task and not surprisingly there were a few tense moments. Barbara (Owen) Scott was asked by the Liaison Officer to confirm her destination:

> I replied, 'I'm going to Seaforth, Ontario.' 'Well, you're on the wrong train,' he said. I was tired and now terrified. 'I was put on this train to Toronto.' 'Yes, but Seaforth is just outside Halifax.' After an hour during which the other brides comforted me (I had only just turned 18), he came back and said I was on the right train. Gordon and his brothers met me at Toronto. Incidentally, on the train mothers with babies were able to heat the bottles in the kitchenette. One girl who was still able to breast feed used the time to make tea for all of us before bed. About thirty years later at a reunion I said there was one person I'd love to meet again, and I related the tea-making incident. Someone who had been on the same *Aquitania* sailing said, 'Well, that was me!'

Old coaches had been taken out of storage to accommodate the sudden increase in passenger traffic. May (Tanner) Collison of Lively, Ontario was in one that was old and dirty:

> For each passenger car, full of girls and their young children, the only bathroom facility was a very small cubicle with a minute hand sink and a toilet. We tried desperately to keep ourselves, the babies and our clothes clean. It was a heartbreaking round of sharing slivers of Pears soap and helping each other to shampoo hair in a sink the size of a soup bowl, and often no hot water. Someone kept asking the porter when would we get to the zoo? I found out she was saying when we would get to 'The Soo', meaning Sault Saint Marie in the Great Lakes area of Ontario.

Jane (Armstrong) Clouthier of Petawawa, Ontario found the train stiflingly hot:

> Many of us were wearing tweed suits, the sun was shining and the heat was on in the train, so they shut it off. I had just got settled that night with my single blanket when the middle part of the bunk collapsed. I called the porter and he fixed it, but he wasn't out of sight before it fell down again. By now it was cold so, being a timid soul, I huddled in the seat trying to sleep. I wished we hadn't complained about the heating.

When Joyce "Terry" (Cotterell) England arrived at Saskatoon, Saskatchewan there were no young husbands waiting on the platform:

> Were we ever worried! Then a big bald man came to me and took my baby. It was my father-in-law who worked for the Canadian National Railway and was allowed on the platform. The rest of the men were downstairs. Anyway, you should have heard the giggles from the other war brides because I had said that my man was tall, blonde and handsome.

Mavis (Howick) Granger, of White Rock, British Columbia was saddened when brides, who had arrived months earlier, came to meet her train. They were homesick and in tears and wanting to talk to someone from home. Gloria Brock remembers with obvious gratitude the porters on her train, one is especially remembered for making jam sandwiches for a bride's birthday.

Patricia (Ramsdale) Hilland of Kamloops, British Columbia remembers:

> Our porter would come bustling into our coach, his face wreathed in smiles, singing at the top of his voice, 'I'm Looking Over a Four Leaf Clover'. I certainly hoped he was right, and that our future held a lot of four-leafed clovers in it.

Joni (Jones) Shuttleworth was also impressed:

> I really don't know how I would have coped without the help of the porters. They just seemed to appear when you needed help.

and Eileen (Powell) Dallas added:

> The porters went out of their way to look after us. I will never forget their kindness.

In the 1940s the job of porter was the only one open to African-Canadians on the Canadian railways. Every other employee was white. It was not until the 1950s that the first African-Canadian was promoted to Conductor.[4]

Doris (Foulkes) Clarkson who came to Lansing, Ontario before moving to Ottawa found the train journey "wonderful". She had no children so was able to relax and enjoy the experience:

> At night I slept in an upper berth, soothed by the haunting sound of the train whistle, and in the daylight I watched the endless miles of open country. We passed through Nova Scotia, New Brunswick, Maine and Quebec's Eastern Townships, stopping along the way to let brides off the train. I did have the most glorious introduction to Canada. October . . . our train seemed to follow the great St. Lawrence River, and I shall always remember the cloudless sky, the clear blue river and the rich red and yellow of the maples. I asked my husband to meet me wearing his uniform, I had never seen him in civilian clothes and didn't want him to appear strange to me. He was at Union Station to greet me carrying a large bouquet of flowers.

The women still aboard the trains watched platform reunions with fascination. Could these men in strange civilian clothing really be the uniformed Canadians we had known in England? My own memory is that the clothing changed as the train moved west. At first, certainly in Ontario, the men wore long tailored winter overcoats and Russian-style fur hats. Further west they sported heavy red and white checkered shirts, buckled black over-boots (as often as not with the buckles flying loose), and close-fitting wool caps with attached ear flaps. Then of course the civilian suits and hats that were part of the demobilization package. The clothing, because it was unexpected, and so unlike that of our fathers and brothers, deepened our feeling of being in a strange land.

Jean Forbes, the daughter of Marguerite (Lee) and Melvin Hunter reported:

> This was the first time my mother had seen my father in civilian clothes and he had on a three-piece suit and a hat. She said he looked like an American gangster! My father lost the hat. I never knew him to wear one during my childhood.

Lille (Phipps) Hodgson, who came to Waterford, Ontario, has a refreshingly different observation:

Seeing my loved one in his civvy clothes made up for any hardships suffered on the journey.

Jane (Beatty) Davidson, Roberts Creek, British Columbia and Margaret (Hall) Alley, Surrey, British Columbia who arrived at the end of track in January 1946, also liked what they saw:

As we came out of the station I saw the old Granville Street Bridge, lovely blue sky with puffs of white clouds. It was cold and so clean, and absolutely beautiful.

Terry and I were on the same train as Joan Small until we reached Swift Current. Bill was at the station, on leave for a few days from the Colonel Belcher Veteran's Hospital in Calgary. His battledress had somehow been stretched over the white plaster body cast that held his right arm almost in the salute position. No shock of civilian clothes for me. Apart from the cast he looked as he always had, except very thin, almost gaunt. I can still feel that unyielding cast as we hugged. It was 2:00 am, snow blowing all around us, and I made a fundamental error. Thinking how nice it was of Bill's mother to have come to meet me, I turned to his sister Vera and said, "Hullo Mother, it's wonderful to meet you at last." Luckily Vera had a great sense of humour.

We stayed for what was left of the night at the Healey Hotel, and next morning the four of us travelled on "the Passenger" (as opposed to "the Freight") along the branch line to Empress, Alberta.

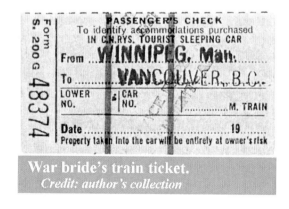

War bride's train ticket.
Credit: author's collection

...anyone would have found the transition from Britain to Canada in the mid 1940s a challenge. The sight of grown men reading comic books typified for one (war bride) a country where even major cities lacked a genuine bookstore.'

The view is also advanced that too much is being made of British war brides in Canada.'Withdraw the attention shown them now and they will want to go home to England.'

from: What to Do About British Brides, *Toronto Star*, September 16, 1946

I didn't know there was any place in the world like it. A far cry from Thornton Heath!

Gwen Grace (Harms) Keele

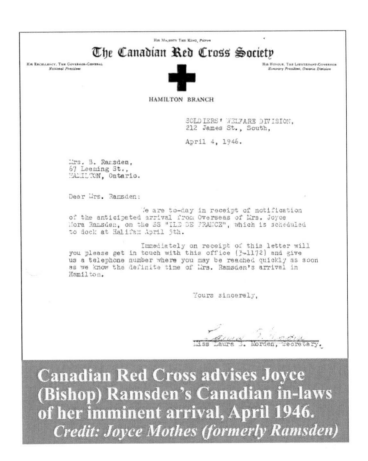

Canadian Red Cross advises Joyce (Bishop) Ramsden's Canadian in-laws of her imminent arrival, April 1946.
Credit: Joyce Mothes (formerly Ramsden)

Chapter 15: A Far Cry from Thornton Heath

Officially, British war brides were warmly welcomed to Canada. Speeches were littered with references to "English Roses" and "the Mother Country", yet not everyone was pleased to see us, probably because not everyone was from "the Mother Country" . . . The Canadian servicemen who had come to Britain were always so friendly that it was a shock to find some that of their countrymen were not. Many Canadian women had spent the war waiting for a local boy to come home, only to find that when he did he had a wife and baby. I was startled to be asked why I couldn't find myself an English husband. I replied that "find" was the operative word. There were not a lot of Englishmen to be found in Britain. On the other hand, for nearly three years the entire overseas Canadian Army had been stationed in my county! I did not allow for my questioner's unfamiliarity with Britain, and back then I was equally unaware of how Canada had been affected by the war.

In her Introduction to Joyce Hibbert's book, *The War Brides,* Mavis Gallant writes of the myths and half-truths that surrounded the newcomers:

> English girls, avid for marriage, were said to leap on any passing Canadian and drag him into blacked-out doorways for goings-on too shameful to describe – the soldier meanwhile clinging to a lamppost and protesting, 'No, no, I'm engaged to a nice girl in Regina!' Torn from his lamppost and his chastity, the Canadian, as the expression went, 'had to marry her'.

(The "goings-on in doorways" sound more like a reference to Piccadilly prostitutes than war brides.)

Empress Alberta, February 1946. Bill Lyster is in a full upper body cast.
Credit: author's collection

Prairie grain elevators.
Credit: author's collection

In small-town Alberta I was treated like a minor celebrity, and always introduced as "our English war bride". These last three words stuck together as if magnetized and entered my vocabulary. It was not until I was taken to task by a Scotswoman for saying "English" when I should have said "British" that I adjusted my perception. Large numbers of English, Scottish, Welsh and Northern Irish lassies fell for Canadian charms.

THE NEW COUNTRY

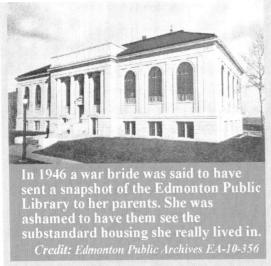

In 1946 a war bride was said to have sent a snapshot of the Edmonton Public Library to her parents. She was ashamed to have them see the substandard housing she really lived in.
Credit: Edmonton Public Archives EA-10-356

The Canada to which we came would be unrecognizable to most young Canadians today. Commercial air travel was severely limited, the Trans-Canada Highway was incomplete. Because Canadian effort had been directed towards building airports, training Allied airmen, and sending war and food supplies to Britain, house building had been neglected so there was an acute housing shortage. Some dicey 1940s landlords would only surrender a key if you crossed their palms with $100 or more. The main form of entertainment was unsophisticated radio programming: there was "Hockey Night in Canada" in winter, baseball in summer, and down home soap operas like *Ma Perkins* that had no sex and actually advertised soap. *The Happy Gang* was on daily with people like Bert Pearl and trumpeter Bobby Gimby (who had gone to school with my husband) and, in the west, cowboy songs delivered with an exaggerated nasal twang. In between, the radio gave us fat stock prices and the CBC (Canadian Broadcasting Corporation) news that seldom mentioned the country we had left. One sign of sophistication was to join the Book of the Month Club. Another difference was that back then I fed a family of three on $15 a week, and could get into a matinee showing of the latest Katherine Hepburn, Spencer Tracy hit for 25¢.

MOTHERS-IN-LAW

Many, perhaps most, war brides began their years in Canada by living with in-laws. Patricia (Collins) McCaskill came to Vancouver, British Columbia, and had a shaky start:

On hearing of our engagement Bud's mother had written asking why he couldn't marry someone from under his own flag! And she herself had English parents! I wrote and asked her not to judge me until she met me. When we arrived in Vancouver we were made very welcome, but Mother Mac spoke of the 'old girlfriend'. I just ignored it and soon Mother Mac was introducing me as Bud's wife, 'and she's an English war bride, you know'.

One war bride tried living in Canada, but wrote from London, England:

> My husband has been back to Canada but I can't go again. I get into a panic just thinking about it, but then I don't expect other war brides who stayed had my mother-in-law to put up with. We often have visitors from Canada. One is a war bride who was originally from Manchester. After fifty-four years in Saskatchewan she still cries her eyes out when we take her to the station to go home, so I guess I'm not the only one who couldn't settle, but I do admire the ones that did.

When her grandson caught measles one mother-in-law surprised her daughter-in-law by rubbing goose-grease on his spots. Another war bride said of her husband's mother, "She was a very cold potato."

Sometimes it took only a small gesture to set things right. Patricia (Ramsdale) Hilland married into a family from Finland, and did all the wrong things in an environment that was strange to her. After losing the bucket down the well, failing to turn the hay with a pitchfork, coping with Saturday night at the sauna, tossing her first attempt at bread-making into the creek, and sewing shut the flap of her husband's winter long johns, she wondered if she would ever please her mother-in law:

> There was a tension hanging over everything. Mom was tight-lipped and Pop stern and even quieter than usual. I had the uncomfortable feeling that it was something to do with us and the pressures of living with a very young family. One evening I saw Mom standing at the sink, peeling carrots. She looked so dejected that I threw all caution to the winds and simply put my arms around her. From such an ordinary gesture a deeper friendship started that was to grow into a very special love for one another over the years.

In many instances mothers-in-law turned out to be the war bride's best friend. My own (Susan) was a remarkable woman who took me in like a prodigal daughter. Her family followed her example so I gained the brother and sisters I'd never had. Everything was done to make us comfortable. There was even winter clothing waiting for Terry. When she heard that I hadn't eaten canned pears in five years she stocked up on Libby's® finest. I consumed so many pears those first weeks that for years I couldn't eat them at all.

Something else concerned Susan. She had an English neighbour everyone spoke of as "Hooky", which I presumed was derived from her surname. Apparently Hooky had once been a saucer short when serving tea, so had reached for the one in her parrot's cage. Susan teased me, saying she hoped I didn't have this "English habit"! I said not to worry, I wasn't planning on buying a parrot. One afternoon Bill's sister saw someone pass the window. "Here comes Hooky!" she said. There were no introductions and over tea I addressed the visitor as Hooky, at which point my new family appeared to go into simultaneous cardiac arrest.

Afterwards I learned that the name originated with one of the Lyster children, and referred to Hooky's slightly down-turned nose, a feature I hadn't even noticed. Later, amid gales of laughter, my gaffe was forgiven (probably not by Hooky!). I realised I had a lot to learn about small town Canada.

Apart from his father, the family of Brenda (Clapham) Carriere's "dashing French-Canadian pilot" spoke no English:

At that time living in Montreal was like going back two hundred years in time. When John visited his mother she would badger him about changing my religion. I suppose she thought she was protecting me as she firmly believed that only Catholics would enter Heaven. He never once put any pressure on me to change. I had one particular friend, a Belgian war bride, one of the most beautiful, talented, vivacious women I have ever met. With her I had to speak French and I made a great effort to learn the language. This surprised many of the English-speaking Canadian women I met who had lived in Montreal all their lives but had never troubled to learn French. There's no doubt that the French were considered rather second-class citizens at that time. Most business was conducted in English. The French had to learn English to get a job.

Another bride who came to Quebec was surprised to find that:

Nobody spoke English. Even the dog spoke French!

Some Maritimers were of Acadian ancestry. Nancy (King) Rioux, of Plaster Rock, New Brunswick, awoke her first morning in Grand Falls, NB, and heard everyone speaking French:

I couldn't understand a thing, but Ivan's mum said everything in English. She really was a lovely lady. Ivan came home with the news that he had been ordered back overseas. The next years were bad until he came home again. I don't know what I would have done without my wonderful mother-in-law.

Although Anne (Bourke) Risley came to "big town" Toronto she felt she had travelled back in time:

I wasn't allowed to wear slacks on the golf course and a hat had to be worn in church. (In England the Archbishop of Canterbury had relaxed the rule for women to cover their heads in church.) There was tremendous division between Catholics and Protestants. Jews were beyond the pale and not allowed to join anything and I remember an awful moment at *The Sword and Anchor* when a prominent local singer was asked to leave because she was black. I was unable to buy Kirby Grips® (hairpins), flannels were face cloths, and nobody knew where the haberdashery counter was. The man in the meat counter was not amused when I asked if he had any brains!

Betty (Woodruff) Cross, of Delta, British Columbia, says that despite Red Cross volunteers on the Canadian train coaching war brides in Canadian vocabulary (don't ask the butcher for a joint of meat but a roast, for instance), she still managed to confuse her new in-laws:

At one of Bob's relatives in Saskatchewan I referred to shell eggs, and they said 'What other kind of eggs are there?' I explained we had only one or two fresh eggs a week and then had to use the powdered kind.

Gertrude "Trudy" (Williams) Flatman started her Canadian life in Saskatchewan where her husband ran a hardware store:

> One day I was looking after the store when a logger asked me for a bastard file. I said I didn't like his language and refused to serve him. Jim explained all the different file names to me and I didn't make the same mistake again.

Our husbands cautioned us not to urge someone to cheer up by saying "Keep your pecker up" (British for "keep your chin up"). Also to forget about asking to be "knocked up in the morning" ("don't let me oversleep"). But we found other booby-traps that even our husbands could not foresee. M. Gwynneth (Bright) Falconer was asked by a neighbour to come for tea and see the new puppies. When asked if she would like one she stopped all other conversation when she said, "I'd love one but only if it's a bitch."

My mother, who rarely said anything out of place, startled Bill during a dinner table conversation about a mutual English friend's career. "He did have a good screw, didn't he!" she said, meaning he was well paid. That Bill was raising a soup spoon to his mouth at the time didn't help. After we had mopped up, my mother said irritably, "It's not safe to say *anything* in this country!" She wanted to know what she had said to cause the commotion, and my brave soldier husband wouldn't tell her. I managed to shock an Empress drug store clerk by saying "I need a rubber and some gum, please." She said icily, "I think you mean an eraser and some glue."

Joyce (Gawn) Crane's husband Bruce had been badly wounded in France after D-Day. When he recovered they were married at Joyce's parish church of St. Paul's. Joyce travelled from Thornton Heath, Surrey, a busy town north of Croydon (on the London to Brighton Road), to rural Manitoba. The farm at Hazelbrook had no running water, electricity or other conveniences. Joyce and Bruce turned it into a real family home where they lived for thirty-eight good years.[2]

Gwendolyn Grace Harms married Dave Keele, RCMP Provost Corps, in 1941. Gwen was also from Thornton Heath. She was married there at St. Jude's Church. This area of Surrey suffered the heaviest bombing in England, and her son David was born "in the middle of one of the worst air raids." Dave persuaded Gwen that she and their child would be safer in Canada. They arrived on the *Empress of Scotland* in July 1944 and went on to Wadena, Saskatchewan, which even today has a population of only 1,500. Gwen's in-laws were openly disappointed that her husband had not waited to marry a local girl, and must have listened to and believed all the myths Mavis Gallant quoted about war brides in her introduction to Joyce Hibbert's book. Alas, all the stereotypes about Canada's "little grey homes in the west" were true as well. The homes were quite often innocent of paint, and the sand-blasting effect of prairie dust storms had weathered them grey with textures like old-fashioned scrubbing boards. The Wadena home had no running water, no phone and an outdoor toilet with Eaton's catalogue standing in for toilet tissue:

I didn't know there was any place in the world like it. A far cry from Thornton Heath! I thought the war would never end, however it did, and Dave came home in August 1945. (After I took a nursing course) I joined Dave who was with the RCMP Detachment at The Pas, in northern Manitoba. We decided that once away from his family we could get along, and I went to work at the local hospital.

Other postings included "the tiny town of Winnipegosis" where their daughter was born, and Wabowden, Manitoba where they arrived in the middle of the night in 50°F below zero weather and had to walk with suitcases and the two children about half a mile along a railway track to the detachment house:

The house had no running water, no lights, no phone and a wood stove and furnace. Willie Etawakeppo fetched wood for us. The only way out of Wabowden was to fly by float plane or take the Churchill train which came through once a week. In 1942 I was diagnosed with T.B. and was told that I must not go back to Wabowden. I didn't know whether to laugh or cry. When I was allowed to go home, home was Dauphin, Manitoba, *very* civilized after Wabowden. After six years we moved to Portage La Prairie.

Gwen's marriage ended and she relocated to Winnipeg with the children:

I was fortunate enough to meet my present husband. We have been married thirty years and very happily. Dave remarried, but he suffered a stroke and died in 1992. We had made our peace, for which I am very thankful.

Lieutenant Ken Rootes.
Credit: author's collection

When Kathleen "Kay" (Davis) Rootes arrived in Edmonton in 1946 her husband was in a military hospital. Ken had been badly wounded while serving in Italy with the Loyal Edmonton Regiment. In 1948 Kay died after a long battle with tuberculosis. As they were both hospitalized she and Ken had not seen each other for three months. Ken spent a total of seven years in the Colonel Mewburn Pavilion, the military wing of Edmonton's University Hospital. During this time he upgraded his education through the Veterans Rehabilitation Act. After several years working in the oil business Ken studied law at the University of Alberta. During this time he married Margaret Haynes of Edmonton. Ken was admitted to the Alberta Bar at the age of 43.

Years after my short stay in Empress, Alberta I wrote down my impressions:

When I first saw the houses
of Smalltown, Alberta
they didn't seem quite fixed to the ground
and when I first saw
a fast-rolling dust storm
I thought the dirt had blown right out
from under them
and when I first saw the false-front stores
I thought the wind had blown their roofs off . . .
At night I listened to the coyotes
howling from the river hills
and tried not to let anyone know
how homesick I was.

Nobody in Smalltown understood
about buzz-bombs
and land-mines,
or why a siren on the radio
still activated my nerve-endings,
and I didn't understand their Great Depression
and so could never belong
to that singular fraternity . . .
　　　　excerpts from Chapbook *Something of Value* [3]

A prairie outdoor toilet.
Credit: Terry Lyster

You make what seems a simple choice: choose a man or a job or a neighborhood, and what you have chosen is not a man or a job or a neighborhood, but a life.
Jessamyn West

The lucky ones took the '$200 cure'.
the author

'What will you do with twenty dollars a month?' he said. I had been counting some cash so I threw a handful of dollar bills in the air, and as they fluttered slowly to the ground I said dramatically, 'Anything I like!'
Ivy (Howes) Riese

Ethel (Cunliffe) Tryon and Marion (Hancock) Roscow, Parksville, BC, c 1975
Credit: author's collection

The author with Pamela (Munn) Pittaway in the garden of "Trail's End" c 1975.
Credit: Bert Pittaway

Chapter 16: Happily Ever After?

All emigrants to North America have adjustments to make. British war brides may have thought that their main adjustment would be to a very different geography and climate, but that was just the beginning. We were all so young, and despite the traumas we had been through our heads were full of certainties. It did not occur to us that the new country we had adjusted to with lesser or greater success would change. When we arrived the Red Ensign was Canada's flag and the Union Jack was honoured. The Red Ensign was dear to our husbands because for the first time Canadians had fought under their own flag. Department stores sold ladies' woolly underwear that was lacy, warm and "made in England" (we had all been taught that "British is Best"). Like the churchgoers depicted in Pierre Berton's[1] *The Comfortable Pew,* British war brides came to a "comfortable" Canada. Few of us could comprehend back then that so many of the things we warmed to were vestiges of colonialism, with little or no meaning for immigrants from many other parts of the world who came before and after we did.

Almost universally we looked forward to a small home of our own where we could take a bath without three or four service girls jostling for the other two facilities and more lined up impatiently outside. We wanted a home that was in no danger of having its roof blown off and where our husbands would came home safely every night.

The homes were a long time coming and homesickness increased. Many war brides took the "$200 cure" (a trip "home"). Once there they found that the country they were homesick for was pathetically slow in recovering because it was financially bankrupt. A continuing shortage of materials meant that as late as 1950 some foods were still rationed. One war bride visitor caused a sensation in that year by asking an English greengrocer for a dozen oranges. They were still sold in ones and twos. Many bomb-damaged buildings still awaited "minor" repairs.

War brides who had been so anxious to get back home found they had changed during their short period in Canada. They were impatient with the old ways and probably said too many times: "That's not the way we do it in Canada!" Despite their joy at seeing family again most were anxious to return to their new home.

The trip home, even in peacetime, had its hazards. Margaret (Innes) Kuhn, (later Bowering), who came to Oyen, Alberta wrote:

> My trip over to Scotland was a nightmare. I was so seasick this time and to top it off our ship hit an iceberg, splitting the deck in half, and I had to spend a week in Newfoundland while it was being repaired. I spent the time sitting in my hotel room knitting Argyll socks.

Whatever happened to Argyll socks?

Not all war brides could afford a trip home, so in 1950 an enterprising group of Liverpool mothers and sisters of war brides held dances, raffles and rummage sales (they had not yet become "garage" or "car boot" sales) so that they could visit Canada. [2]

All this was happening against a background of the best rehabilitation benefits ever offered ex-servicemen. The much maligned "demob" clothing may have been a flop, but Canadian veterans received a resettlement allowance of so much for each day served in

Canada and a higher rate for service overseas. Educational opportunities were available, with a monthly living allowance (about $60 a month for a single man, or $80 if he was married) for the time the veteran was in college or university.

Writer Barry Broadfoot, a veteran from Nanaimo, British Columbia praised Canada's treatment of its servicemen:

> It was a popular sport to curse MacKenzie King . . . as a fumbler and a dodderer but he was, in fact, a very shrewd operator. He brought out the very best DVA (Department of Veterans Affairs) education program in the world. It didn't just apply to university. It applied to trade schools and all sorts of other things like that. . . . They were out to give us the time that we had lost during the war and to set us back on the road.[3]

Barry, like so many of his fellow students, was the first member of his family to attend university. He become a newspaperman and the acclaimed writer of many books including *The Veterans' Years*, and *Six War Years*. Another veteran, Alec Colville also praised the government scheme:

> One of the most wonderful things that someone in the Federal government had the brains to think up was that if a veteran wanted to have an education, there it was.[4]

D. David Small, ex-RCAF Radar Mechanic, was one who took advantage of the higher education offered. An ambitious fellow, he not only enrolled at the University of British Columbia, but formed a small company to supply the University with biological specimens. His wife the former Joan Watts of Leeds, Yorkshire became involved in the enterprise:

> I found myself being a foster mother to tubs of earthworms that were being raised in shredded newspaper and fed on pablum and oatmeal. There were also wee frogs being raised to puberty in a baby's bathtub. I learned the fine art of pickling starfish and sand dollars and how to inject coloured latex into the veins, arteries and nervous systems of dogfish. All this took place in my mother-in-law's garage.

Meanwhile Dave and his business partner were out collecting new specimens. Later on the family lived in a tent with their young daughter while Joan and Dave built their first home. Neither had ever wielded a hammer before.

The 1940s Veteran's Land Act (VLA) followed a Canadian tradition dating from the 17th century of settling ex-soldiers on the land. The Act made five acre lots available to veterans, based on their length of service and need. Government loans were available with very generous repayment terms. In 1950 the programme was extended so that veterans could build their own homes. By the time the programme was terminated in 1977 over 140,000 applications had been received. Some never did get to the top of the list but only because they were already well established.[5]

Not long after I became engaged to a western Canadian I had an unsettling conversation with a man from eastern Canada. "So, you're going to Alberta," he said. "Did your fiancé tell you about the dust storms? Did he tell you the prairies are so flat you can stand in Alberta and watch your topsoil blow all the way to Ontario? If a horse bolts you can still see it running three days later." I turned on my best frigid English voice and said "He has told me all about the prairies," making a mental note that I should ask him about the dust storms.

One bride who arrived in Alberta in the spring of 1946, would have been mystified by the suggestion that Alberta was flat. My bearer of bad news failed to mention that the road west of Calgary rises through foothills to the grandeur of the Rocky Mountains. Pamela (Munn) Pittaway came to The Waterton Lakes National Park area in the south west corner of Alberta where flat prairie runs smack into towering mountains without any transitional foothills. When Pam's husband Bert was demobilised in 1945 he followed in his father's footsteps and joined the National Parks of Canada. Pam arrived holding 3-month-old Michael in her arms, with 2 1/2-year-old Anne in tow. Michael was meeting his father for the first time. After a short visit with Bert's family in Waterton township Pam moved to her new home:

> Bert's first posting as a Park Warden was to a remote two-bedroom cabin at Belly River, which was our home for the next two and a half years. We were five miles from the US border, and five miles from our nearest neighbour, a farmer outside the Park boundary. In September the snow began to fly, winds piling it into drifts and isolating the little cabin until the following May when a crew would arrive to dig out the road. In those days the Park Service had no mechanised road clearing equipment.

In Pam's new world flour and sugar came in 100 lb. sacks, sufficient for the winter's bread and other baking. There was a cow in the barn, chickens in the hen house, and wild animals as well. It was commonplace for Pam to see a bear ambling down the path to the chicken house. Water came by the bucketful from a nearby creek, and in winter thick ice had to be broken with an axe before the bucket could be filled:

> Bert was often away on border patrol, or delivering his Parks Diary to HQ at the Townsite, fifteen miles away. He travelled on skis or snowshoes; after May he rode one of his two horses. He always left a large stack of wood cut to length for the cook stove and the old "Herald" heater, a horizontal monster always greedy for wood. My parents came for six months in 1947, and really loved this part of Canada with its beautiful scenery.
> After Bert's retirement we revisited Belly River. It was rather sad . . . The cabin and other buildings had been bulldozed; only the cool house with its cement foundation remained, reminding us of the time a skunk made its home underneath, and Bert captured it with predictably smelly results.

Living conditions improved slightly in 1949 when Bert was transferred to the Waterton River District. The new cabin was within walking distance of one of the park gates. The cow and chickens were gone, but Bert still had his two horses, Rainbow and Silver. It was here that Pam, while unsaddling Silver, was kicked on both sides of her left leg. Bert was away and she could do nothing but self-medicate. She had trouble with that leg for the rest of her life.

Collecting water was slightly different in Waterton River. It still came from a creek, but Pam hauled it using a shoulder yoke from which hung two wooden buckets. It was a windy area, and the water would swirl around in the buckets and spill out. In winter her drenched clothing froze and crackled as she walked. Often as a senior she'd still feel an ache in her shoulders from that wooden yoke.

Eventually there was a posting to Banff Township and the first true home comforts, but Bert's retirement was hastened when he was injured in a fall during a hazardous mountain rescue. The Pittaways came to a log home in Qualicum Beach they named "Trail's End", where Bert's snowshoes were part of the living room décor. Not long after Bert died Pam was diagnosed with cancer. She coped with this as bravely as she had all the other challenges in her life. I had known Pam for many years and when she died I lost a very dear friend.

In her Internet story, "*Down North*", Jean Watts told of equally isolated locations. Jean's husband, Dick, served on several Royal Canadian Signals' stations in the far north:

> We were at a greater distance from Ottawa than Ottawa is from London . . . A fascinating experience – one that I have greatly valued.

Jean writes of reindeer herds, trappers' cabins, and of the wooden "Cathedral of the Snows", Aklavik's All Saints Cathedral. It has a beautiful altarpiece depicting a group of Inuit (in Jean's time known as Eskimos) in their traditional dress. Jean raised two children in the north as well as several rare Tahltan Bear Dogs.[6]

She also tells of a fledgling Mountie who was required to travel with a sled and a team of sled dogs. He was flummoxed when the lead dog sat down in the snow and refused to budge. In the extreme cold this could be a life and death situation. After a lot of pulling and shouting he remembered something about having to let the dog know who was boss. In desperation he bit the dog's ear. It got to its feet and he had no further trouble.

Much has been written about women being forced back into the kitchen after tasting the financial freedom of wartime jobs, but that can only apply to North American women.

British family homes were subject to unwanted alterations by the Luftwaffe, and grew dingy during the war years of shortages, but that only made them more precious. Many of our wartime jobs in Britain took us out of our homes into institutional living with absolutely no privacy. There was a distinct resemblance between service life for women, and girls' boarding schools. We slept in dormitories that in the WRNS were called cabins. We were watched over by Wren Petty Officers and a Wren First Officer with all the determination of a Head Mistress, or in my case nuns and a Mother Superior. My WRNS uniform was only slightly different from the one I wore in school, from the flat lace-up shoes, black cotton stockings, blazer, and shirt and tie, to the regulation hat.

Instead of school insignia my WRNS hat bore the legend "H.M.S." (Although abbreviations were used extensively in World War II, punctuation was often demanded.) Service pay was pitifully low. As a Wren Writer (a specialised category) I received ten shillings twice a month (about $2.10 Canadian at wartime exchange rates). My father subsidised me extensively all through my time in the service.

My first house in Canada was a prairie shack in small-town Alberta. I would not have survived without my father-in-law who came every morning to start my coal and wood stove. He delivered the laundry which my thoughtful mother-in-law had taken care of, and he dug a path if there had been heavy snow. After Bill's release from hospital we rented a house in Regina for the winter of 1946-7. Here the dripping taps formed icicles overnight, the damper in the coal and wood cook stove was stuck shut, so that our Christmas turkey was in the oven for hours and hours. The furnace accumulated coal gas that exploded at odd intervals delivering blue smoke instead of heat. One memorable winter night we hung a blanket over the entrance door that had no weather-stripping. It developed a frosty door-shaped image. We had a visitor who could not drive home because of the blizzard, so we unpinned the blanket for his makeshift bed.

We moved several times between Edmonton and Regina and eventually bought a house in North Vancouver where our children grew up. All these homes had full modern conveniences. In the late sixties we found a neglected house with a view on Vancouver Island and renovated it as a retirement home. Bill had a sign made with the words "Sussex Downs". He claimed that as an infantryman he had crawled over every inch of them! It still hangs outside my front door.

Ex-servicewomen meet at the Island Hall, Parksville, BC, c 1970. Among them three WRNS war brides (first l.) Joyce (Bishop) Ramsden, (seventh from l.) Iris (Turner) Page, and (tenth from l.) the author. To my l. is ex-WRNS "Tiger" Timms.
Credit: author's collection

Soon after Betty (Barber) Fouchard arrived in Ottawa her new family gave a reception for their son and his wife:

> The dining room was decorated as if it was a wedding reception and we even had a wedding cake. It was quite a feast and certainly made up for the wartime wedding in Britain and made me feel so very much a part of this wonderful family.

For many of us the '60s and '70s were the creative years. We took yoga and art classes, spinning and painting lessons. Some of us had a flirtation with Women's Lib or at the very least listened to Helen Reddy singing "I Am Woman". I remember telling a mystified Bill, "It's *my* turn!" which he decided had something to do with my being an only child! Ivy (Howes) Riese, from Stockton-on-Tees, Durham spent 40 years in the far-northern community of La Ronge, Saskatchewan before retiring to Victoria, British Columbia:

Walter and I ran a small movie theatre in La Ronge. In winter there were no tourists and many local people would be away tending their traplines, so I had more leisure time. I became an avid reader of the American feminist magazine *MS*. The articles pointed out that women were being taken advantage of in many ways. I realized that our home, business, vehicle and bank account were all in my husband's name. With more prodding from Editor Gloria Steinham, I decided I had to do something about it. If Walt ever tired of me and our life together he could give me the heave-ho. I was interested in Irene Murdoch, the Saskatchewan farm wife who, after working for twenty-five years, taking the place of a hired man, was deserted for a younger woman. She then found out that she had no legal rights to the farm. Women everywhere were enraged. I started campaigning for some changes in our own business, namely some cash for myself. Walt couldn't see the need. I threatened to quit my unpaid job as cashier, bookkeeper and maid-of-all-work. No money, no work, I said. Walter thought that everything was just fine and couldn't see the need for change. But since he couldn't get anyone for less he gave in. 'What will you do with twenty dollars a month?' he said. I had been counting some cash so I threw a handful of dollar bills in the air, and as they fluttered slowly to the ground I said dramatically, 'Anything I like!' [7]

Most of us survived the siren call of Women's Lib. Perhaps we were too complacent, but we felt we had effectively established that women could do the jobs previously held by men.

Women of our age had been heavily influenced by American movies, and by the 1950s were impacted even more strongly by American magazines and television. The CBC had some excellent dramatic programming, but was hampered by lack of funds and the drain of talent to the US. Television more than movies influenced the meals we cooked or purchased ready made (I was thrilled with the idea of TV dinners, but usually reused the trays with my own version), where we ate them, the clothes we wore and what we did on Saturday nights.

We survived the New Look and the mini-skirt. We survived Trudeaumania and the metric system (many of us still think in pounds and ounces, feet and inches) and could sing "O Canada" without having to think about the words. We encouraged our children to be good Canadians, but did not let them forget their mothers' roots!

May 28ᵗʰ 1945

Usually it was the war bride who had wedding clothes issues. Newly commissioned Art Angus wore battle dress because his dress uniform was held up in transit.

Credit: Dr. Lynn Angus (daughter)

Doreen and Art revisit St. Christopher's Halton, Leeds, Yorkshire in 1995, their golden anniversary year. Doreen died in 1998.

Credit: Dr. Lynn Angus (daughter)

Can't get away to marry you today
My wife won't let me.
    English music hall song

. . . every nation has its proportion of trouble-makers, and 'single men in barracks' are no more likely to grow into plaster saints during the Second World War than they were when Kipling wrote. But the impression sometimes created by the more lurid London papers was unjust to the (Canadian) Army.
    Colonel C.P. Stacey, *Six Years of War*

The *News of the World* became known as the Unofficial Canadian War Diary.
    Ben Malkin

Chapter 17: Crimes, Mischiefs and Misdemeanors

PRANKS

When Canadian troops were first in England they were young, bored and homesick. They wanted to take the stuffy English down a peg or two, the result being a rash of practical jokes. It was usual for babies to be left outside in their large English prams when mothers shopped. This certainly happened in Aldwick, at least it did until the day a mother came out to find a messy baby in her spotless pram, and her ultra-clean baby in a grimy one. At the height of the invasion scare our local paper reported that police had been called to the telephone box by the Aldwick duck pond. The "suspicious characters" reported to be lurking inside turned out to be irate ducks. Canadian pranksters were suspected in both instances.

Anxious to keep their troops amused as well as occupied, the officers of a prairie regiment arranged for concerts at an Aldwick country club. Regular entertainers soon palled so a fairly harmless strip-tease artiste was hired to wind up the next production. There were intensive rehearsals with a spotlight that had to be extinguished at a crucial point in the lady's act. On the night everything went as planned. The stage was plunged into total darkness . . . but immediately every man in the front row switched on a powerful flashlight.

Obviously the Canadian Army needed to focus the minds of these men on the reason they were in England. Soon military exercises with names like "Waterloo" and "Bumper" caused mass movements of troops around the country, giving rise to the term "the highly mobile Canadian soldier". The men claimed they had tramped over every inch of Britain which was almost true, and some boffin worked out that Canadian army boots lasted for 200 miles on British roads. During one of the largest of these exercises British umpires pasted a note on a bridge, "Consider this bridge blown". Undaunted, a Canadian participant crossed it out, and wrote "Consider I have mended it." [1]

Adrien Demers, a Canadian lance-corporal stationed near Guildford, Surrey, England went AWL (absent without leave), letting his war bride believe he was still in the Army. In 1945 he pleaded guilty to being AWL for 1692 days, twelve hours and twenty minutes.[2]

Whenever a Canadian serviceman was in trouble with the law he appeared in a British court that was attended by British reporters, so that Canadian wrong doings appeared regularly in our newspapers. The notorious *News of the World* was happy to add Canadian offenders to its roster of black market racketeers, wayward vicars and shady doctors. This happened so often that the British government, anxious for good relations with the newcomers, instructed the newspaper to omit the word "Canadian" from future reporting, on the grounds that they identified no other troops by their country of origin:

It seemed that whenever a Canadian got in trouble with the authorities (the *News of the World*) had to print the story . . . it became known as the unofficial Canadian War Diary.[3]

American GIs, unlike Canadian troops, came across as the best behaved troops in modern history. This was because, except for major crimes, their discipline and punishment was handled by US authorities. The British press had no access to the proceedings so, in the main, GI misdeeds went unreported even by the *News of the World.*

BIGAMY

When the first Canadians arrived in 1939 bigamy was a prime topic of conversation in British homes. Memories stretched back to World War I. Everyone had something derogatory to say, usually recalling an aunt who couldn't go to Canada because she had discovered her dashing Canadian had a wife and ten children in Saskatchewan. C.P. Stacey reports that some cases of bigamy came to light early in World War II after which marriage regulations were considerably tightened. I was mortified when I was told that the "husband" of a slight acquaintance already had a wife in Canada. Was the informant truthful or a trouble-maker? Perhaps the man had obtained a divorce? I'd been shown photographs of the English wedding, with the bride's family gathered around the happy couple outside the church. Did the bridegroom look a trifle smug? It was hard to tell. I lost touch with them. It was only when I was on my way to Canada that the war bride, if indeed she was one, came strongly to mind. Had she received news of her sailing, or was she still at home, her life in tatters? I was never to know, but I've thought of her many times.

Many British girls asked outright about the man's matrimonial status before accepting a date. Asking such a question may have seemed wise, but expecting an honest answer if the guy was indeed a philanderer showed a certain naiveté. The best, though not infallible plan, was to write a friendly letter to the young man's mother.

A few wives had to face desertion, and even that could be a two-way street. When it came time to go to Canada some wives refused to leave. A few made the journey but when they reached Halifax received one of those "dreaded white envelopes" [4] with the news that their husbands no longer wanted them, or (on a wartime sailing) had been killed in combat.

Joan Weller, arrived on the *Aquitania* in April 1946:

> One girl attempted suicide. She had learned her husband was seeing another woman.[5]

STOWAWAY BRIDES

For some reason stowaways carry a slight aura of romance and daring about them. Some are desperate people, unable to come up with the cash necessary to make a journey by ship or plane in the normal way, or in wartime unable to obtain passage any other way. Marie Bourassa, a young Scottish war bride, who admits she was a naive young woman, believed her husband Red had been sent to New Zealand. She decided she would be closer to him in Canada so she applied and was given passage on the *Rangitata*, but when she arrived at Radville near Regina, Saskatchewan found that Red was still in Europe.

162

Marie made her way back to Halifax, took the advice of some merchant seamen and dressed herself as a cleaner in an overall and with a scarf tied turban-fashion around her head and walked without challenge aboard the *Pasteur*. Crew members smuggled food to her during the journey. On arrival at Southampton she walked ashore again dressed as a cleaner and took the train to Glasgow.

Once home she found she had again missed Red. She was in Scotland several months without a passport, an identity card or a ration book and with her Dependent's Allowance cut off. Eventually she got in touch with an officer in Red's regiment. The Canadian authorities were not well pleased with Marie. They had a thick file on her. However the upshot was that she "paid" for her second trip to Canada on the *Mauretania* by caring for the child of a war bride who had been killed. The war bride's husband was returning to Canada on the same ship. It's reasonable to assume the baby was the year old son of the unfortunate Lillian Miller, the war bride under the heading "Murder". [6]

Flight-Sergeant Albert Rosso of Stratford Ontario worked his passage to Britain after his release from the RCAF to see if he could hurry his wife's transportation to Canada. In June 1945 finding he was unable to change the priority system, Rosso boarded the *Empire McRae* to return to Canada. His wife Irene Rosso and her 16 year-old brother stowed away on the same ship, but became so ill that they gave themselves up. Being married to a Canadian Irene was not deported, but her brother was sent back to Britain. In October 1946 Mr. and Mrs. Rosso met another Atlantic liner that was carrying their 17 month-old son, Leonard in the care of the Canadian Red Cross. He had been left with his English Grandmother when his mother came to Canada. Mrs. Rosso was in tears as she held Leonard. "I've almost gone to pieces waiting for this day to get our baby," said her husband. [7]

MURDER

In 1946 Lillian (Kemp) Miller, a young war bride awaiting transportation to Canada, was found dead near her home in Kent, England. Her husband, who had already been repatriated to Canada and was waiting for her to join him, was recalled to attend the inquest. The verdict was "Death by asphyxia through manual strangulation by some person unknown." [8] Her grieving husband dropped three red roses into the grave when Lillian was buried in a Canterbury cemetery. She had carried red roses at their wedding on October 17, 1942. Her husband returned to Canada on a war bride sailing of the *Mauretania,* this time with his young son in tow.

In a double tragedy Jean (Kelly) McAllister, who came to Ontario from Scotland in 1946, was put on trial in November 1948 for the shooting death of her husband, John, earlier in the year. There was evidence that she had suffered mental and physical abuse from the former naval officer, after she had undergone a hysterectomy. She was convicted of manslaughter, with a strong recommendation for mercy, and was sentenced to three years in prison. [9]

The Dutch people, during the Liberation, are said to have believed that Canadians were on a par with the angels. In reality some Canadians fell short of that elevated position.

Before starting his criminal career Edwin Alonzo Boyd served in World War II. When he was repatriated he had a British bride, a young family, and a liberated German Luger. For a time he drove a streetcar (tram), but one day, wearing a disguise, he robbed a bank. After a few profitable ventures he was caught and incarcerated in Toronto's Don Jail. Later Boyd and two accomplices formed The Boyd Gang. Boyd was caught with a suitcase full of money and for some inexplicable reason was housed in the same cell as the other two gang members who were awaiting trial for murder. All three escaped using, according to one account, a hand-made wooden key.

The escape triggered the biggest manhunt in Canadian history, Boyd being described in the press as "Canada's Public Enemy Number One". When all three gang members were caught the escape was the subject of a Royal Commission. Boyd received three life sentences, the other two gang members were executed.

Boyd was released in 1966, changed his name and went to live in British Columbia. He drove a bus for the disabled and married one of his passengers, becoming her caregiver for the next thirty-five years.[10]

ALCOHOLISM

It is impossible to write of the war bride experience without mentioning alcohol and the problems connected with it. Not technically a crime (although those close to the situation might disagree) substance abuse, whether the substance is alcohol during and after World War II, or drugs in the Vietnam conflict, is a wartime legacy.

More than one war bride has said that the man who came back to her at the end of the war was not the same one she had married. I'm sure that many non-war brides have made the same observation.

In the 1930's two problem drinkers in Akron, Ohio found a way of keeping each other sober, and Alcoholics Anonymous was born. It couldn't have happened at a better time. Canada, along with many other nations, was about to witness an escalation of serious alcohol dependence among young men who had witnessed the horrors of modern warfare. Problem drinking can be enormously threatening to marriages and relationships with children, not only for the obvious reasons, but because the victim jeopardizes his reasoning powers, his health and his future. There were even problems among veterans who had never been in battle situations. As one understanding daughter of a war bride put it:

> Who knows what demons my father had. He drank a lot and was very abusive to both my mother and me, and my mother's genteel upbringing didn't prepare her for this kind of life. She mentioned a car where the floor was so rusted she had to sit with her feet on the seat, and so cold in winter she would do anything rather than ride in it. My sister was born but died two days later. By the time my brother was born the marriage had gone sour. My grandparents in England had said 'You made your bed, now you must lie on it.' Eventually my uncle sent the money for us to return to England. In an attempt to keep my mother in Canada my father refused to allow my brother to be taken out of the country. I was still a baby when we sailed sometime in 1947, and my mother discovered she was again pregnant. The new baby was given up for adoption, there was a divorce and the rest, as they say, is history. I was raised thinking I was an only child, and it was not until I was a married

woman that I learned I had siblings. I found my brother with the help of the Salvation Army, and came back to Canada in 1969 to reunite with my Canadian family. I was also able to trace my sister.

Another daughter wrote in one of a series of letters:

I'm glad the deep and loving commitment Mum and Dad had for each other came across to you. It is interesting that despite the intermittent times where alcohol caused financial problems and social embarrassment, vehement differences in opinions, etc. both my mother and father were always deeply in love. Sometimes out of like, but always there was love. When I was in high school friends commented on the fact that my parents walked hand in hand. My father never saw my Mum as anything but beautiful. During those years Dad was working in northern Saskatchewan so was home for ten days out of five weeks, they used to exchange cassette tapes. I have listened to a few of the tapes and the love is unmistakable.

The complications of alcohol sometimes made it impossible, not only for the marriage to survive, but for the wife to make a success of the balance of her life, as this anonymous war bride reported:

I have had a hard life as my husband died an alcoholic. He did not believe in insurance or pensions, but Veteran's Affairs helps me out, thank God.

Another war bride came with her baby from a very small town in England to an equally small town in western Canada. She was happy to be reunited with her husband but he was not the gentle fun-loving man she remembered. He had a serious alcohol addiction and under its influence was violent and vindictive. After a severe beating she ran from the house with her baby. She was taken in by strangers in a state of collapse. The Red Cross arranged for them to return to England via New York. (Her parents were forced to sell some of the contents of their home to repay the cost.) While awaiting a ship she was further distressed to be referred to as an Alien. (Forty-six years later her eyes still flashed when she used the word. I explained that this rather unpleasant term is the one used by the United States government to distinguish anyone in their country who is not a citizen, but I'm not sure she heard.) When she reached her English home she was found to have internal injuries from the ill-treatment and required immediate surgery. Although it is unlikely that she will ever forget the circumstances of her first marriage, she has been happily wed for the past fifty years to someone she says was a gentle man when she met him, and remains so today.

Some veterans who went through a phase of heavy drinking were able to stop and restructure their lives as this war bride attests:

My Tom had a terrible drinking problem for a few years. I thank God he was able to quit for the last thirty years of his life. He died in 1989 and I felt my life had come to a complete standstill - I have never quite recovered. My son Danny died in 1994 which was a terrible shock - we never expect to outlive our children.

WAR BRIDES AS "HISTORIC TREASURES"?

In the late 1990s *The Montreal Gazette* printed a column headed: HISTORIC TREASURES. The columnist, Eileen Travers, posed a rhetorical question: "What do pioneering feminists, war brides, and The Main have in common?" ('The Main' is the colourful Boulevard Saint-Laurent dividing Montreal into east and west.) Her answer? Nothing, except that all three had just been given national historic status by the Canadian Heritage Department.

She identifies war brides as the '48,000 British women who married Canadian soldiers' during World War II (thereby omitting over twenty other nationals who were part of the 48,000, and transforming several thousand RCAF and RCN husbands into soldiers).

But it is nice to be honoured, and amusing to think that years earlier some of us received information from the Department of Mines and Resources. In fifty years war brides had gone from 'Resources' (we surely weren't Mines!) to 'Historic Sites and Monuments!'

> the author

In later years war bride Betty Oliphant and Celia Franca were not on speaking terms, a fact mentioned in many sources - even in Miss Franca's obituaries - but unknown to me when I contacted Miss Franca.

> the author

(Gwladys Aikens) was completely unaware of the enormity of her crime. As a member of QAIMNS/R she was subject to Army discipline, so found herself awaiting court martial proceedings.

> Gwladys (Rees) Aikens, *Nurses in Battledress*, 145

Miss Oliphant played a big rôle in establishing high standards of dance teaching in Canada

Good luck with your project.

Sincerely,
Celia Franca

Celia Franca's note dated June 25, 1999.
Credit: author's collection

Chapter 18: Some *Really* Excellent Citizens

Many war brides merit special mention, and this chapter celebrates only those whose stories I've been able to discover, there must be dozens more I know nothing about.

BETTY OLIPHANT

Nancy Elizabeth (Oliphant) Grover was trained in classical ballet in 1930s England. Too tall to make ballet her career, she opened The Betty Oliphant School of Stage Dancing and Dramatic Art, above the Twinings Tea Emporium in Wigmore Street, London. The outbreak of war forced its closure. She worked briefly for the Ministry of Pensions and drove an ambulance. In 1942 she married Frank Grover, a Canadian Fusilier. Two daughters were born in England, one of whom was injured in an air raid.

"Miss O", Betty Oliphant.
*Credit: Harry Palmer, Calgary Photographer
reproduced by special permission*

Betty came to Canada on the *Aquitania* in 1947. She and Frank separated soon afterwards. Betty's early years in Toronto were a struggle. She had three people dependent on her as her mother had also come to Canada. However her talents were soon recognized. As Betty Oliphant she became associated with the fledgling National Ballet of Canada, and together with director Celia Franca co-founded Canada's first National Ballet School. In 1988, the Betty Oliphant Theatre opened its doors on Jarvis Street, Toronto. Among many other honours Betty has been made a Companion of the Order of Canada.

Known to all as "Miss O" (to some as "the formidable Miss O ") Betty numbered among her pupils Karen Kain and Frank Augustyn. It was her single-minded dedication that made her formidable. Her prickly relationship with Celia Franca was well-known, well known that is to everyone but me. I had met Miss Franca briefly at a dance recital and took advantage of that slim connection to ask if she would write a few words about Betty's contribution to Canadian ballet. This she was gracious enough to do.

Betty was in her eighties when we corresponded. In her lifetime she endured concern about her daughter's wartime injury, the illness of her second daughter that was serious enough to delay her entry into Canada, two divorces, intermittent and sometimes severe depression, as well as a stroke. When we spoke on the phone I valued her encouraging words about the outcome of my own stroke. At that time she was coping with badly impaired eyesight, but with the help of one of her daughters she wrote to me of her early days in Canada:

> I was offered two very important jobs: first to arrange the ballet dream sequence in the Canadian Opera School's first production *Hansel and Gretel*; secondly to arrange the dances for the *Mother Goose* pantomime which was shown at the Royal Alexandra Theatre in Toronto, and his Majesty's Theatre in Montreal, for three consecutive years. The first year I worked under Dora Mavor Moore; the last two years under Wayne and Shuster. From that time on my career went from strength to strength, culminating in the founding of the National Ballet School. Had I remained in England I would never have had the opportunity to develop a world famous (ballet) school, or to become a Companion of the Order of Canada, etc.

My favourite story about Miss O was told by writer John Fraser in the *Globe and Mail* shortly after her death. He had been entrusted by Mikhail Baryshnikov to deliver to Betty a battered pair of ballet slippers. They were the ones he had worn at the Bari Opera House in Italy in 1987 for his final performance of *Giselle*. When Betty saw them her response was immediate: "They're Misha's, aren't they!" Fraser says they were things of no great beauty, having conformed to every bunion, but he was impressed with a woman who knew her dancer's feet so well she could recognize their imprint in a shoe! These slippers are preserved in The Shoe Room, in the Betty Oliphant Theatre lobby, Toronto.

Betty's memoir *Miss O, My Life in Dance* was published in 1997, with an introduction by Baryshnikov. In her last months she was working on a book that outlined her approach to teaching. Betty died at Saint Catharines, Ontario aged eighty-five on July 12, 2004, with her daughters at her side.

ELEANOR CAMPBELL

Eleanor (Benson) Campbell was born in South Africa. Her husband, Gray Campbell wrote of that time:

> When little Eleanor was born her mother held her in her arms while the wagons rumbled by relentlessly, carrying the corpses of the victims in the terrible 'flu epidemic of 1918.[1]

Eleanor's family returned to Yorkshire, England, where early in the war she met Canadian Gray A. Campbell, RAF pilot of "Lancaster C for Charlie". They were married in St. John's Anglican Church, Moor Allerton. Gray wrote:

> When we married in June of 1941 we simply wanted a chance to live together, with a desperate, hurried feeling that we were not to be cheated out of whatever marriage had to offer, in spite of war. There was no time to consider the future. You couldn't see further than the next few days or weeks . . . It was a real war-time marriage, but neither the vicar nor anyone else threw it at us. We were together two months, then separated for seven. I faced the choice of being posted to Kenya to instruct or going back to Canada. I couldn't take my wife to Kenya. I couldn't get her to Canada either, but we didn't know that and after running into sticky red tape I had a stroke of good luck. While flying a kite (RAF slang

for "aircraft") from Halifax to Calgary I ran into L. B. Pearson at the Chateau Laurier cafeteria. When I told him the British were holding up Eleanor's passport he agreed that she was a Canadian and managed to reunite the Campbell family.[2]

Eleanor crossed the Atlantic in the spring of 1942, the riskiest year for Allied ships. Gray describes her experience:

(it was) horrendous . . . sailed in convoy on Polish SS *Batory*, converted to wartime troopship. Had to sit on life jacket – no deck chairs – and sleep in clothes. A very rough crossing.

On the Canadian train Eleanor asked directions to the washroom. It was occupied by a Group Captain's wife and child, so she smiled at them and went about using soap and towels. Only then did she discover that she was in the woman's private compartment. Eleanor termed this "Lesson No. 1."

A year after they settled in Canada Gray was recalled to England to make thirty-two more bombing trips over Germany. Upon his discharge he and Eleanor acquired a prairie ranch where she raised the chickens, ducks and turkeys. Some years later, Eleanor's health suffered, so they came out to British Columbia's Saanich Peninsula north of Victoria, with four children in tow. The Campbells met war veteran John Windsor (who was "undergoing plastic surgery and learning to be blind!") and his war bride, Pam. Gray drove John to creative writing lectures at the fledgling University of Victoria. John's manuscript of his war experiences was sent off to a Toronto publisher and returned without even a note. Gray had just won $229 in a TV quiz show, so he and Eleanor impulsively decided to publish Windsor's book. Eleanor came up with the title, *Blind Date*. At that time the publishing industry was virtually confined to eastern Canada. There was even a name for it: "The Eastern Mafia".

The pages of John Windsor's book were turned out, four at a time, on an ancient hand-set press owned by the *Sidney Review*, and Gray's Publishing was in business. By the end of the year more than 3,000 copies of Windsor's book were in print. Eleanor was a full partner in the venture, and son Dane, twenty, helped with distribution. The business operated from a converted chicken coop and eventually hit pay dirt:

The Pacific Gardener by Art Willis came out in time for the snowdrops in 1974, and sold 5,000 copies . . . the last time I looked over 100,000 copies were in print.[3]

Gray's Publishing office and staff in the former chicken house: Gray, John Barclay, Eleanor, son Dave and the dog Ketchup.
Credit: Diane Campbell

If the gardening book brought in much needed capital, an earlier reprint of a book by another neighbour, Capi Blanchet, became a west coast classic. First published in Edinburgh, *The Curve of Time* is an idyllic memoir of summers Blanchet and her children spent aboard the *Caprice* exploring the waters off Vancouver Island. Like *Pacific Gardener*, it is still in print. Gray's Publishing became a legend for struggling writers like myself. Gray lived on to semi-retirement and received recognition for his great contribution to west coast publishing. At the inauguration of the Gray Campbell Distinguished Service Award he spoke of his war bride:

> It was my partner of nearly 59 years who urged me into all this. She also created some of our best titles, suggested illustrations and designed covers . . . I give credit to Eleanor for pushing me into the biggest risk of our lives, Lew Clark's *Wildflowers of British Columbia* in 1973. It turned out to be a spectacular success and at the time I couldn't distinguish a daisy from a dandelion.

Both Grey and Eleanor are gone now. I treasure notes from them both, Gray's giving me permission "willingly and enthusiastically", to use material from *Butter Side Up*, and Eleanor's recalling the washroom incident.

MOLLIE GILLEN

My phone call reached Dr. Mollie (Woolnaugh) Gillen in an Ontario rest home in November 2004. At ninety-seven her voice was strong, and we had a lively conversation. One of a handful of Australian-born war brides, Mollie was orphaned in Sydney when both her parents succumbed to the 1918 'flu epidemic. With a 1930 degree from Sydney University Mollie moved to London, England where she met her first husband, Canadian Orval John Gillen. She came to Canada on the *Nerissa* in 1942.

Mollie's two children were born in Montreal. In Toronto she became an associate editor with *Chatelaine*, Canada's premier women's magazine, and was an early president of the University Women's Club. *Chatelaine's* editor, Doris Anderson, suggested Mollie submit an article on L. M. Montgomery whose centennial was imminent. The assignment led to Mollie's acclaimed biography about the author of *Anne of Green Gables*, *The Wheel of Things* (1975). *The Masseys, Founding Family* followed. Mollie's 1989 study, *The Founders of Australia: A Biographical Dictionary of the First Fleet*, was hailed as a significant contribution to Australian history and led to an honorary doctorate from Sydney University; to Mollie receiving the Order of Australia, and ultimately to a terrible tragedy. In the early 1990's Mollie married Phil Murphy. According to journalists Linda and Bill Bonvie,[4] Mollie and her new husband flew to Sydney, but before passengers were allowed to deplane regulations decreed that the cabin must be fumigated. Despite strong protests that Mr. Murphy suffered from allergies, the spraying took place. Mollie's husband suffered a severe reaction and died later that day.

CATHERINE MERRIMAN

Catherine "Taffy" Merriman, was from Pwltheli, Wales. She served with the WAAF in Bomber Command, and married writer and outdoorsman Alec Merriman. She came with their daughter to Langford Lake, British Columbia. Taffy accompanied her husband on his extensive fishing trips; exploring Vancouver Island and gathering information for Alec's column "Outdoors with Merriman" as well as the seven books on fishing and outdoor life they co-authored. Alec's book, *Outdoors with Merriman* is dedicated:

> TO MY WIFE TAFFY
> my constant companion, inspiration, fishing partner
> and helper on the outdoor trips that make up this book.

JOYCE HIBBERT

For many years Joyce Hibbert's 1978 publication, *The War Brides* was the only book available on the subject. It was the outcome of a reunion where Joyce passed out questionnaires to war brides. She had undertaken research at the National Archives, and in her introduction mentions that Barry Broadfoot's book *Six Years of War,* as well as the recent International Women's Year inspired the project. In 1985 she published *Fragments of War.* Joyce came to the Eastern Townships of Quebec. In 1999 I made several efforts to contact her, eventually learning she had passed away. Her husband Eric kindly gave me permission to make liberal use of the material in her book.

PEGGY O'HARA

In 1983 Peggy (Fiddimore) O'Hara published the informative *From Romance to Reality, Stories of Canadian WWII War Brides.* This book with the really great title is particularly strong on ship information and photographs. Peggy also drew on information from escort staff who are now almost impossible to locate. With her permission her title was used for a documentary on Canada's war brides produced by Kiss the Bride Productions, based on an original script.

GWLADYS AIKENS

The war as experienced by Welsh-born Gwladys M. (Rees) Aikens was a dangerous affair. She served with the Queen Alexandra's Imperial Military Nursing Service Reserve (QUAIMNS/R), leaving Greenock, Scotland on the *Strathallan* for service in North Africa. She tells the story of the ship being torpedoed and her subsequent rescue in *Nurses in Battledress* (1998). In pitch darkness she found her way to a lifeboat. It was overcrowded and on board was *Life* magazine photographer, Margaret Bourke-White. Next morning she watched Bourke-White busily taking pictures that later appeared in *Life* along with her account of the sinking (somewhat embellished, Gwladys thought).

In Algiers Gwladys was billeted with about thirty other nurses in what had been a harem. "It was exquisite," she writes, "with rich mosaic floors". By September 1943, she was in Italy and on December 2nd was on staff at the British 98th General Base Hospital writing a letter for a patient. She heard gunfire, which she thought odd, since the battle line was miles away to the north, but then it became obvious that Bari harbour was under attack by Luftwaffe bombers. Gwladys and another nurse went up to the flat roof of the hospital for a better view. Just as they arrived a powerful explosion shattered every window in the building. Seventeen US ships in the harbour were destroyed. The extra-violent detonation was from the Liberty cargo ship *John Harvey*. It carried ammunition, military stores, and a secret stash of two thousand 100-pound mustard gas cylinders. There were no survivors from the *John Harvey* and no one to warn port authorities that a poisonous cloud of smoke and mustard gas was drifting over the city. The next gruelling hours at the hospital are detailed in Gwladys' book. All the area hospitals were soon overcrowded with survivors from the other ships, who had been thrown or had jumped into the water. They were given the standard treatment for bunker oil contamination. The fact that the oil was mixed with mustard gas was unknown for many hours. Victims exhibited huge water-filled blisters and suffered horribly. The eventual death toll among service people and civilians was estimated to be 1,000. Gwladys wrote:

> I am pretty sure Marion, one of my QA friends, was killed in the Bari Raid. She was on the Bari docks making arrangements for a number of wounded to leave by boat for the UK that night. She is seen on the far right of the picture on the cover of my book. [5]

Gwladys met her future husband, Robert Aikens, a captain in The Royal Canadian Army Medical Corps, in Italy. They were married after returning to the UK. Their honeymoon destination was unknown to the bride's mother so a letter that arrived for Gwladys could not be forwarded. Therefore she missed information about a new posting. She checked in late, but as a member of QA she was subject to Army discipline. She found herself awaiting court martial on a charge of desertion. An armed guard escorted her to the hearing, and one has the feeling that the presiding officer had his tongue in his cheek. It was close to the end of the war so until she was discharged Gwladys was given into the custody of her new husband, much to her chagrin and his amusement.

JOYCE DUNN

Joyce Dunn (1925-1997) was born in France to British parents. When war threatened the family returned to Britain where she married Canadian Raymond Dunn. She came first to Calgary, Alberta and then to British Columbia where she worked as a journalist and wrote *A Town Called Chase* which went into a second printing. Joyce was a valued member of a local writers' group, where she mentored many fledgling authors. After Joyce died of Lou Gehrig's Disease (ALS) her friends and associates created The Annual Joyce Dunn Memorial Writers Competition. The contest is now part of the International Writers Conference held annually at Shuswap Lake, British Columbia. Joyce's autobiographical book *War Bride* was in manuscript form at the time of her death.

OLGA RAINS

Olga (Trestorff) Rains is a Dutch war bride who has become well-known because of her efforts to reunite Dutch War Children with their Canadian fathers. After the war Olga came to England on the *Lady Rodney* and then on to Canada aboard the *Mauretania*. She suffered near starvation during the Nazi occupation years, and by 1945 was too sick to join in the Liberation celebrations. She gradually recovered and it was then she met her life partner, Lloyd Rains. In the post-war years they made many trips to Holland, and at one parade of Canadian veterans Olga noticed a small group of Dutch people holding signs. They represented the children fathered by Canadian servicemen who had been left in Holland with their unmarried Dutch mothers. Olga, with Lloyd's dedicated help, has made it her mission to reunite as many of these War Children as possible with their Canadian fathers through the organization "Project Roots". Among many other honours, Olga has received the Knight's Cross from the Queen of the Netherlands. She is the author of *We Became Canadians, Children of the Liberation* and *The Summer of '46*. In 2004 she and Lloyd collaborated with Melynda Jarratt in writing *Voices of the Left Behind, Project Roots and the Canadian War Children of World War II*.

HETTY MACAULAY

Hetty (Smith) Macaulay worked as a stenographer at Canadian Military Headquarters, Trafalgar Square, one of many English civilians employed there. She was there when a bomb exploded in Pall Mall East behind the adjoining Canada House, and was bombed out of three homes in East Finchley. She met Norman Macaulay of La Ronge, Saskatchewan at a skating rink before he left for France, Holland and Germany. Hetty's son, Angus, spoke to me of his mother:

> She was a trained classical pianist and singer, and was a bright and cheerful person. She came to Canada in a Lancaster bomber and said she could see the ground through the cracks in the bomb-bay door.

Norman and Hetty spent some years in remote areas of Saskatchewan. When it was time for their children to attend school they relocated to Norman's northern home town of La Ronge, Saskatchewan. Here they built and operated a tourist resort on the shores of Lac La Ronge.

The Macaulay's life-long dedication to their community and to the well-being of northern youth was honoured by the Saskatchewan government in 1999 when a prominent point on the lake (near the site of their resort) was named for them. This distinction is usually bestowed posthumously. The citation credited the Macaulay's with:

- Starting the first Scout, Cub and Girl Guide organizations in La Ronge
- Organizing the local chapter of the Royal Canadian Legion and the Ladies Auxiliary
- Norman becoming first Chairman of the Northern School Board on which he served for ten years

- His serving as Chairman of the first Northern Community College in the communities of La Ronge and Sandy Bay in 1975
- His becoming the first Northerner to be elected to the Legislative Assembly of Saskatchewan in 1975

Hetty fully supported Norman in his political career, campaigning with him and accompanying him on trips to several international conferences in London, England. Sadly Hetty's health prevented her from attending the 1999 ceremonies. She died not long afterwards in Kelowna, British Columbia.

LESLIE DALE-HARRIS

Leslie Ruth (Howard) Dale-Harris, known to her family as Doodie, is the daughter of the renowned movie actor Leslie Howard (*Gone With the Wind, Pygmalion, The Scarlet Pimpernel, Petrified Forest* etc.). At the age of ten she acted with her father in radio shows, and had a small part in his wartime film *The First of the Few* (released in the US as *Spitfire*). When a Canadian artillery regiment pitched tents in the grounds of the Howard estate at Stow Maries, Essex the actor declared open-house for the officers. He seemed dismayed when his beloved daughter became engaged to Robert Dale-Harris of Toronto, even though he liked his future son-in-law. Howard complained that he was always powerless when it came to the women in his family. As mother and daughter made plans for the wedding he protested that he and his wife had managed to be married without spending a fortune on fabric and flowers. As a mild token of protest he wore a bright blue tie with his formal clothes for Doodie's wedding in May 1942, and as they reached the church playfully suggested to his daughter that they return home and play cards instead of going inside. As the ceremony began and he heard his cue ("Who gives this woman?") this consummate actor fluffed his two-word line!

Sadly Leslie Howard was killed in June 1943 when his plane from Lisbon was attacked by eight Junkers 88s, and crashed into the Bay of Biscay. His son Ronald believes that the anti-Nazi content of some of his father's films may have antagonized Hitler (*The Thirty-Ninth Parallel*, is one instance). Another theory is that German spies in Lisbon could have mistaken the actor's business manager and travelling companion, who had a slightly Churchillian appearance, for the British Prime Minister, and attempted an assassination.

After the war Doodie came to New York and then in March 1946 travelled with her husband and daughter Carolyn, to Toronto. Robert was by then a Lieutenant Colonel. Two more daughters were born in Canada. Doodie's book, *A Quite Remarkable Father,* was published in 1959. After reaching *Time's* best-seller list it went on to be published in many countries around the world.

Doodie's brother, Ronald, best remembered in North America for his portrayal of Sherlock Holmes in a 1954 TV series, published *In Search of my Father*. Robert Dale-Harris died in 1982, and Doodie later remarried.

THE REV. MARGARET SHEFFIELD

Two war brides have realized a very special calling after coming to Canada. The Rev. Margaret (Sayer) Sheffield grew up in Bromley, Kent, where she was fascinated by stories of Church missionaries. She served in the Woman's Land Army and later married John Sheffield, a young Canadian soldier. Twenty-nine years after arriving in Canada Peggy lost her husband to cancer. For the next several years she served as a lay reader. Then in 1983 she informed her bishop of her decision to seek ordination, and on June 16, 1985 was ordained into the Anglican priesthood by the Rt. Rev. John F. S. Conlin, Bishop of Brandon, Manitoba.

THE REV. MARGARET WHEELER

Margaret Wheeler vividly remembers seeing the flames from the "Baedecker" raid on Coventry from a location in Yorkshire. She met and married Les Wheeler who was serving in England with the Canadian Army. Peggy arrived in Canada at St. John, New Brunswick with her first two children, eight more were born in Canada. When Les died they had been married for thirty-eight years. After her ordination Peggy served for five years at St. Peter's, Tyrconnel, Diocese of Huron, Ontario. She retired to Grandview on the shores of Lake Erie.

BARBARA BARRETT

Barbara B. (Mickelthwaite) Barrett, CM, came from Huddersfield, Yorkshire to Curling, Newfoundland. From the beginning she showed a deep interest in her fellow war brides, writing a "War Brides" column for the *Western Star* to keep them in touch with things "back home".

While still in England Barbara had studied drama at Bishop Otter College, Chichester. For well over fifty years she has directed, adjudicated, and taught drama. She is a playwright, and has supervised over a thousand theatrical productions. For nine years she was the artistic director of the St. John's Summer Festival and became widely known as "the Mother of Newfoundland Theatre". (When we corresponded in 2001 she was again in rehearsal.) In 1995, in recognition of her many contributions to Newfoundland's theatre, and for her other community work, she was made an Officer of the Order of Canada. Barbara co-edited *We Came from Over the Sea*, a selection of Newfoundland war bride stories, published in 1996. That same year the English magazine *This England* awarded her the Silver Cross of St. George. The accompanying article noted that she was Presiding Officer at the Canadian Citizenship Court in Newfoundland, where she administered the Oath of Allegiance to the Queen to new Canadians.

The following women, although not war brides, are notable for their talents in recording the many facets of the war bride story:

MELYNDA JARRATT

Melynda Jarratt hardly needs an introduction, having been mentioned throughout this book. She is a New Brunswick historian, researcher, and writer. Her credits include her work as consultant on the war bride documentary, *From Romance to Reality,* radio discussions and television interviews, usually in support of war bride issues. On numerous occasions she has given evidence before Government Standing Committees on Citizenship issues as they affect war brides and their overseas born children. Melynda has a wide statistical and historical knowledge of Canada's war brides. Her published books are listed in the Bibliography.

BEVERLEY TOSH

Professor Beverley Tosh is a sensitive, dedicated Calgary artist who empathizes deeply with war brides in the global sense. She grew up in New Zealand, the child of a Canadian mother and a New Zealand airman father. When her parents separated

Bev Tosh with the author, Royal Victoria Museum, May, 2008.
Credit: Terry Lyster

Winifred Rose and the author, Royal British Columbia Museum, Victoria, May 2008, in front of Bev Tosh's paintings of the two war brides on their wedding days.
Credit: Terry Lyster

Bev and her sister accompanied their mother on the long sea journey back to Canada. The girls were being taken away from home, family and friends, from everything they knew and in Canada they were in completely strange surroundings. That their experience mirrored her mother's voyage to New Zealand, was not lost on Bev.

Bev's series of war bride paintings, "One Way Passage" began with an oversize 80th birthday head and shoulders portrait of her mother. Measuring 7 1/2 ft. by 5 1/2 ft. it is currently on a five-year loan to Ottawa's new War Museum where it is prominently featured in the entrance lobby (at times it has been on tour with the main exhibition).

The paintings that have followed are five-foot, full-length portraits of Canadian war brides in their wedding attire, some in uniform, others wearing two-piece suits, or traditional white, painted on rough plywood. Despite the unpromising background, the war brides depicted come through with remarkable presence, as if they are looking at you through the mists of the intervening years. To mark the Year of the War Bride the original collection of sixty portraits was displayed at the Pier 21 Museum. When "One Way Passage" was at the Royal British Columbia Museum, Victoria for the Summer of 2008, the collection had grown to eighty-three. I am tremendously honoured that Bev included my own wedding-day portrait. In Calgary she is represented by the Masters Gallery.

DEBBIE BEAVIS

Debbie Beavis has been one of the most informed researchers of passenger lists. She has transcribed British Board of Trade information, making it available for a fee to family history researchers and those interested in special groups such as war brides. Debbie's well received book, *Who Sailed on the Titanic? The Definitive Passenger List* was published in 2002 by Ian Allan. Her "listserve" is now in the hands of Patricia Tanner, webmaster of WeddingsPastAndPresent. Debbie has helped me considerably with several late war bride friends about whose data I knew very little.

ANNETTE FULFORD

Apart from a few memoirs very little has been written by or about World War I war brides, but their story is now being pieced together by Annette Fulford. Her interest was sparked when she inherited a sixty-eight page letter written by her grandmother, a war bride of World War I, describing in detail her 1919 journey to Canada. Annette has over forty genealogical articles to her credit. She has supervised museum displays of World War I war bride ephemera, and has been associated with the Langley Centennial Museum web site catering to genealogists and family historians.

JUDY KOZAR

In *Canada's War Grooms, and the Girls who Stole their Hearts,* Judy Kozar tells of marriages between British Commonwealth Air Training Plan airmen and young Canadian women.

JACKIE ALCOCK

Jackie Alcock, daughter of a Newfoundland war bride, is researching the war brides of Newfoundland and Labrador and collating material on her website.

I met again the girl I had known briefly on the ship. To see each other again was pure heaven - 'Do you like it here? - 'No, I hate it!' - 'So do I.'
Sheila Anketel-Jones, East Sussex, England

I quickly found that it wasn't a good idea to complain to Canadians about Canada, and quite rightly so, but complaining to other war brides was fine!
Nancy (Bennett) Sutherland, Milton, Ontario

These girls are my best friends to this day.
Sheila (Seery) Waslzak, Saskatoon, Saskatchewan

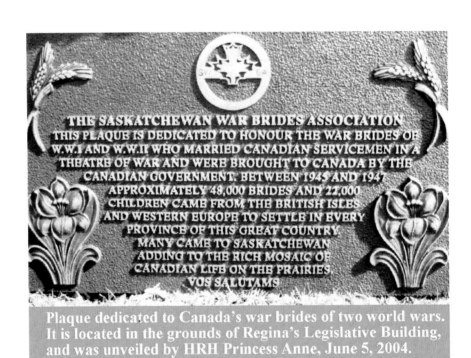

Plaque dedicated to Canada's war brides of two world wars. It is located in the grounds of Regina's Legislative Building, and was unveiled by HRH Princess Anne, June 5, 2004.
Credit: Kay Garside, Saskatchewan War Brides Association

Chapter 19: War Brides Clubs and Associations

By November 1945 there were 32 war bride clubs functioning in England and Scotland, most of them promoted by the Canadian Wives Bureau and formed with the assistance of the Canadian Red Cross or the Salvation Army. The intent: to make Canada less of a mystery to us, but of course there were instances of brides headed for Montreal who found themselves learning about remote farms in Saskatchewan, while others who really were going to those remote farms were given leaflets describing homes in the affluent Montreal district of Westmount.

One of the earliest clubs in Canada, and certainly the one that has been kept going without a break since 1945 is ESWIC, standing for England, Scotland, Wales, Ireland and Canada. If this sounds exclusively British it must be remembered that at that early date the only Continental women free to marry Allied personnel were those who had taken refuge in Britain, or who had been trapped there when war was declared.

Because of its location in Canada's capital city, ESWIC has enjoyed the patronage of successive British High Commissioners' wives, along with invitations to the official residence, Earnscliffe. Representative war brides have been included in many important Ottawa functions such as those honouring members of the Royal Family and the February 2001 visit of the British Prime Minister, Tony Blair, and his wife Cherie.

Charter member, Jean Spear, has been an enthusiastic member and record-keeper for ESWIC since the beginning. She was also one of those interviewed for the 2001 documentary, *From Romance to Reality*.[1] Jean received the Queen's Golden Jubilee Medal in 2002, and was named in the Queen's New Year's Honours in 2006 under the Diplomatic Service and Overseas List where she was recognized with an MBE (Member of the Order of the British Empire) for Services to UK/Canadian Relations.

In the presence of
Her Majesty The Queen
and His Royal Highness The Duke of Edinburgh

The Right Honourable Jean Chrétien
Prime Minister of Canada
and Mrs. Aline Chrétien

request the pleasure of the company of

Mr. and Mrs. George Spear

at a dinner
at the Canadian Museum of Civilization, Gatineau
on Sunday, October 13, 2002
at 6:00 p.m.

Jean Spear MBE and her husband George.
Credit: Jean Spear

Dr. Gwen Service was a charter member of Halifax's PADAGEANS Club. The name stands for the patron saints of Ireland, Wales, England and Scotland: PAtrick, DAvid, GEorge and ANdrew. Before marrying Canadian Raymond Service, Dr. Service was a staff doctor with a Surrey (England) hospital. She came to Canada in 1946 on the *Queen Mary*. In Canada she worked for 18 years with Dalhousie Student Health Services, and as late as 1988 was teaching courses in anatomy. Hazel (Clements) Oliver of Lunenburg, Nova Scotia visited two original PADAGEANS in Ottawa following the 2006 Remembrance Day service. Hazel came to Canada as a fiancée and was married at All Saints Cathedral, Halifax in June 1947. I believe the PADAGEANS Club still functions although I've been unable to find any details about it.

Joan (Palmer) Watson who came to Lasalle, Quebec is a member of the Acorn Club:

> Our club was originally started by two World War I war brides. It folded in the early 'sixties but in 1982 we started up again. We are about sixty strong, meeting every Monday except for July and August. We raise money for the vets at St. Anne's (Veteran's Hospital) and the poor of Montreal. I am also a member of the New Brunswick Club.

The Rose and Thistle Club met every Thursday afternoon at the YWCA on Harvey Road, St. John's, Newfoundland. It seems to have been inspired by Barbara Barrett's weekly newspaper column mentioned in Chapter 17.

Undoubtedly many clubs began spontaneously when two war brides got together over a cup of tea or coffee, decided to meet again and invite others to join them. Some tended to be social gatherings with no other stated purpose. The spirit behind them is evident in Sheila Anketel-Jones' account, even though this instance did not result in the formation of a club:

> Going across to Halifax on the Dartmouth ferry I met a girl I had known briefly on the ship. To see each other again was pure heaven - we danced around in a circle hugging each other. 'Do you like it here?' - 'No, I hate it!' - 'So do I.' - We talked all day, mostly sitting in the ice cream parlour, and somehow everything became more bearable. We could say things to each other that we could not say to our husbands - we loved them and had no wish to hurt them, but obviously we were not the happy creatures we had been in England.

Some of us had no access to clubs and many had conflicting attitudes towards them. Some felt that total immersion in Canadian ways and friendships was essential to speed assimilation, others believed that the companionship of other war brides was a necessary safety valve to cope with homesickness and loneliness. Both attitudes were valid, depending on the personality and situation of the individual. I chose the first option, mostly because I wanted to become fully Canadian, but also involvement with a family and a family business left me little spare time. Eventually I joined the Vancouver Island Association and attended a number of war bride reunions. It was then I truly appreciated the deep bonds of friendship that long-term membership in these organizations provided.

Sheila (Seery) Walczak of Saskatoon, Saskatchewan was one of the many thousands who found the company of other war brides comforting:

> In the early days Johnny worked long hours and was only home at weekends. I missed home and family, but here I met other war brides. We could visit and exchange stories of the war, swap recipes, baby-sit for each other, and make available a shoulder to cry on if necessary. These girls are my best friends to this day.

Referring to mature women, or even the young war brides, as "girls" (and young men in the military as "boys") is something with which Melynda Jarratt, Canadian and from a different generation, feels uncomfortable. I understand Melynda's point, yet "the girls" is a British term of friendship, even "old girl", coming from a British male, is (was?) - unbelievably - a term of endearment. "The Boys in Blue", "When the Boys Come Marching Home", "Fly Boys", "The Boys in the Back Room" (meaning boffins, or civilians in charge), and many other references are so much part of the time that I find it impossible avoid either term.

In the mid-1970s Saskatchewan war brides Gloria (Berry) Brock of Abernethy and Bette Frame of North Battleford decided that as most war brides had been in Canada longer than they had lived in their homelands there might be interest in a reunion. On April 3, 1975 Regina's bus station rang with non-Canadian accents as forty-seven war brides met before making their way to a luncheon hosted by the province's Minister for Highways and Transportation. The Saskatchewan War Brides Association was formed the following June, with Gloria Brock, President, Helene Smith, Vice-President and Kay Garside, Secretary. It is apt that Saskatchewan should take this lead since 800 or more servicemen from that province are said to have made overseas marriages, more per capita than any other province.[2]

Gloria encouraged other provinces to follow suit, and was soon travelling across western Canada as Manitoba, Alberta, British Columbia and Vancouver Island formed their own chartered associations. Another first for Saskatchewan was the design of the war bride pin, which has been adopted by other associations. It is a gold circle (the wedding band) and a gold bar (the distance the women travelled) with a white-edged red Maple Leaf dividing the initials of the particular association.

Joyce Hibbert, war bride author of the 1978 book *The War Brides*, was invited to Saskatchewan's 1979 Regina Reunion. She was presented with a tablecloth designed and embroidered with maple leaves and double wedding rings by Agnes Chouinard of Gravelbourg.

The English wartime vocalist Vera Lynn visited Saskatchewan at Gloria's invitation. She invited author/cartoonist Ben Wicks to the 1990 reunion, where he gathered material for his book *Promise You'll Take Care of my Daughter*. His title comes from the words spoken by Gloria's father to John Garside, RCAMC, at the time of their January 1944 marriage.

Associations have not been mere social clubs. Apart from charitable work, members have taken care of their own, visiting war brides in hospital, providing comfort at times of bereavement or other distress. The Association produced a booklet to guide the war bride or her husband through the practical steps necessary for the transition after losing a lifetime partner.

John Brock, because of his unstinting support of Gloria's work, has been voted an "Honorary War Bride" by the Saskatchewan Association.

MALE WAR BRIDES

John Brock may have been an "Honorary" war bride, and Cary Grant may have played a Male GI Bride, in a screwball 1949 movie, but Canada had a real male war bride. He came to the country's attention when his image appeared on the Canadian ten dollar bill, standing to attention near Ottawa's war memorial. Robert Metcalfe died at the age of 90. He was born in England, served his country with the British Expeditionary Force in France, was wounded and evacuated from Dunkirk. He then served in North Africa and in Italy where he met his Canadian wife, a lieutenant and physiotherapist in a Canadian hospital. They were married first by the Mayor of the Italian town and then by a Canadian padre. He and his wife settled in Chatham, Ontario where he went into local politics. Don Chapman wonders whether Robert ever had citizenship issues!

There was a warm feeling of remembrance and many a sigh at the 2000 Alberta Reunion in Lethbridge, Alberta when Joan Waterfield read the poem she had composed for the occasion:

THEY'RE PLAYING OUR SONG
'I'll Be Seeing You in all the Old Familiar Places'
Brings to mind so many faces,
And a musical trip to those wartime years
Recalls for us both joy and tears.
A brief encounter, a remembered friend,
The lasting love that would never end,
We are touched again when we hear a song
And sometimes it will makes us long
To return again to our youthful Spring
That in our Autumn still makes us sing.
There's the 'Nightingale Singing in Berkeley Square'
That made even the dark days fair,
And 'Yours 'til the Stars Lose Their Glory'
Was the start of many a romantic story.
And in a world gone helter-skelter,
'You are my Sunshine' brightened many a shelter.
We beat the blackout blues, made many a nighttime rock
With a cheery 'Oi!' and 'The Lambeth Walk'.
And there were Bogey and Bergman to make us cry
When they parted forever to 'As Time Goes By'.
And, yes, we danced for all to see

To 'The Boogie Woogie Bugle Boy from Company B'.
'In the Mood', 'Begin the Beguine'
Were special to the Palais scene.
'The More I See You' was kind of dreamy,
Reminds me now of a lad in the 'Reemie'.*
Slow dancing to that 'Satin Doll'
Takes me back to Pilot Paul,
And then there was 'Sweet Tangerine'
to make my friend Ena the Ballroom Queen.
The silly songs demand some notes
With 'Three Little Fishes' and 'Mairsey Dotes'.
'String of Pearls', 'Serenade in Blue'
'There Will Never Be Another You'.
'That Old Black Magic' wove a certain spell.
Eyes would meet and who could tell
If this was the beginning, the very start
With one who was 'Always in my Heart'?
When so many of us were far apart.
Yet we could dream when the war would be over
With Vera Lynn and 'The White Cliffs of Dover'.
Yes, we were young perhaps not too wise
But we had 'Stardust' in our eyes.
Now the years behind us are very long
But always treasure you special song.
Have that echo from our wartime past
Be something of you that will ever last,
And let your melody be always a part
Of the music, forever, in your heart.

Submitted to the author by Joan Reichart
* REME (Royal Electrical Mechanical Engineers), or more likely RCEME (Royal
Canadian Electrical Mechanical Engineers)!

ESWIC's 50th reunion, 1995, at Earnscliffe. Jean Spear (centre front with
rosette) is to the right of Lady Bayne.
Credit: Jean Spear

The Committee of the Montreal Overseas War Brides Club.
Front row centre, Joan Watson, President c 1999.
Credit: Joan Watson

Kay Young, President of the Alberta
War Brides Association, at the
AWBA Reunion Banquet, Calgary,
September 2003.
Credit: author's collection

War brides of Cornwall, Ontario, children's Christmas party, 1950.
Credit: Edith Edwards

Jeanne (Marchais) Pfannmuller, Calgary 2003.
Credit: author's collection

Cath Cuddy and Peggy Bell buy toys for war bride's children, 1950's.
Credit: Peggy Bell

Welcome to Okanagan Valley War Bride's Reunion Penticton 1998

A ceremony in Halifax on Thursday (February 5, 2006) marked the 60th anniversary of the first all war bride sailing. Although Mother's Day is still a few months away, many Islanders this week had cause to thank their mothers for the incredible leap of faith they made at the end of the Second World War. Thanks for the trip, Mom.

> Gary MacDougall, journalist, writing in *The P.E.I. Guardian* February 2006
> (Gary is referring to the trip he shared back in the 'forties with his mother, Isabella [Tennant] MacDougall)

After years of filming prize-winning Canadian documentaries, Richard Stringer began work on the one story he had always wanted to put on film.

> the author

The Oxford Companion to Canadian Literature describes John Ralston Saul's novels as having "the intrigue of Graham Greene and the social relevance of Dickens and Balzac."

> the author

Senator Romeo Dallaire, son of a Dutch war bride, came to Canada aboard the *Empire Brent* in 1946. He discovered that he was not a Canadian citizen in 1971 when denied a passport while serving in the Canadian Army.
Credit: Wikimedia Commons, unrestricted use

Chapter 20: The Next Generation

In Chapter 5 the babies and toddlers were arriving at their destinations aboard the Canadian train. Within a few years they were joined by Canadian-born brothers and sisters. When these children graduated from high school, they had a good chance of going on to university. Now that they have made us grandmothers and great-grandmothers, we are estimated to have upwards of a million descendants in Canada. The following few represent hundreds more who have made significant contributions to their home and native land.

THOMAS BURKE

Thomas J. Burke made an excellent start by choosing good grandparents. His grandfather, Charles Paul, served overseas in World War II, and while in England married Jean Keegan of Coulsdon, Surrey. When Jean arrived in New Brunswick with her daughter she was met by her husband and the Roman Catholic priest from the Maliseet Indian Reserve, who escorted her the rest of the way in a canoe. She became the first non-aboriginal woman to become a permanent resident on the Reserve which is located north of the town of Perth. Her first years were spent in poverty, in a house with no modern conveniences, but despite this she resolved first that she would become fluent in the Maliseet language, and second that her children would be well educated. Five of them earned university degrees. Her husband Charles was elected Chief in the 1960s, and awarded an honorary Ph.D. for his work in the community. Living conditions gradually improved and in 1971 Jean and Charles moved to Fredericton the capital city.

Twenty years later Jean was diagnosed with cancer. Her three sisters arrived for one last Christmas reunion before she died early in 1992. Her funeral Mass was conducted in English and Maliseet.

Thomas J. Burke, best known as "TJ", earned his law degree, then became the first MLA (Member of the Legislative Assembly) to represent the newly formed riding of Fredericton-Nashwaaksis. "TJ", is the son of Jean's daughter Cindy. He remembers his grandmother as "the glue that held the family together."

By 2006 "TJ" was Attorney General and Minister of Justice in the New Brunswick provincial Liberal government. He was the first Provincial Government member to introduce a motion recommending that the Province of New Brunswick declare 2006 "The Year of the War Bride", which it did.

ROMEO DALLAIRE

Roméo Louis Dallaire, of the 85th Corps Bridge Company married Catherina Vermaesen, a Dutch nurse in Brussels, Belgium. Their first child, named for his father, was born in Denekamp, Holland. In November 1946 Catherina and her infant son travelled to England. After a few days in London they boarded the jinxed *Empire Brent* that was involved in a collision with a cattle boat (Chapter 12). When they returned to Liverpool

Catherina and young Roméo were escorted with other Dutch war brides to a London hostel until the ship was repaired.

General (now Senator) Roméo Dallaire embarked on a career in the Canadian Army. As a young Captain about to have his initial posting overseas he applied to renew his passport and was informed that "since he had not filed for retention of his citizenship by age twenty-four, he was not a Canadian citizen." [1] Like all the other overseas-born children of war brides, he had never heard of this requirement. In order to obtain the passport to go overseas with his regiment Capt. Dallaire was required to prove his Canadian Citizenship!

In 1984 Dallaire was charged by the United Nations with heading up a peace-keeping mission in Rwanda, a country that was just emerging from civil war. He was in charge of 2,000 troops, his mandate being to oversee a peace accord between the Hutus and the Tutsis. It was an impossible task, and when the war began anew he and his men witnessed a blood bath as civilians were tortured and beheaded just outside their compound. On his return to Canada General Dallaire was diagnosed with Post Traumatic Stress Disorder (PTSD), as were many others who had served with him. Later he was told by Canadian Forces medical officers he was not responding to treatment. He was advised he must forget Rwanda (in much the same way Bill Lyster was told he must forget World War II. If only they could have been taught how to do that!).

His final medical report stated that he would no longer be in command of troops. "My whole life had been commanding troops." he says, "That's when I realised the impact of what Rwanda had done to me."

Dallaire is credited with maintaining the safety of 20,000 Rwandans who had sought his protection, but he takes little solace in that. Slowly, with the help of his wife Elizabeth, and his children, General Dallaire has rebuilt his life. While in recovery he wrote of his experiences in *Shake Hands with the Devil, The Failure of Humanity in Rwanda,* for which he won the Governor General's Award for Non-Fiction. Since his retirement from the Canadian Armed Forces he has worked to create understanding of the ramifications of PTSD. In March 2005 he was appointed to the Canadian Senate.[2]

RICHARD STRINGER

Richard Stringer arrived in Victoria British Columbia with his mother Clare (Donnelly) Stringer, a Registered Nurse from London, England in August 1946. His mother's happiness at being reunited with her husband Wilfred, a surgeon with the Royal Canadian Navy who was stationed in Esquimalt, was short lived. He died not long afterwards from hepatitis. Mother and son moved to Winnipeg where Richard grew up hearing stories about his grandfather, Bishop Isaac Stringer. The Bishop and his wife Sadie were missionaries in the western Arctic, living for some years on the remote Herschel Island in the Beaufort Sea. They were so isolated that their first two children were delivered at the mission house by their father who had some medical training. Although a traditional missionary, the Bishop also documented on film the now vanished way of life of the native people.

After years of filming prize-winning Canadian documentaries, Richard began work on the one story he had always wanted to put on film, his grandfather's. The title, *The Bishop*

Who Ate His Boots, refers to the time the Bishop and a native guide became hopelessly lost in the wilderness. Their lives were saved by making a kind of soup from a spare pair of sealskin boots.

In 1990 the late author and broadcaster Pierre Berton, who grew up in the Yukon and knew the Stringers, told Richard how much he had enjoyed the Bishop's 8mm films. He also said he believed Charlie Chaplin's famous boot-eating sequence was inspired by the Bishop's adventure which was highly publicized at the time.

Sadly Richard died in Victoria on July 27, 2007 after a long and brave battle with cancer. The filming of *The Bishop Who Ate His Boots* is complete. Family, friends and colleagues are doing the final editing. They hope that it will be released soon.

Richard's career in feature films, TV movies and documentaries has been recognized by a Gemini award (2000) and Canadian Society of Cinematographers Awards in 2000 and 2003. [3]

PAUL KEDDY

Dr. Paul Keddy, holder of the Edward G. Shlieder Endowed Chair for Environmental Studies at Southeastern Louisiana University, is the son and grandson of World War I and World War II servicemen and their British war brides. He studied at York University, Ontario and Dalhousie University, Nova Scotia. A life-threatening illness interrupted Professor Keddy's career for almost a decade during which time he wrote for his then infant children, *If I Should Die Before You Wake, Instructions on the Art of Life,* (1990). The book has found a larger audience who appreciate Keddy's reflections on living and dying without regret. His next publication was *Earth, Fire and Water, An Ecological Profile of Lanark County,* (1990), winner of the Lawson Medal and the Gleason Prize. It was followed by *Wetland Ecology, Principles and Conservation* (2000).

DAVID CLAYTON-THOMAS

David Henry Thomsett was born to Freda and Fred Thomsett in Surrey, England in September 1941. His father was away fighting in Italy and by war's end had been wounded twice, and highly decorated. David came to Toronto with his mother when he was four. Fred Thomsett was repatriated and over the years there was friction between father and son. David left home in his teens, to emerge some years later as David Clayton-Thomas, a prominent figure in Canadian music even before becoming the lead singer of *Blood Sweat and Tears.* Later he struck out on his own as a singer and song writer. Among his hits are the unforgettable "You Made Me So Very Happy", "And When I Die", and "Spinning Wheel". David continues to give concerts around the world. He has sold over 30 million albums, and in 1996 was inducted into Canada's Music Hall of Fame. David makes his home in Toronto, and has long since reconciled with his father.[4]

Internationally known, award-winning writer John Ralston Saul is the son of Beryl Ralston, a wartime member of the prestigious First Aid Nursing Yeomanry (FANY) (2nd Hampshire Company) and William John Saul, who was a Canadian exchange officer with the British Army in North Africa. On D-Day William Saul landed with the Winnipeg Rifles during the first wave. He was later wounded in Holland. John's mother, came to Canada in 1946 on the *Mauretania II*. His father embarked upon a distinguished post-war career with the Canadian Army. John was born in Ottawa in June 1947 and was named for his uncle, John Ralston, an RAF pilot who was shot down over Germany at the age of 19.

Susan Lyster (the author's grand-daughter) with His Excellency, John Ralston Saul and Jorge Castillo, Chilean journalist (now a Canadian citizen). The occasion was a reception in Santiago, Chile, 2001, honouring Chilean poet, Pablo Neruda, attended by Adrienne Clarkson, then Governor General of Canada. Susan was an employee of the Canadian Embassy in Santiago that summer.
Credit: Susan Lyster

The boy grew up on military bases in Alberta, Manitoba and Ontario. He married broadcast-journalist Adrienne Clarkson not long before she was appointed Canada's twenty sixth Governor General, and thus became the first winner of a Governor General's Award (for non-fiction) to be an occupant of Rideau Hall (traditional home of Canada's Governor General).

Internationally respected for his philosophical writing, Saul is also a novelist.

The Oxford Companion to Canadian Literature describes his novels as having "the intrigue of Graham Greene and the social relevance of Dickens and Balzac."

How does a person become an admired Canadian? Shoot the winning goal in the Stanley Cup final? Triumph as the Canadian Idol? Jump from a great height attached to the world's longest bungee cord? Be articulate and the possessor of a remarkable intelligence? The last will most likely get you nowhere. John Saul stepped into the thankless task of spouse of a Governor General, a role previously taken by a long line of invisible women and a few invisible men.

Saul became the target of sniping criticism, and of articles like Philip Preville's "What exactly is John Ralston Saul's Job?" something that was never asked about previous regal spouses. Saul made changes during his stay at Rideau Hall. He caused the mansion's wine cellars to be stocked with the finest Canadian wines. He supervised the transformation of Rideau Hall's flower gardens. He continued something he began in 1998, promoting understanding between Quebec students and French Immersion students by bringing them together for the annual "French for the Future/François pour l'avenir" conference on the theory that first-hand knowledge is superior to long-distance prejudice. He carried out his role as consort with dignity and occasional boredom.

Most children who came to Canada had a good life. They had educational advantages usually denied their mothers either because of the war, financial constraints or because they were not open to women. I was delighted to find that journalism was available at Pitman's Business College, however it was open to male students only. My father would not have let me take it even if it had been available. He was convinced that a secretarial course would be of more use to me. He was a loving man and I know he had my best interests at heart. Many war brides embraced what used to be called "Continuing Education" after our children were grown. Others earned university degrees, but in most cases it was our sons and daughters who have gone ahead in fields we only dreamed of.

Terry earned a degree in Architecture from the University of British Columbia, was a planner for three municipalities in the Vancouver area. He was an early advocate of solar energy. Too early perhaps, the average Canadian in the 1970s could see no advantage in it. He has co-authored several books on the subject. He was project manager for the WindSong CoHousing development which won a Georgie award from the Canadian Home Builders Association of BC for Best Environmental Achievement.

Joni Shuttleworth of Qualicum Beach, was thrilled when in 2004 her story and wedding photograph became part of a large plaque in the Maritime Quest Museum Exhibit aboard the magnificent new liner *Queen Mary II*. This particular exhibit commemorates Canadian and American war brides who sailed to North America on the *Queen Mary I*.

Joni came to Canada with her five month-old son Bill on the *Queen Mary I* in June 1946. The story of her wedding photograph becoming part of the luxury cruise vessel appeared in a March 2004 issue of *The News*, a local Qualicum Beach newspaper, together with a photograph of Joni and her husband Dixie. Sadly it was followed a week later by the obituary of their son Bill, who had passed away on March 13. Joni graciously gave me permission to reprint Bill's obituary in memory of all those children who have predeceased their war-bride mothers as babies on the journey to Canada or later in life.

Dixie and Joni Shuttleworth.
Credit: Joni (Jones) Shuttleworth

SHUTTLEWORTH
William "Bill"

January 9, 1946 - March 13, 2004

Bill was born in Preston England, January 9, 1946 and came to Canada with his mother at the age of 5 months. Bill retired from the RCMP as a corporal in 1979 to pursue a career as a commercial pilot and flight instructor. Bill had a zest for life, discovery and learning. His passions were flying, photography, electronics, computers, shooting, geocaching, ham radio and animals of all types, especially his cats, Cardo, Missy Miss and Tia. Bill's special talent and quest in life was to bring joy, humour and laughter into the lives of everyone he met and was delighted when he accomplished this.

Bill passed away peacefully in his sleep on March 13, 2004 after a long and courageous battle with cancer at the age of 58. He is survived by his loving mother and father Joni and Dixie Shuttleworth, his sister and best friend Dianne, nephews Nathan and Joel Murdoch, niece Jillian Shuttleworth, Aunt Beth Shaw, and cousins Kerry, Pete and Sheldon Shaw and many, many friends.

At Bill's request there will be no memorial service. In lieu of flowers those who wish may make a donation to the North Island Wildlife Recovery Centre in Bill's name.

Bill's family would like to heartfully thank Dr. Kevin McNeil, Dr. Chris Edwards, The hospitilists group, Dr. Spry, emergency room nurse Lois, and the entire nursing staff of the 5th floor palliative care unit at the Nanaimo Hospital for the wonderful care and compassion they showed to Bill and his family. Thank you also to Dr. Brian Altenkirk and Dr. Morag Atherstone.

192

She remembers
what a beautiful woman she was
and the man that she loved …
In the silence after
all the tears and laughter
and time …
she knows life has not passed her by …[1]
    Shari Ulrich

I always had a slight feeling that I was living someone else's life. I am neither fish, flesh nor good red herring – too Canadian to be a good Englishwoman, too English to be 100% Canadian! But I have played the hand I was dealt (after seeing those blue eyes there was no turning back) the best way I could.
    Sheila "Jane" (Beatty) Davidson

Don't call me a war bride, I'm a war granny now.
    Vicky (Pickering) Golder

Temple Store, Parksville, BC has been associated with two war brides. Olive May (Parritt) Walton and her husband Frank ran it as "Green Briar's Café". Doris M. (Hogben) Johnson (founder-member of the Vancouver Island War Brides Association) and her husband Al ran it as "Al's Corner Store".
Credit: author's collection

194

Chapter 21: "She Remembers . . ."

"She remembers what a beautiful woman she was . . ." The words are not quite the same without the melody and the magic of Shari's voice. War brides, you rightly say, were no more, no less beautiful than any other group of young women in their late teens and early twenties. But women in love do have a special aura, and we were definitely in love. There had to be some compelling reason for doing what we did. The years have flown, the buzz of that busy life with home and children and jobs and careers is behind us. "In the silence after all the tears and laughter" we look back and remember . . .

When we came to Canada the historic Canadian Pacific and Canadian National Railways were the only completed links from coast to coast. The Trans-Canada Highway (TCH), with its trademark green maple leaf signs, was still a work in progress. In some places it was necessary to detour into the United States to get to the next part. Miles of it in the Canadian west were not blacktopped, making for a heart-stopping ride through the mountains (made even worse by winter snow and ice). The TCH was never a unified project but cobbled together by all nine provinces of the time. (Quebec did not come in until after Saskatchewan's section was finished.) The first Canadian phrase I heard on arrival in Alberta was "Is it a Federal, Provincial or Municipal responsibility?" TCH was a Provincial responsibility, and we all know about the camel being a horse designed by a committee. Prime Minister John Diefenbaker tamped down a representative square of asphalt and declared the Highway open on September 3, 1962. (Tommy Douglas, Premier of Saskatchewan had already opened the bit across his province in 1957.)

The TCH is not a single highway. At Portage la Prairie, Manitoba, roughly the half-way point, it branches off north-west winding all the way to Prince Rupert, British Columbia. In fact apart from some short sections and the run from Montreal, Quebec to St. John's, Newfoundland, it is two highways (in parts of Ontario, three).

Close by the sea in Victoria British Columbia is a large Mile Zero monument. Why Mile Zero should be at the western end is a Canadian puzzle, when the oldest part of the road is surely in eastern Canada. There is also a Mile Zero at Prince Rupert, and surprisingly another one seven thousand miles away on the Atlantic end at St. John's Newfoundland. Only in Canada!

In 1967 we celebrated Canada's Centennial, and realised yet again what a young country we had come to. Centennial projects across the country stressed the Arts. Many civic centres, theatres, and museums were built, as well as hockey arenas. The Canadian free spirit was alive and well when the town fathers and mothers of St. Paul, Alberta, chose to build a UFO landing pad as their Centennial project. On July 1, 1967 our whole family joined the thousands in Vancouver's Empire Stadium to celebrate the Centennial and heard the words of the late Chief Dan George, Hereditary Chief of the Coast Salish people. He was a poet and knew how to write the words, he was an actor and knew how to speak them, and he told of a history going back far, far longer than a hundred years.

In 1978 the two historic railways that had conveyed us to our new homes, the Canadian Pacific Railway and the Canadian National Railway were amalgamated into Via Rail – a singularly unimaginative name, I felt, with none of the romance of, say, the Canadian Pacific. With that change another part of the war bride story disappeared.

The year 2005 marked the sixtieth anniversary of the end of the war. The Canadian Government proclaimed it also to be the Year of the Veteran. We watched, often with tears, televised reports of elderly veterans taking part in ceremonies overseas and here in Canada. One image was of surviving Victoria Cross winners, travelling by car because of their age. All the events were moving because we knew that many of these men were getting together at this type of event for probably the last time.

When Vicky Golder said that it was time she was called a war granny she was unconsciously echoing a newspaper report that appeared in 1948. It posed the question, "How long a war bride?" and gave the definition of a bride, "One just wed or about to be wed".[2] But even in the new Millennium we were indelibly lodged in the Canadian memory as "brides", however many wrinkles, hip replacements and great-grandchildren gave evidence to the contrary, and we began taking pride in the term.

A COMMEMORATIVE ENVELOPE

In 2005, the Year of the Veteran, Canada Post issued a war bride commemorative envelope so obviously there was not going to be a war bride stamp in 2006 the 60th anniversary of the year most war brides arrived. Commemorative envelopes have regular stamps and small line drawings, and are not available at post offices. They have to be specially ordered and usually only come to the attention of stamp collectors. I began to feel angry on behalf of all the women I had interviewed, but then I realised we were in august company. Canada Post made it known it would not be issuing a stamp to mark Queen Elizabeth the Queen Mother's hundredth birthday! (Public pressure brought about a change of heart in that instance.) When a series of Endangered Species stamps for 2006 was announced I thought, "Great, they haven't forgotten after all," but we didn't make that one either.

It began to look more and more as if the year 2006 would slip by as the decades had since 1946, without a nod of recognition. Ten years earlier someone else had been concerned. Estella Spergel quotes columnist Catherine Ford:

> So many of these women blended into the landscape of Canadian life that they remain barely noticeable today. My mother and the thousands of women brought to Canada as war brides did nothing spectacular except uproot their entire lives to follow their Canadian husbands . . . it might have been nice if somebody had noticed: if the arrival of war brides to Canada had a least been remembered by a larger audience than their now middle-aged children.[3]

Melynda Jarratt and I knew we could not sit back and be part of the silence. I added to my website the words: "Remember 2006 is the Year of the War Bride", and was awed by the power of the computer to spread the message, but it was Melynda Jarratt who used her many skills to set the ball rolling. With a miniscule budget she campaigned for recognition and eventually six provinces proclaimed 2006 to be The Year of The War Bride. The Federal Government remained strangely silent. Melynda's valiant efforts were rewarded in February when the Pier 21 Museum hosted a celebration to acknowledge the arrival of the first all-war-bride ship. Because Terry and I had been aboard when the *Mauretania II* docked on February 9, 1946 we were invited to the celebration along with Alan Hitchon who had been on the sailing with his mother Helen. Sadly Helen had died the previous year, but Alan's father and his siblings were in the audience when Alan spoke. Afterwards, Dan McKinnon, Nova Scotia folk singer/composer sang his tribute to War Brides, "Kith and Kin" from his CD "Fields of Dreams and Glory". The lines of the chorus brought a lump to many a throat:

> Goodbye years of hunger I thought would never end
> Goodbye tears of sorrow each time I lost a friend
> The endless days and blacked-out nights when fire rained from the sky
> Goodbye my land of kith and kin I'll love you till I die.[4]

It was at this celebration that Melynda and I met for the very first time.

Many special events followed right across Canada, including a War Bride train that travelled from Montreal to Halifax in November with war brides and many husbands. Eighteen couples renewed their marriage vows in a special ceremony at Pier 21.

The Year of the War Bride became a time for taking stock of our lives; of looking back on the hardships and the good times. Joyce (Ing) O'Donnell wrote a memoir with the ingenious title, "Rejoyceing". She says she has never regretted her decision to marry and come to Canada.

The late Joan (Bates) Burton had travelled to many overseas postings with her Army husband:

> They were happy years that I miss to this day. Postings included one for NATO where our house was on a fiord in Oslo. We were in Egypt and Pakistan, as well as many Canadian cities. Summing up, I love Canada and count my blessings for such a happy life.

Nancy (Etches) Fussell of Delta, British Columbia looked back to the 1940s:

> One of the chances I took was at eighteen marrying a man I hardly knew. It never should have worked out, but nearly fifty-six years, six children, fifteen grandchildren and one great grandchild later we are still together and happy.

Annie (Smith) Reed of Acton, Ontario felt that her story was hardly exciting enough to be told:

> It is simply a tale of young love sought, found and still in bloom, albeit a little droopy at times.

Mary (Mallinson) Talbot wrote from retirement in Athabasca, northern Alberta. (The town predates the railway as it was once the terminus of the Edmonton-Athabasca Landing Trail). She speaks for so many of us:

I always think that I have been lucky to have grown up in England and then to live in Canada as well. My life has been richer for it.

Even when things did not go so well many women said they were glad they had come to Canada. Margaret (Hall) Alley of Surrey British Columbia told me:

After the divorce I learned how to type and do other office work. I worked on bookkeeping machines until the first computers came in, when I retired.

Jane (Sinclair) Jones of Musquodoboit Harbour, Nova Scotia was divorced in 1969:

He met someone younger, the usual story. However I feel Canada has been good to me and I'm glad I came. I do not think I would like to go back to Scotland, too many changes. As long as I can afford to go home each year to renew old friendships and visit the family I am content.

A war bride who wishes to be anonymous lost her British husband in the sinking of the HMS *Niger* in 1942 on the hazardous convoy route to Russia. Their daughter was born after her father's death:

I met my second husband when he was on leave and looking for his Scottish roots. We were married in Dundee in 1945. I can honestly say it was the best decision I have ever made and I have never regretted it. Life in Canada was difficult at the beginning as my second husband was not as upstanding as I presumed. The second-best decision I made was to divorce him. However I fell in love with Canada and my in-laws were supportive and still are.

For many it was difficult to put the war behind them as they continued to live with its effects. Evelyn (Weaver) Payne now lives in Coleman Alberta, but came first to Natal British Columbia:

My husband lied about his age and was in England by the age of seventeen. We were married in 1944 and he was immediately sent to Europe. We saw very little of each other until I arrived in British Columbia. He had been wounded and sent home in May, 1945 after extensive surgery to his right arm. They told him that after the age of thirty-five he would be unable to use it but he proved them wrong. He died in 1986 and I still live in the house we bought in 1949.

Irene Hunt, who lost her first love, a British policeman, in that Buckingham Palace bombing, married Joseph Hunt who served in NW Europe with the Queen's Own Rifles of Canada. He was repatriated to Ontario apparently unscathed:

Before we moved to London, Ontario, our youngest daughter died, two days before her seventh birthday, with leukemia. I honestly think my husband never recovered from the shock. In the six years in London, we made a happy life for ourselves, made a lot of new friends, and in our third year there were blessed with another baby girl. Unfortunately when she was three years old my husband had a very severe breakdown. He lost his job and within a few months we had lost everything. Finally I managed to get him into the veterans' section of Sunnybrook Hospital.[5]

The doctors were never able to find the real reason for his breakdown but they certainly succeeded in bringing him back to face the world. However he was a changed man and quite different from the man I had married. They found him a job where he would be out of doors all the time and not have to cope with many people. In 1984 he became seriously ill and was not able to work again. Strangely enough he then became his old self. He amazed the doctors and survived three episodes until two years later when he succumbed again to illness, this time not surviving. I came to Canada with an open mind, was homesick until going home for the first time after five years. After that I settled and am happy to say this is my country now.

Megan (Powell) Ouderkirk wrote in 2003:

To sum up my feelings on being a war bride I have to say that attitude plays an important role in whether or not you will make a good life in a new country. Wanting to do the right thing and learning how to get along are prime requisites. Of course a loving husband and family helps.

Doris Clarkson is a pragmatist:

Has my life been different because of the decision taken so long ago? Difficult to say. I have lived *this* life and I know *this* man . . . the life that might have been is pure fiction. At times there was the longing to 'go home' but the stoicism that was British bred always surfaced and life in Canada continued. British I was born and the land of my birth will forever be dear to me, yet when we stand to be counted, I am proud to be Canadian.

Dorothy (Kent) Hartland is grateful for the life she has had in the Kootenay area of British Columbia:

. . . and for the dear husband who taught me his way of life which at first was much removed from my own, but which now seems so natural. I have never looked back and never will. Thank you George, and thank you Canada.

Margaret (Innes) Kuhn from Balillieston Scotland, came to Oyen Alberta:

The best gift I ever received was the gas clothes dryer George bought for me the day I brought our fifth child, Heather, home from the hospital. George and I had forty wonderful years together.

Lottie (Wallwork) Gillis wrote in 1999:

In a month Gill and I will celebrate our 54th wedding anniversary, and consider ourselves lucky to still be together. Had our ups and downs, but no regrets to have married my Canadian, changed religion (she became a Roman Catholic), way of life, family and country.

Barbara (Micklethwaite) Barrett, who has contributed so much to theatre and journalism in Newfoundland expressed her gratitude:

> Newfoundland has offered me lots of opportunities, and a chance to experiment. It's a great place to develop dreams.[6]

Patricia (Collins) McCaskill has memories of visiting England through membership in the Overseas War Brides Parents Organization:

> Staying three months in England, seeing my kin again and my lovely England, shedding my nagging homesickness (then) wanting to get back to my husband and home. My husband was with the Vancouver Fire Department. He was a hard worker and after 33 years retired as District Chief. Bud loved England and he and I went back several times for holidays. Bud was my life and I have been a very lucky lady.

It is ironic that one of the last war brides I traced lived out her life in seclusion about five miles from my home. In August 2004 Parksville's Craig Heritage Museum advertised a six-week showing of the late Olive Walton's folk art collection. Intrigued, I attended opening night and saw an astonishing display of hand crafted items. Representatives from the local war bride's group were there, but had no knowledge of Olive either. Born Olive May Parritt at New Bilton, Warwickshire, she married Frank Walton, RCAF, on January 2nd 1943; she was 21 and he was 33. Perhaps the age discrepancy troubled her parents. Perhaps they thought the couple should not move away to Canada. What ever the cause, there seems to have been a rift that was never resolved.

Frank and Olive settled in Parksville in a primitive dwelling. Water was carried from a

From Olive Walton's folk art collection displayed at thr Craig Heritage Museum, Parksville, BC, 2004.
Credit: author's collection

nearby creek (there was a pump in the kitchen but it wasn't connected to a water supply). The Walton's ran the Green Briar's Café (later the Temple Store) located on the Old Island Highway. They had no children and Olive seemed withdrawn, always deferring to her husband. After a fall in the store, she became a complete recluse. Frank cut her hair because she declined to go to a hair dresser. He went to work at the Post Office and Olive's hours at home were filled with creating dozens of colourful rugs, cushions and place mats from oddments of bright yarn. She painted the radio cabinet, kitchen table, chairs, side tables, trays and canisters using left-over paint. The designs were intricate and accomplished with a sure hand. Often they included the names "Frank" or "Olive". It is difficult to reconcile the woman who wore no makeup and had the drabbest of clothing with the riot of colour that surrounded her.

Olive was devastated when Frank died in 1990. She lived until March 2004 in a modest apartment where to her surprise heat came "from the wall" instead of a labour intensive fireplace.

War bride Sheila "Jane" (Beatty) Davidson was born in Saskatchewan. Her mother had married a Canadian but "it had been a disaster", so mother and child returned home to England where Sheila was raised. (Sheila's mother was not a World War I war bride). She wrote from Roberts Creek, British Columbia:

When I met my husband-to-be it was (and I did not tell this to my children for years) a pick-up! It was the winter of 1943 and I was a nurse at the London Hospital for Sick Children, commonly called the Great Ormond Street Hospital. I had a morning off, and stopped for coffee. The café was crowded and I sat at a table for two opposite a raised newspaper. I'm a print fiend and of course was reading the back of the paper when suddenly it dropped and I was caught out looking into the two bluest eyes I had ever seen. I was embarrassed, he was courteous, if amused. One thing led to another and we ended by strolling in the park for half-an-hour before I returned to work and he caught his train. I heard no more until mid-January. It turned out he was, I guess 'dumping' is the word, a previous girlfriend. The hospital rules were rigid, in at ten or else, so our meetings were few but intense. On Valentine's Day the hospital gave a ball (our first since before the war) and I invited Norm. He arrived with an enormous bunch of carnations and a proposal. I had to ask permission from Matron, married nurses were unknown in those days when all nurses lived in. When told my fiancé was a Canadian she said, 'Well, at least he isn't an American, nurse.' We had 44 years together and three children, and a good life even if it was not one I could ever have imagined. We had our ups and downs, but more of the former than the latter. I lost Norm on the last day of 1988, and you know what? It is not the sick old man I remember and grieve for, it is the young love with whom I strolled through London's parks and kissed in the back of taxis before arriving back at my hospital at the statutory 10 pm.

I have lost count of the number of times I have quoted Sheila's last sentence - it still brings tears to my eyes.

What we got here is . . . failure to communicate.

Strother Martin as, 'The Captain', in the Paul Newman movie, *Cool Hand Luke*

. . . you ceased to be a Canadian citizen on March 30, 1967 because you did not reside in Canada on your twenty-fourth birthday, nor had you applied for retention of your citizenship . . .

Extract from a letter received from Citizenship and Immigration Canada by Sheila Walshe, daughter of Canadian serviceman and a British war bride [1]

Most people probably thought Robert Goulet, who died suddenly this week, was a Canadian. He wasn't. Oh, he thought of himself as Canadian, grew up here and reached stardom as a Canadian, but his efforts to have his citizenship established remained tangled in Bureaucratic red tape. He died in hospital as another 'lost Canadian'. . . . Don Chapman, founder of the 'Lost Canadians' group recalls when Goulet was in Toronto last year receiving a star on the Walk of Fame, he commented to Prime Minister Stephen Harper who was accompanying him: 'This is great, but what I really want is my Canadian citizenship.'

Peter Worthington, columnist, *Toronto Sun*, November 2, 2007

Joe Taylor with the author following Joe's citizenship ceremony, in Vancouver, BC, January 24, 2008.
Credit: Stuart Lyster

Chapter 22: Failure to Communicate: War Brides, Citizenship and Passports

CANADIAN CITIZENSHIP

Prior to 1947 there was legally no such thing as Canadian citizenship. Native-born and naturalized citizens were British subjects. In 1977 the current Citizenship Act came into force. It removed special treatment for British nationals and the remaining discrimination between men and women (and) provided that Canadians could hold dual citizenship.[1] (None of the changes in 1977 were retroactive.)

A typical war bride arriving in Canada from Britain and other countries in the 1940s did not travel on a passport. The substitute was a numbered Canadian Travel Certificate issued by the Canadian Wives Bureau in London, England under the authority of The High Commissioner for Canada, Canada House, London, SW1. This Certificate was good for one trip only. Consequently not many were retained, leaving us with few documents to prove we had arrived on a war bride ship. For several years this seemed of no importance. War brides were British (even those from non-British countries became British Subjects by marriage to a Canadian). From the beginning we voted in all three levels of government, held jobs, paid income taxes, owned property and paid property taxes. When we reached sixty-five we drew old age pensions. One war bride was a Citizenship Judge, another who lived in a remote area of British Columbia was licensed to perform marriages. When the first Citizenship Act came into effect on January 1, 1947 it contained a specific clause stating that war brides were Canadian citizens. It said nothing about our children who had been born abroad, those 20,997 children who came with us on the Atlantic liners as toddlers or babes in arms. We had no reason to doubt that they too were citizens.

Our status is confirmed by Canadian Order in Council #858, dated Ottawa, February 9, 1945 which defines a dependent:

> 'dependent' means the wife, the widow or child under eighteen years of age of a member or former member of the Canadian Armed Services who is serving or has served outside Canada in the present war.

and further states:

> Every dependent who is permitted to enter Canada pursuant to section two of this Order *shall for the purposes of Canadian immigration law be deemed to be a Canadian citizen if the member of the forces upon whom he is dependent is a Canadian citizen and shall be deemed to have Canadian domicile if the said member has Canadian domicile.*

> (italics are mine)

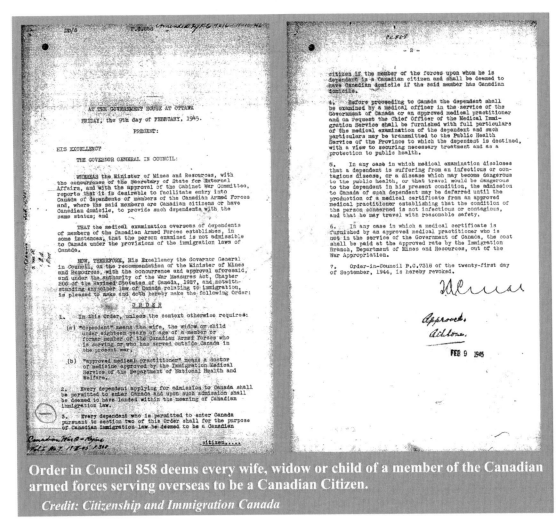

Order in Council 858 deems every wife, widow or child of a member of the Canadian armed forces serving overseas to be a Canadian Citizen.
Credit: Citizenship and Immigration Canada

Even before the first Canadian Citizenship Act of 1947 the word "citizen" was widely used in numerous government documents and in speeches, letters and statements by prominent Canadians when referring to war brides and their husbands. This was confusing as the legal status of a person born in Canada before 1947 was "a British Subject domiciled in Canada". A woman's nationality at that time was determined by that of her father or if married by that of her husband.

Early in my research I requested information from Citizenship and Immigration Canada as to the status of war brides upon marriage, and upon arrival in Canada. To my surprise they were unable to supply it. After a number of unanswered enquiries I received a package of papers critical of the development of citizenship in Canada, and of anomalies contained in the two Citizenship Acts, (1947 and 1977) as well an almost illegible copy of Order in Council #858 (illustrated above).

PRE-1947 REFERENCES TO "CITIZENS"

I welcome these young women (war brides) who will be returning to Canada with their husbands as citizens of our country.
Canadian Lieut. General P.J. Montague, Chief of Staff, CMHQ, September 26, 1945 [2]

Canada's wartime Prime Minister, William Lyon Mackenzie King addressed war brides aboard the *Queen Mary,* on August 31, 1946 congratulating Canada on the splendid addition being made to its citizenship. [3]

To quote a brochure 'Dock to Destination' circulated to war brides: 'As soon as the ship docks Canadian immigration officials will come aboard. These men will complete the formalities for your entry to Canada which automatically makes you a Canadian citizen.' [4]

Thus one result of the Army's long sojourn in Britain was to bring to Canada a large group of new and in general most excellent citizens.
Colonel C.P. Stacey [5]

PASSPORTS AND CITIZENSHIP

As explained earlier, right from the beginning war brides voted in all three levels of Canadian government, paid taxes etc. At first we had no problems when we applied for passports, and things seemed to be even better when the first Citizenship Act came into effect on January 1, 1947. A clause in the act specifically stated that War Brides were Canadian citizens, however we still lacked a document of citizenship. We naturally assumed (never, never assume!) that our overseas born children, having two Canadian parents, were also citizens.

Early in 1972 Bill heard a rumour that Canadian residents who were not born in Canada should apply for proof of Canadian citizenship, and urged that Terry and I do so. Remembering how careful my father had been to ascertain my status after marriage, at first I refused. "I have the same status as you," I told my husband, "and I don't see you applying for proof of citizenship." "My motto is if the government wants you to do something, do it," he replied. ("He was in the Army too many years!" I thought, but didn't say so.) He had the last word, "OK, but don't complain if you find you will not be eligible for the old age pension!" That did it. By the time I was sixty-five I might be badly in need of it. So I gave in, ungracefully. I wrote away and received Citizenship Certificate No. 1-507594 dated June 13, 1972. Terry did the same. I don't know how many times I have blessed Bill for his sometimes irritating habit of crossing every "t" and dotting every "i".

There must have been others who applied when I did or a little later, but the only war bride I know who did so is Audrey (Beasley) Waddy, who in 1976 volunteered to assist people in Duncan British Columbia, who had to apply for Citizenship. (The people she was assisting were not war brides.) Her supervisor asked if *she* had applied, and when

Audrey said, "I'm a war bride, I don't have to," replied "Oh yes you do!" so of course she did. Note that as a warbride she would be applying for proof of citizenship. [6]

Gertrude "Trudy" (Williams) Flatman, came to Victoria British Columbia. I found her story so different and so disturbing that the full text of her 10-page letter (dated November 6, 2000) was attached to the brief I submitted to the government Committee on Citizenship and Immigration in Victoria. The following is a greatly edited version:

> The only upsetting thing about my story was brought about by the government. My sister had been injured when my parent's home was bombed, but nothing appeared too seriously wrong at the time. She married an American Navy officer, and moved to Vermont, USA. After her second son was born an insidious paralysis started throughout her body and she became bedridden. Her husband appealed to my parents (in England) and they sold everything and moved to Vermont. During the first winter the husband disappeared. My parents were too old to find work in the US so Dad returned to London hoping to be able to earn enough to take my sister and the boys back home.
>
> Meanwhile my mother came to visit us (in Canada). While she was here my Dad fell from a building and died. We couldn't bring my sister and her boys to Canada because her boys couldn't leave the US without their father's consent. We then applied to have my mother made an emigrant because she was on a visitor's permit. They would only allow us to have the visitor's permit extended for three months periods.
>
> On one of the renewal visits utter chaos reigned – there were hundreds of refugees being stamped in with impunity and I lost my temper. I demanded to see the supervisor and called my husband to join me. My husband said he was well able to provide a home for my mother, but they refused *on the grounds that I was a war bride!* They said they had seen too many marriages broken this way with the parent or parents becoming 'wards of the state'. I was given an alternative. I could get a job and hire my mother as my housekeeper which would ensure that she would be a wage earner and no threat to the state! I was to pay her an adequate salary and submit receipts from her to their office each month. So for 18 years she lived with us and became the beloved Nana for my children. I never regretted the situation but I hated the necessity because of a government order. I also missed a great deal of the younger years of my children. My mother was safe and we no longer had to fear she would be deported, which was the other alternative they gave me.

The earliest case to come to my attention of a British war bride being denied a passport was that of Mrs. Rose Roy, 75, of Edmonton, Alberta. The City of Edmonton Archives provided a copy of an article from the *Edmonton Journal* dated March 30, 1993. According to it, Rose's first husband, a Petty Officer in the Royal Navy died at sea when she was 24. She later married Canadian Louis Phillippe Roy, and came to Quebec in 1946. Her marriage certificate, his Identification Card, her birth certificate and their 1985 divorce papers were not enough to convince bureaucrats that she had married a Canadian. Rose is quoted as saying "I'm very angry. I was belittled by these people. I was degraded because I'm a war bride. I have to depend on my ex-husband once again because (Debra Presse, court manager at the city's federal Multiculturalism and Citizenship offices) said to me, 'how do I know you're a Canadian?' She's calling me a liar." Rose was still planning to travel to London to visit her older English siblings, but had applied to the British High Commission in Vancouver to renew her British passport. My best efforts to track down the rest of Rose's story have been unsuccessful.

Citizenship and Immigration Canada may have been fully aware of our citizenship but not all employees in Canadian Passport Offices seem to have been informed. (The Passport Office is a separate entity, not part of Citizenship and Immigration.) Much distress could have been avoided if women who said they arrived in Canada between 1941 and early 1948 had been asked by Passport Officers, "Were you a war bride?" War brides and government officials were about the only civilians given permission to cross the Atlantic during those years. The Passport Officer could then have explained to war brides that all they required was *documentary* proof that they were citizens, and have explained how to obtain it. Instead these women were told, "You have no proof you are a Canadian citizen, therefore you cannot be issued a passport."

A few similar problems dated from as early as the 1950s.[7]

Incidents prior to the attack on the World Trade Centre that were reported in the news media were quickly resolved. [8] It was after that tragic event that war brides, their overseas-born children and many other Canadians in no way connected with war brides, ran into trouble. Border regulations were tightened, birth certificates, passports or other proofs of citizenship were required in order to cross into the US. Immigration Canada added a puzzling sentence to its website about this time: "A passport is no proof of citizenship".

After August 1944, the responsibility for movement of war brides passed from the Immigration Branch of the Department of Mines and Resources to the Department of National Defence. The newly opened Canadian Wives Bureau corresponded with us directly concerning our forthcoming voyages on paper headed "*Repatriation* of Civilians" (italics are mine).

Canadian Travel Certificates state that the bearer is travelling to Canada "under the Free Passage Scheme" of the Canadian government. The Certificates do not resemble a passport, being pieces of beige cardstock folded in half to make four pages. They are numbered and carry a photograph of "the bearer", and her signature (photograph and signature authenticated by a round embossed stamp - "Canadian Military Headquarters London" - that encompasses both signature and corner of photograph). Details of any children travelling with the war bride follow.

Rosemary (Jeffries) Bauchman remembers hearing information about status aboard the *Pasteur* in May 1945:

> We were told that as we stepped ashore we became Canadians as a tribute to the Canadian servicemen who were our husbands.

Linda (Whipp) Hanson of Oakbank, Manitoba was on the *Aquitania* in June 1946:

> I remember that we were in the middle of the Atlantic when the Captain announced that by a special Act of Parliament all war brides were automatically Canadian citizens as of that date. Several years later somehow I learned that I had to apply for my Canadian citizenship and I went to the Citizenship Court in Brandon, Manitoba. The judge explained that we were in a different category than the others who were applying because we were already Canadian citizens through this special Act of Parliament but the problem was that

we had nothing in writing to show (that we were), so I received my citizenship papers right there.

The Captain of the *Aquitania* was referring to the first Citizenship Act that did not actually come into effect until January 1, 1947. Linda was lucky to meet the Citizenship judge who clarified the situation for her.

THOSE BAFFLING RUBBER STAMPS

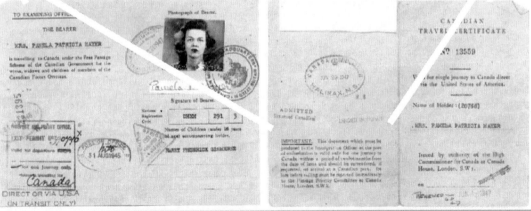

War bride Travel Certificates were routinely stamped "Landed Immigrant", (see text). This one, inexplicably, is stamped "Admitted Returned Canadian" *and* "Landed Immigrant".
    Credit: Harry Mayer

War brides left Britain as British Subjects, and once on Canadian soil we had the same status as our husbands. Shortly after arrival at Pier 21 Halifax, every war bride ship was boarded by Immigration officials who applied a rubber stamp "LANDED IMMIGRANT" to page four of each war bride's Travel Certificate. Today war brides would understand the phrase to mean an official status, but at the time, if we thought about it at all, we took it at face value, we had *landed*, and we had *immigrated* to a new country. Every Certificate I've seen, and I've seen hundreds, is stamped in this way. One that is even more puzzling is the photocopy I have of Pamela Patricia Mayer's Travel Certificate. It is stamped LANDED IMMIGRANT, but has a second stamp: ADMITTED Returned Canadian. (Surely a contradiction in terms?)

Immigration officers advised a handful of war brides to retain their Certificates as they were "proof of Canadian citizenship", yet page four instructs: "This document . . . should be surrendered, if requested, on arrival at a Canadian port." Many of those that were not handed in were lost or discarded. But what about those rubber stamps? A possible explanation is that from the time the Canadian Immigration officer stamped a war bride's Travel Certificate, until the time she set her little foot on Canadian soil she was stripped of her British status and was subject to quite different rulings. For instance, only as a Landed Immigrant could she be refused entry on the grounds that she was "undesirable".

When the second Canadian Citizenship Act became law in January 1977 it was intended to rectify many problems in the 1947 Act which it did, but none of the new rulings were made retroactive, therefore leaving many Canadians with unsolved citizenship problems.

When Newfoundland became Canada's tenth province in 1949, Newfoundlanders became Canadian Citizens under the following Statute:

Statute Law Amendment (Newfoundland) Act, 1949
S.C. 1949, chap. 6

46. The Canadian Citizenship Act, chapter fifteen of the statutes of 1946, is amended by adding thereto, immediately after section forty-four thereof, the following section:

44A. (1) a person who was a British subject on the first day of April, nineteen hundred and forty-nine and
(i) was born in Newfoundland;
(ii) was naturalized under the laws of Newfoundland; or
(iii) had Newfoundland domicile on the said first day of April;
is a Canadian citizen

Through Don Chapman, who runs a website called Lost Canadians, I began to hear of overseas-born children of war brides being informed they were not Canadian citizens. An obscure amendment to the 1947 Act decreed that these people were required to be in Canada on their 24th birthday and furthermore to confirm that they wished to retain their Canadian citizenship, otherwise it was lost. I have yet to learn of even one of these "children" who knew of this amendment at the time when the knowledge was of such importance to them. Sheila (Cross) Walshe certainly didn't. Her mother took her back to England and led her to believe that her father had died. However she traced him to the Okanagan Valley, British Columbia, met him in 1991 and she and her husband purchased a mobile home there to be near him. Ever since then she has been trying to get her Canadian status recognized. In 2003 she was told her case was "on hold" pending the Joe Taylor case (below). In the meantime the Walshes were living on pensions and savings as they had no permits to work. Sheila continues her story:

> It was shortly after this that, thanks to a great Canadian, Don Chapman, my husband got Federal Health cover, and we both got temporary residency . . . then on October 4th, 2007 in a special and private ceremony, my Canadian status was restored. So I now work for the Ministry for Children and Families, and I stride into each day as a very proud Canadian.

Into all this confusion stepped Joe Taylor, named for his Canadian soldier father who fought in the Normandy campaign. Joe, through no fault of his own, had a complicating factor. Twice his father had applied for permission to marry Joe's mother, twice he was turned down owing to service priorities including the run-up to D-Day and the Normandy landings. Joe was five months old when his father finally had leave from Northwest Europe as well as permission to marry.

Joe came to Canada with his war bride mother on the *Queen Mary* in 1946, to a father who had been completely changed, most likely by his wartime task of operating a Wasp flame-thrower. A nastier piece of modern weaponry would be difficult to imagine. Turning it on enemy troops is an experience that is almost guaranteed to give its operator postwar stress and nightmares. (Stacey describes the weapon as "spurting long jets of shriveling flame" and "a weapon much feared by the enemy".) Like so many in the same position Joe's father self-medicated with alcohol. Under its influence he became abusive to his wife. Unable to tolerate her situation, and with the help of the Canadian Red Cross and her parents, she took Joe back to England.

ONE-WAY OR TWO-WAY PASSAGE?

Joe Taylor and his mother returned to England on a Canadian passport. His English grandparents sold part of the contents of their home to reimburse the cost of the fare.[9] Yet Canadian Red Cross Worker, Eleanor Wallace Culver, writes: 'war brides could return, fare paid, within a certain time frame.'[10]

Joe grew up in a loving English home, aware that unlike other boys he had a father in far off Canada. He vowed that as he was a Canadian citizen he would return to Canada to find him. He first tried in the 1970s but was given the wrong forms and incorrect information. He renewed his efforts in 2002 and at that time was told he had lost his Canadian citizenship because he was not in Canada on his 24th birthday and did not at that time confirm that he wished to retain his citizenship. When he challenged this he was told that he was not a Canadian citizen anyway because he was born out of wedlock, which according to Canadian law of the time would give him the nationality of his mother. Unbelievably, in 2002 Canada, where great numbers of children are born to unwed parents, and in defiance of the United Nations Charter of the Rights of the Child to which Canada is a signatory, Joe was labelled "illegitimate".

I first met Joe on April 8, 2005 when we both gave evidence before a government Standing Committee on Citizenship and Immigration in Victoria, British Columbia. I followed his case with deep interest. He sued the Canadian government for wrongful denial of his citizenship. The presiding judge, Justice Luc Martineau, issued an 88-page summation of his findings which were in favour of Joe on all counts. Justice Martineau instructed Citizenship and Immigration to restore his citizenship and he was awarded costs, but Joe's triumph was short-lived. The Canadian government appealed and Justice Martineau's findings were overturned. Meanwhile the case attracted wide attention. It was the subject of broadcasts, articles, and dozens of Letters to the Editor in the Canadian media. Joe's last hope was to take his case to the Supreme Court of Canada, but while he was working towards this the Minister of Citizenship and Immigration, Diane Finley, had a change of heart. She decided to use her discretionary powers to grant his Citizenship. On January 24, 2008, in a colourful ceremony attended by many of Joe's friends and supporters, including Don Chapman, Melynda Jarratt and myself, Joe was sworn in as a new citizen of Canada.

For over sixty years Joe's mother had been reluctant to return to the place that represented so much unhappiness, despite the fact that Joe and his wife owned a home in British Columbia. When she did, Joe was not sure that she would agree to come to see me but she did. I met a small woman in her early eighties, happy for many years in a later marriage with a man who "was kind when I met him and is kind to this day". The story of her first arrival in Canada spilled out almost as soon as she was through my door. I like to think that it was helpful for her to discuss the past with someone who knew of all kinds of difficult experiences and that it brought her some resolution.

Joe's dilemma being solved was one thing, but there were still hundreds, perhaps thousands of Canadians without citizenship. It was entirely possible to have Canadian ancestry going back four of five generations and to lose your citizenship because your father took you to live in another country. This happened to Don Chapman. You could be born in Canada of Canadian parents, have never left Canada, and lose your citizenship because of some action taken by your father. Or to be the only one in a group of siblings who did not have citizenship. Unbelievably there were even First Nations men and women whose citizenship was in question.

Don Chapman, tireless advocate for all Canadians who have been denied their citizenship, including "born overseas" children of war brides.
Credit: author's collection

Don Chapman identified nine different categories and worked ceaselessly to help them, assisted by Melynda Jarratt, and many, many supporters. Then, after years of disappointments, of Bills that were started on their way through Parliament and crashed when there was a change of government, in the spring of 2008 Bill C-37 went through three readings in Parliament, three in the Senate, all the way to the Governor General where it was signed into law. In April 2009 the benefits will be available to 99% of the "Lost". Much has been accomplished. More needs to be done. Of foremost importance to war brides, the citizenship of their overseas-born children is secure. We all owe Don Chapman a tremendous debt of gratitude for his dedication. His e-mail address is:

<dcinbc@yahoo.ca>

I have one more reason to hark back to the label, "Landed Immigrant". On the first day aboard a ship bound for Canada war brides received a ship's newspaper that had information about the ship's size, speed, etc., about activities on board, daily lotteries in which the number of nautical miles traversed were guessed, and a statement that the ship was under strict military discipline. This was followed by a stern warning: women passengers were forbidden to fraternize with any males on board except crew carrying out their normal duties. Breaking this rule, it cautioned, carried a heavy penalty. With few exceptions (widows and fiancées) we were on our way to rejoin our husbands so the warning seemed superfluous in the extreme. The ruling was not specifically directed at war brides. Ships under military discipline have always segregated the sexes. As we have seen, even married couples were not allowed to share accommodation.

On arrival in Halifax Canadian Immigration officials came aboard to facilitate our entry into Canada, which according to the "Dock to Destination" leaflet "automatically makes (the war bride) a Canadian citizen".

On February 9, 1946 I stood with a small group of war brides near the Purser's office on the *Mauretania II*, watching those bound for points in eastern Canada leave the ship. Those of us travelling to the west were to spend one more night on board. Suddenly the Tannoy above our heads came to life. A voice that been giving bulletins all the way across announced that two or three – I don't recall the exact number – war brides had been discovered consorting with the crew, despite the warning of serious consequences. Their husbands had been informed, and the war brides involved would not be going ashore today or tomorrow, but would remain on board and return to Britain when the ship sailed. "How *could* they!", someone said, annoyed that our good name had been sullied. "And them so seasick," said someone else, wonderingly.

Let me pause here to say that I don't enjoy bringing up this subject. I'm uncomfortable with it, but my interest in the role of the Immigration Branch, or perhaps I should say, the laws and regulations as they existed in the 1940s, is greater than my discomfort.

The topic of a few "sinning" war brides being sent home without leaving the ship always seemed to come up when groups of war brides got together, and is referred to in many books of war bride reminiscences. (One dear, trusting soul said to me, "It could never have happened on my ship. The war brides quarters had armed guards on the doors." It had never crossed her mind that guards could be bribed, or even consorted with!) This situation has also been remarked on by Aubrey Jeffries, Fourth Engineer on the *Lady Nelson,* (see Chapter 12). Jeffries says in part:

> There were some of the war brides who had to return, didn't get off. Either they had been abandoned, they didn't have anybody to go to, or else they didn't like what they saw. I think we took back twenty-four.

Twenty-four is a large number out of a total of 150 or 300 or even 450 (Jeffries is not clear whether he refers to one sailing or two or three) to decide either that they "didn't like what they saw" when all they saw was Halifax from the ship, or "they didn't have anybody to go to" when the Canadian Red Cross had worked tirelessly before we left England to confirm that we *did* have someone to go to. "Abandoned" I could agree with, remembering those Dreaded White Envelopes. The phrase "who had to return" doesn't sound like freely-made decisions. What Jeffries' observations do is to establish that someone other than a war bride knew that a number of women did not go through the landing process and were returned to the UK.

Let's leave Aubrey Jeffries' vague recollections and go to someone who has seriously researched Canadian war brides. She is the late Estella (Halfin) Spergel who wrote a 1997 paper, "*Topics in Canadian Social History*", for Professor Ian Radforth, vice-principal of University College, University of Toronto. Estella's grandson Ben kindly sent me a copy. Estella refers to Millie Craig, a Scottish war bride she interviewed who sailed on the *Andes* in 1944:

> Her own accommodation was comparatively comfortable because she had been assigned to a four-bed stateroom, complete with its own bathroom in what had previously been the ship's officers' quarters. As the wife of a soldier in the category 'other ranks', this allocation was unusual and Milly believes was made mistakenly, especially since one of the other three occupants of the stateroom was also a Mrs. Craig, but an officer's wife. About the third day out to sea Milly was told to report to the officer responsible for their group . . . who accused her of 'fraternizing', a serious charge because, if proved true, the bride was not allowed to land in Canada but was returned to the U.K. On Milly's denial, she was told that she had been caught, *in flagrante delicto* by two sailors who had reported the matter to him. It was cleared up when the sailors told the officer he had accused the wrong Mrs. Craig. He had simply assumed that if there were two Mrs. Craigs, the culprit must be the

wife of the ordinary soldier. Milly says she never saw the other woman again and has no idea what happened to her. (pp 40, 41)

Estella addresses the topic again a few pages later:

The rule against fraternization was never changed. If anything it was strengthened when the mass movement of dependents began. No doubt 'saints and sinners' should be added to that list of words, 'dependents', 'wives', 'war brides' . . . (p 44)

and then speaks of her own voyage on the *Andes*:

Fraternization . . . could be very tempting for the young and foolish especially those travelling without children. When Peggy Turnbull and I were aboard the *Andes* in November, 1944 . . . there were rumours among the brides concerning one of our party getting 'caught' with a fellow passenger, a Canadian airman. The general assumption was that it was nothing but idle gossip until, being curious why a soldier was standing guard outside one of the cabins, a crew member confirmed that what we thought to be rumour was indeed, fact. The culprit had to remain inside that cabin for the rest of the trip and would be sent back to England probably on the ship's return voyage. (p 44)

Could these unpalatable stories have any connection with those "Landed Immigrant" stamps? It's possible. Only a Landed Immigrant could be turned back at the gate, so to speak, by being declared "Undesirable". On page 79 of Ben Wicks' book, *Promise You'll Take Care of My Daughter* is a story that supports this possibility. Joan Georgina Weller was on the *Aquitania* when it docked in Halifax, in April 1946:

When we arrived a few of the brides were not allowed to land but were returned to England as "undesirable aliens" having been found in the lifeboats with returning servicemen.

If true it was an incredibly cruel method of refusing a British Subject entry to into a country of British Subjects. Incredible in the light of the giant effort being made to reunite the partners in marriages that the 'war had made'; cruel because of the irreparable harm it would do to those marriages. I would like to believe it is not true, but what other possible reason could there be for turning 44,000 war brides into Landed Immigrants for such a brief period of time?'

One day I heard Maureen Forrester sing 'O Canada' and found myself remembering when there was only one anthem for me.

Betty (Stitchbury) Ramshaw

He came to dinner. He did, after all, own half the chicken.

Ibid.

. . . after much struggling with a girdle, nylon stockings, high heels and dodging of mosquitoes, I adjusted to the pleasures of outdoor plumbing.

Ibid

Mr. and Mrs. Ramshaw, December 22, 1945.
Credit: Betty (Stitchbury) Ramshaw

Chapter 23: Betty's Story

Betty Doris (Stitchbury) Ramshaw was born in London, England. When she met her husband, Arthur C. E. Ramshaw, 8th Recce, Canadian Army, she lived at 1 Chestnut Villas in the village of Thundersley, Essex. When they married their names became part of church records that date back to 1569. Betty sailed on the *Aquitania* in the summer of 1946, her destination: Nokomis, Saskatchewan. Betty still lives in Nokomis. Her story made me laugh, nod in recognition, and at times moved me to tears. It still moves me, not because Betty's story is necessarily typical, or the most extraordinary one I've received, but because there is something of every war bride in it. Betty has what my creative writing instructor called "Voice". Distinctive. Indeed it's a Voice you'll not soon forget. Betty exemplifies the stubbornness and the willingness to hang on despite what life flings at her, and the sense of humour that was the basis for all successful war marriages. What better story with which to end this larger one.

> O, Canada, my home and native land. You were not always my native land. No, I didn't want to come here, I didn't even know you were here, and I can't say I knew anyone else who knew you were here. But now you are my country; my roots are here and they go deep.
> Betty Ramshaw

One day I heard Maureen Forrester sing "O Canada" and found myself remembering when there was only one anthem for me: "God Save The Queen." When was that?

The war was over. Troops were returning to their homelands, things were winding down. I was still working in a factory making uniforms; there had been no halt called to production. I was twenty years of age.

Hadleigh, a small town five miles from Thundersley, Essex where I lived was having its weekly dance. Mary Smith, Violet Kerns, and yours truly decided we should go. After all, once the boys went home there would be no more dances and the excitement of having ten men to every girl would be a thing of the past. (At the beginning of the war partners had been so scarce that young women danced with each other.) It was the usual dance, the bar along the wall, smoke hanging in the air. Everyone smoked in those days, it was sophisticated! One of the soldiers from the army barracks had been in the *Wagon and Horses*. He wove his bleary-eyed way across the dance floor towards me. I have a way of attracting drunks and other wild things. I hated drunks, and I went as fast as I could in the other direction. I was not fast enough, and was caught in the arms of the man with a smiling face and the fastest pair of legs I've ever known. He whirled me on to the dance floor. There was no escape.

"I'm going to marry you," this grinning stranger informed me. I thanked him politely, but I must have been too polite. No matter how hard I tried I couldn't get rid of him. We danced again and again. As the night wore on he sobered up.

We bought two raffle tickets on a chicken, and guess what, we had numbers eight and eighty-eight, and it went to the couple with the most eights. He came to dinner. He did, after all, own half the chicken. We fell in love and within eight weeks we were married in the little Saxon church of St. Peter's. That was December 22, 1945. On January 18, 1946 my new husband was on his way back to Canada.

After he left my life went on as usual. I went to work. I wrote letters every day. Before long my wedding and my new husband became a pleasant dream. The weeks passed. I had written to various boys all through the war years, and soon my husband was just like one of those boys. Memories fade fast when you are young.

Then the bubble broke. It was June, 1946 when the letter came. Those unseen controllers of my fate whose sole purpose was to remind me of my duty, dragged me back to reality. I would be leaving for Canada from Southampton on July 26 aboard the *Aquitania*. It was too soon! I had known this was going to happen, but like Scarlett O'Hara I preferred to think about it tomorrow.

My two brothers, Frank and Ron, were home now from the war. They had never met Art and I couldn't understand why they were so interested in Canada. I certainly wasn't. I had been married five months and had never looked at a map. Did you know that Canada is pink? *Saskatchewan*, now that was funny. We practised spelling it. "See, that's where you are going. Extreme climate." More laughter. What was so funny? The enormity of what I had done was beginning to penetrate my consciousness. Where was the sympathy?

The responsibility was mine. I had made a decision in December, and it was assumed I was aware of the consequences. No one gave me the comfort I was seeking. They didn't think I needed any. I don't want to leave. Dear God, I had forgotten what he looked like!

There was planning to do, letters to write. A farewell party from my friends at work. Go to London to buy a trunk and a new suitcase. Mum bought me a warm coat. So much to do, so many pictures to store in my mind. Green trees, my church, summer rains, my beloved family. I needed to store it all.

It was hard to sleep, hard to eat. Dear God, help me. I was only twenty years old and had made a commitment before God to love and follow a man I could barely remember.

My brothers were concerned that Arthur would be no good. I was their only sister and would be miles away from their help. Money was put into my savings account. I was told, "Give him a fair trial, but if he hurts or abuses you, come home. Give him a year, if he's all right, keep the money, make good use of it." What a sacrifice they made. It wasn't much by today's standards, but $500 in 1946 was a great deal of money. I felt better. I had a way back.

July 25, 1946 - I said goodbye to Mum, Dad, and my youngest brother in the passageway of our house. Facing forward, not able to look back for fear of breaking down, I boarded the bus to the railway station with my brothers. My trunk had left earlier in the week.

My heart broke that day. Ron, tears streaming down his cheeks, ran beside the train, holding my hand 'til he could follow no longer. Frank, silent, would see me safely to a large building in London's West End. We checked in and he hugged me. We couldn't speak, there were no words. I don't believe we expected to see each other again. A promise to write was all the commitment we could make. For the first time in my life I was totally alone. I didn't like it, but I couldn't cry. Unshed tears gathered into a solid lump in my stomach.

Next day we wives and children of Canadian soldiers left by bus for Southampton. I was glad I didn't have any children. I never looked back when we sailed. I turned my face to the sea and wept. Gracie Fields was singing, "Now is the hour, for us to say goodbye" on the intercom. I still weep when I hear that recording.

Leroy, the black porter, came through the rail car calling "Regina! Regina!" This was my stop. The customs officer in Halifax had smilingly told us we were very welcome and were now Canadian citizens. I didn't care. I was having a hard time trying to remember what Art looked like. I had a photograph, but could not form a clear memory of his face. There were other things to worry about. People dressed differently here. The houses were strange, all wood. There was so much sky and the heat was overpowering.

Art was standing on the platform in a new brown suit and wide-brimmed hat. He was grinning from ear to ear. "Oh my God, who is this man? I know, it's the hat. I will know him without the hat." Art obligingly put the hat on and off several times. It was no use, he looked different and I didn't know him out of uniform. Art is the most patient of men, and I know he loved me dearly. He had to, to put up with me. We spent three days in Regina, visiting friends, eating food I had forgotten existed. I was getting reacquainted with Art and listening to people talk. Canadians have a nice accent.

The hot days of August, the noises of the Exhibition crowds, broke for a time the grief of parting. I would be all right. I had found my man again. "Let's go home," Art said. It was harvest time, there was hay to haul, stoves to buy. STOVES????????? Plural???

A home. The stuff that dreams are made of. My home would have a curved driveway, green leafy trees, flower beds with roses, and smooth green lawns. I would wear nice frilly aprons, and my floors would gleam with wax. I would be a good wife and have perfect babies. I was happy too that I would never have to work again.

We arrived in Nokomis on August 6th. The air shimmered with heat. I was dressed in a grey wool suit, a girdle and high-heeled shoes. I refused to take my jacket off and spoil my appearance, I was going to meet the family and had to be properly dressed. That day I learned that your eyelids can sweat. The family was at the station to greet us. After some handshakes and pleasantries somebody yelled, "Nell's making dinner, let's go." I was hustled into a khaki-green '29 Chevy and my trunk was thrown onto a truck. Amid sounds of yelling back and forth, the revving of motors and in that terrible heat I forgot my homesickness. I would have sad days and nights, but I would settle down.

"There's the house, what do you think?" We had driven three miles out of Nokomis. "Where?" I couldn't see any house. Art tapped the glass, "There." I scanned the horizon. Surely not. All I could see was a hip-roofed barn. "I don't see it." He was pointing at the building sitting on top of the hill. "That's it," he said.

It was a house all right, unpainted, and the windows blank. The yard, untended for twenty years was brown with dead grass. Trees with dead white limbs pointed to the sky.

A driveway, cracked in deep grooves like a jigsaw puzzle, circled the house. "Dad built this place; it's well built. Going to need some work, but you'll see. One of the best houses around here."

Art rambled on. He was home, he had been born in this house. He pushed open a broken screen door on to a tiny porch. "It stops the wind," Art said. "Good place to keep the slop pail. Keeps the flies out of the house." Art regaled me with stories of flies in the syrup pail, and memories of his childhood. The house door was heavy. After much rattling and twisting it ground open. Brown, brown, brown. Walls, ceilings - every room in that house was painted chocolate brown. Old Charley, Art's Dad, told me years later that it didn't show the dirt, " 'sides the paint was cheap!"

I was hot. "Where's the bathroom?" I asked. "Oh, you'll have to go outside 'til we fix something up." I was not sure what he meant, so I said again, "I have to go to the toilet."

"Sure, go behind the garage, There's no one around."

Where to go. There was a ramshackle shed north of the house and behind that the drooping remains of an outside toilet. The floor boards were broken and cobwebs hung in all their undisturbed glory. My high heels dug into the broken boards. No, I couldn't go in there. After much stumbling around I found a spot where I could not be seen and after much struggling with a girdle, nylon stockings, high heels plus mosquitoes, I adjusted to the pleasures of outdoor plumbing.

We worked on the house for the next month. First a toilet. Dig a hole . . . the old one had been filled in years ago. The old outhouse was scrubbed and calcimined white (a water-based paint similar to whitewash but made with zinc oxide and glue). It was clean. It was also a two-holer. For some unexplained reason this was important. Maybe, I reasoned, large families had a bearing on this, maybe they liked sharing. Anyway, we had a two-seater.

Next the house. To cover the brown walls we decided on wallpaper. Bill, a local man, agreed to do the job. The paper was pale green, with dropped ceilings of cream. Bill was firm. "You stay out of my way. I'll tell you when it's finished." We put in the time grading forty miles of Highway 15 and were paid eighteen dollars a day for the two of us.

We were allowed back in the house when the job was finished. The rooms were beautifully papered. Neighbours told me later that Bill only worked when weaving drunk. Art had bought chickens and cows early in the spring, so we covered the gaping hole in the barn with straw. Chickens, cows and horses don't mind living together. There was the odd murder of a chicken or two, but nothing to get excited about. Over the years we raised thousands of chickens and turkeys in that old barn. As Art said, his Dad built it well.

Now, about stoves. We chose a McClary Royal Charm, a Quebec heater and at least a mile of stove pipes. Mac was handsome, all black and white enamel, and a woman hater. Art could take a piece of paper, a handful of wood, one piece of coal, and Mac would glow with satisfying heat. I tried to please him. I would clean the ash out of his belly, lay sticks carefully on puffed up pieces of paper, and Mac would blow out my match, sulk, puff black smoke in my face, or better yet, burn so fast and hot he'd make the pipes glow red, and I'd have to lay wet rags in the firebox and put him out. In the dining room his cousin from Quebec was also contrary, sulky, dirty and miserable. I promised them both a quick trip to the junkyard when things improved.

What about language? No trouble there? Don't you believe it. I was laughed at good-naturedly about knocking Art up in the mornings. I learned that cows had tits. That there were all kinds of Sons of Bitches. That God damned everything that didn't work right. That there were lots of Holy Cows. But best of all was Bull Shit. It fit everywhere. At first I was totally shocked, but eventually I learned to accept it as pure Canadiana. It came in beautifully when the dining room ceiling came down during a dinner party.

Yes, I was fitting in nicely. I travelled by sleigh, in a wagon box hitched to Dick and Rosie who would fart merrily at every opportunity, in a 1929 Whippet Coupe, and on my favourite, Alice Chalmers, our little yellow tractor.

My family emigrated to Canada in 1947 and Canada you gathered more of me to you. I had no reason to leave you now. The land was broken up, crops grew and failed, grasshoppers ate their way through years of my life. The sun burned the earth, and those never-ending winds blew and blew. There were times when I hated you. You were hard to please, Canada, yet I always loved you.

I would like to say we prospered in those early years, but we didn't. The only travelling we did was to the credit union to borrow money. Three times we went broke.

We had nowhere to go and no money to go with, so we worked where we could. Art worked on the CPR track and cleaned barns, I took in sewing. We did custom killing at Christmas when everyone raised turkeys. We went to Moose Jaw and worked. We had our babies. But you know what, Canada? We became tough and survived. We raised three children, all good citizens. You must be proud of them. We bought land. We never asked for charity!

Do you know what you are to me, Canada? You are a beautiful, harsh, loving, giving, taking, hurting, healing builder of strong sharing men and women. I'm not worried about Distinct Societies, or Quebec leaving. We are in the process of growing up, that's all. You will mould us in the way we should go. It doesn't matter what our ethnic background is. We have proved that this land has men and women ready to die for her. We are one people, a mix of the finest. We are Canadians.

POSTSCRIPT

UNIFICATION OR SCHISM?

Some changes in Canada between 1946 and the Millennium have been discussed in the body of this book, with the notable exception of the unification of Canada's three services.

Most veterans of World War II deplored the loss of the Army's regimental system and the distinctive uniforms of the three services. By 1965 many who had made service life their career retired in protest, including military historian J. L. Granatstein. The Unification Bill passed into law in April 1967.[1] From then on there was to be "one force with a common name, a common uniform and common rank designations".[2] Soon the services were wearing a green uniform made from cloth previously used for gas station attendants.

Canadian war brides in the 1960's were usually employed, juggling work with demands of home and family, even involved with their children's wedding plans (weddings were still a part of Canadian family life at that time!) Unification was a subject that disturbed our husbands profoundly, and I, for one, remember it mainly as a subject to be avoided if at all possible. Only now, after studying so much about World War II, do I realize what was lost by it.

About the Author:

British WREN Eswyn Ellinor fell in love with Calgary Highlander Bill Lyster and came to Canada as a war bride in February 1946. Businesswoman, alpine gardener, weaver, genealogist and writer; she advanced reform of Canadian Citizenship laws. Eswyn fought stroke and cancer to finish this book. She died in July 2009 knowing that her loving family would make sure it was published.

Appendix I: Names of War Bride Ships

WARTIME SAILINGS:

Documented war bride sailings to Canada date from 1942. However, as the first marriages took place in January 1940, a few brides could have made the journey before records were kept. Ethel (Cox) Coulter is recorded on the Vancouver Island War Brides Association Boat Boards as arriving on the *Baltrover* in September 1941.

At the beginning the transportation was handled by the Immigration Branch of the Department of Mines and Resources. War brides reported to Canada House in London for their documents and instructions. During this period small groups of war brides were given the few spaces available on what were basically troop ships. This list shows the names of some of these ships but is by no means complete:

Andes, Aquitania, Aria (may not be a valid name), *Ariguani, Arcadian, Athlone Castle, Baltrover, Batory, Bayano, Britannic, Cavina, Drottningholm, Duchess of Bedford, Empress of Canada, Empress of Scotland, Franconia, Ile de France, Jamaica Producer, Letitia, Liverpool, Pasteur, Manchester Shipper, Marine Falcon, Mataroa, Mauretania II, Monterey* (August 1942 from Greenock unidentified war bride, wife of government official), *Mosdale, Myrmidon* (to New York. Bride took train to Canada), *Nea Helas, Nerissa, Niew Amsterdam, Queen Elizabeth I, Queen Mary I, Rangitata, Samaria, Scythia. Sitma* (may not be a valid name), *Stockholm, Tabina, Tortugero, and Volendam*.[1] These sailings were made under strict secrecy. Information is only available from the war brides concerned.

War Bride transportation ceased between April and July 1944. No civilians were allowed to leave Britain during the build-up to, and following the Normandy Invasion.

POST D-DAY SAILINGS:

From the beginning of August 1944, the Department of National Defence took over the repatriation (as they termed movement of servicemen's dependents) from the Immigration branch. As part of this new initiative the London branch of The Canadian Wives Bureau was opened. At first the numbers moved continued to be small, and almost ceased between May 1945 and January 1946 while Canadian troops were being repatriated. February 5, 1946 saw the first dedicated war bride sailing, indeed the greatest number of war brides were moved in 1946. These well supervised and escorted sailings continued until the end of 1947. The limited number of ships involved in this phase of the transportation did yeoman service. They were the *Aquitania, Ascania, Athos II, Cavina, Drottningholm, Georgic, Gripsholm, Ile de France, Lady Nelson, Lady Rodney, Letitia* (renamed *Empire Brent* in late 1946), *Queen Elizabeth I, Queen Mary I, Samaria, Scythia, Sitma, Stavangerfiord, Tetela, Willem Ruys,* and *Vollendam*.[2]

1948 SAILINGS:

For a short time after this the responsibility reverted to the Immigration Branch of the Department of Mines and Resources. After that the war brides made their own arrangements. Some of the ships involved in unsupervised sailings include: *Ascania, Beaverbrae, Beaverburn, Columbia, Empress of Canada, Franconia, Georgic, Ivernia, Queen Frederica, Mauretania , Saxonia*.[3]

Note: A small number of war brides travelled by air.

Appendix II: Number Crunching

WAR BRIDES

Non-Canadian women who married Canadian servicemen serving overseas,
1940 to 1950:   48,000-50,000
British women included in those figures: 44,000+

WAR BRIDES WHO CAME TO CANADA:

45,000 (43,454 in Canadian Wives Bureau records + those who came before and after escorted passages were in operation. To that figure should be added a small number who travelled by air, fiancées who travelled in 1947-8 and were not included in CWB figures, and a few American women who married Canadian servicemen temporarily in the US or serving with the US forces).

The total number of war brides will probably never be known, but it is safe to say that it is somewhat larger than the accepted figures.

CHILDREN OF CANADIAN SERVICEMEN:

The children who came to Canada with their war bride mothers under the government passage scheme, based on CWB records numbered: 20,997
A few may have come before or after supervised sailings.

CANADIAN SERVICEMEN

Wartime population of Canada: 11.4 million[1]

Armed Forces: 780,000[2]

Killed and missing: 43,000[3]

Wounded: 53,174[4]

Appendix III: World War I Brides

Surprisingly, the 54,500[1] dependents who came to Canada after World War I is not far short of the 64,451 dependents who came after World War II.

It is fair to say that whatever difficulties we encountered must have been worse for our predecessors. At least we had the post-war boom years, not the devastation of crop failures, of even more isolated and primitive living conditions, bank failures and the later Depression. (Annette Fulford refers to a 1919 booklet,   "Information for Wives of Soldiers coming from overseas", issued by "the Repatriation Committee" that was offered for sale on E-Bay in October, 2006. It contained a welcome to war brides, addressing them as "citizens"!!) Canada did not have Dominion status in 1914, and responded to Britain's need much as Newfoundland did in 1939.

Of the few First War brides I have traced, all were British; all but one (who came a year earlier) sailed for Canada in 1919. They usually came with their husbands who had their own separate sleeping quarters but seem to have been available to assist with children during the day. The ships included the *Melita, Cassandra, Empress of France, Minnedosa, Corrian, Adriatic, Scandinavia, Grampion* and *Tunisian.*

The following may serve to bring those earlier wives into focus. Irving Latimer, a Corporal with the Royal Canadian Regiment was wounded at Vimy Ridge. After recovering he married Englishwoman Dorothy Clode. They sailed to Canada in 1919 on the *Minnedosa*, docking at St. John, New Brunswick. Their son Russell was born in Radville, Saskatchewan where, according to Russ, the small family nearly starved to death. They moved to Jerseyman Island at the western entrance to Arichat Harbour, Cape Breton, Nova Scotia. Irving and Dorothy were "Keepers of the Light" there for 25 years. As a home it was uncomfortable, and void of neighbours, electricity, or telephone; groceries were a rowboat ride away. Fresh water was hauled by boat from another part of the island. The light-keeper earned $68 a month.

Dorothy raised four sons who became successful in business, banking and the military, and one daughter who died at the age of 13 due to lack of adequate medical attention. This loss was the only Canadian experience from which Dorothy never fully recovered. She always referred to Jerseyman Island as "that God-forsaken hole."

Dorothy Abraham, another WW I war bride who came to a lonely island off the coast of British Columbia, read of the second generation of war brides who were about to arrive in Canada in 1946. She wrote in her memoir, *Lone Cone*, p 98:

So, to every war bride of today, I send a wish that you may be as happy in this great land as I have been. You will find it very different, of course: Canada is a young country, comparatively, with little or none of the traditions of the Old Land, and there will be many things you may not like at first, and perhaps be inclined to criticize. You may be homesick, as I was many a time, and many problems and difficulties will arise; but as brides we promised 'for better, for worse,' . . .

Appendix IV: GI Brides

> . . . the sudden influx of Americans, speaking like the films, who actually lived in the magic country, and who had plenty of money, at once went to the girls' heads. The American attitude to women, their proneness to spoil a girl, to build up, exaggerate, talk big, and to act with generosity and flamboyance, helped to make them the most attractive boy-friends.
>
> from a Home Office survey. Calder, *The People's War,* 311.

(Almost as much is said here about British attitudes towards women, as about American!)

Jenel Virden's Definition of English GI Brides:

> . . . women who met American GIs stationed in Britain in the Second World War and then married and immigrated to the United States, as well as fiancées of GIs who traveled to the States, married, and became permanent residents.
>
> Virden *Good-bye, Piccadilly,* 1.

It is difficult to establish the exact number of GI Brides as estimates differ widely. Colonel Stacey believed that the percentage per capita of marriages was higher in the Canadian forces.

Virden's book deals exclusively with British women who married GIs (but Shukert and Scibetta's book reveals there were marriages with 28 other nationalities). GI Brides were not lodged in London-based hostels, but were processed through a former GI Base at Tidworth, Hampshire that was close to the southern port of Southampton. Little seems to have been done to ready it for women and hardly anything to accommodate babies who slept in improvised army footlockers. However it was the last-minute medicals that were particularly difficult to take. While Canadian Brides were examined in the privacy of a doctor's office, GI Brides were treated as their husbands had been when they passed through this facility:

> We walked to the (Garrison) theatre, undressed - completely undressed, even if you were menstruating - . . . put on a robe if there was one available, and walked onto stage. We waited in line to go to the doctor who was seated center stage. There he examined us, but the only thing I remember is him shining a flashlight between my legs, evidently to check for venereal disease. The back of the theatre was filled with American army officers, who were watching the proceedings.
>
> Shukert and Scibetta, *War Brides,* 51-2 (see also Virden, *Goodbye Piccadilly,* 71).

The mother of one GI Bride brought conditions at Tidworth to the attention of her MP. When a number of American babies died on the voyages to New York the situation at Tidworth tended to be blamed.

> Virden *Goodbye, Piccadilly,* 73-4.

Although there were many similarities between the experiences of American (GI) brides and Canadian brides there were also significant differences.

NUMBERS	American	Canadian
Number of men who served in Europe(most spent many months in Britain.):	61 Divisions	5 Divisions
Longest time in Britain (plus short time while being repatriated):	1942-1944	1939-1944

SIMILARITIES		
Both War Bride groups came to vast countries about which they knew little. Shipboard and train experiences were roughly the same.		

DIFFERENCIES		
Number of marriages:	Estimates of British/GI marriages range from 70,000 to 100,000	48,000 or higher
UK lodging before boarding ship:	Tidworth, Hampshire, a former US army base through which returning GI troops had been channelled; little changes were made to accommodate women and children	Comfortable hostels staffed by the Canadian Red Cross
Medicals:	Virden speaks of the "ignominy of the physical exam at Tidworth	Last minute medicals were conducted in the privacy of an Army Medical Officer's office
First all-war bride sailings after repatriation of troops:	*Argentina,* January 1946	*Mauretania,* February 1946
Fiancées (travelling to US to be married):	Fiancées had to enter US under a quota from their respective countries; British quota was large, but brides from small countries encountered difficulties	The Canadian Wives Bureau offered minimal assistance to fiancées; passage was withheld until every wife had sailed

Monica Dickens (a granddaughter of Charles Dickens) was well-known and loved by British readers for her articles in "Woman's Own" and for her books, especially those of her experiences as a cook-general in *One Pair of Feet*, (1939) as a nurse in *One Pair of Hands*, (1942), and as a GI bride in *An Open Book* (1978). She married a US Marine officer, Roy Stratton, and called herself "an ageing GI bride" (she was 36). She describes her arrival in New Jersey:

Dismayed, terrified of marriage after being independent for so long, I sat clenching the seat of the car and thinking, ugly, ugly, ugly . . . I wasted a lot of time comparing, looking for things that were like England and criticising things that were not. I wasted a lot of energy arguing about pronunciation and the choice of words. I wasted a lot of emotion being home-sick.

An Open Book, 128-9.

Transatlantic marriages are desirable, but, not easy. When you criticise a country's customs, the other person gets defensive, even if they agree. It takes about five years for this to wear off.

Ibid, 131.

(Monica Dickens returned to England after her husband's death in 1985.)

Virden mentions a case of fraternization between a War Bride and a German prisoner employed at Tidworth and several cases of fraternization on board ship, but gives no indication of the consequences, if any, to the Brides involved. The men, however were threatened with "instant dismissal".

Canadian Brides came to the "Mother Country"; there had been no War of Independence to change that perception. Canadians would win their "independence" by legal means, by inventing a new flag and removing the "Royal" prefix from various agencies, but not from the Royal Canadian Mounted Police, the Royal Canadian Legion, or the Royal Bank of Canada.

Appendix V: War Brides Clubs and Associations

There has never been a national or umbrella organization of war brides clubs or associations. All clubs were separate entities. Many had been disbanded by the time this list was compiled. Apart from Melynda Jarratt's records it has been pieced together from multiple other sources, and may contain inaccuracies.

BRITAIN	name	location	time frame	sponsor, founder, or members
England	Maple Leaf Clubs	London, Kent, etc.	wartime	
	Princess Alice Clubs	Brighton, Chichester, etc.	"	Named for widow of Canada's Governor General Lord Tweedsmuir
	Rose and Maple Leaf Club	Nottingham	"	
	Waiting Wives Club	Ealing, London	"	
	War Bride Clubs	Aldershot and Farnborough, Birkenhead, Birmingham, Blackpool, Bournemouth, Bradford, Bromley, Chichester, Croydon, Leamington, Lincoln, London East and South East, Manchester, Nethy Bridge, Portsmouth	"	
Scotland	Canadian Wives Club	Aberdeen, Dundee	"	
	Heather Clubs (2)	Glasgow	1944	Helena Hammer, member
Wales	War Bride Club	Cardiff, Swansea	"	Joan Louise Pearce, founder
CANADA				
Alberta	Alberta War Brides Association	Calgary	1979	Pat Douglas, founding President
				Doreen Kamis, Secretary
		Edmonton		Kay Young, President
		Lethbridge		
		Medicine Hat		
British Columbia	Comox Valley War Brides			Maisie Godin
	Fraser Valley War Brides Club			Kathy Ballentyne
	Greater Vancouver War Brides, Zone 2 (based		pre-2006	Yetty Foulds, President
				Bea Ackerman, contact person
				Jessie Sinclair
			2006	Ivy St. Cyr, President

			2008	
	in Burnaby)		2008	
	North Vancouver War Brides, Zone 1			Winifred Rose, founder and President
	Imperial Order Daughters of the Empire (Vancouver)		1946 and later	The IODE took an interest in war brides and welcomed them to their meetings
	Kamloops Overseas War Brides			
	Okanagan Valley Overseas War Brides Association		1984 1992	Joan Dedels, founding President Joan Jennens, President
	Vancouver Island War Brides Association		1979	Edith Hineker, founding President, Doris Johnston, founding member Audrey Waddy, long time member
Manitoba	British Wives Club	Winnipeg	1946	Vi Pearn joined this very active club when she arrived in Canada
	Manitoba War Brides Association		1983	Lil Bird, founding President Celia Knight, President Mavis Jackson, President Rev. Canon Peggy Sheffield, Secretary
	War Brides of Brandon name changed to British Wives Club			"Name changed when a charter flight to Britain was planned in order to have more people qualify." Peggy Bell
New Brunswick	New Brunswick War Brides Association		c 1980	Doris Lloyd, founding President. Isobel "Zoe" Boone, President
Newfound-land	Rose & Thistle Club	.		YWCA, Harvey Rd. St. John's Club active until 1960
	The British War Brides Association of Newfoundland & Labrador			Barbara B. Barrett, CM, founder
	British Wives Club (perhaps the same as above)			
Nova Scotia	Nova Scotia War Brides Association (NSWBA)			Joan Schnatre, President
	PADAGEAN Club,	Halifax		Dr. Gwen Service, early member

	Halifax & Dartmouth Area WB Association			Scotia Branch, Royal Canadian Legion Margueríte Turner, President
	King's County Overseas WB Club (Chapter of NSWBA)		1990	Irene Griffin and Eileen Folley, charter members
	Upper Stewiacke War Bride Club		1947	Still operating in the 1990s
Ontario	British War Brides*	Toronto	November 1943 May 1947	Margaret Brenner, President. (Henrietta Reid assisted, then left for Ottawa.) Mrs. Vincent Gallant, President
	British Brides' Club*	Ottawa	1943-44	Organized by Henrietta Reid of Ottawa
	Club 45	Kingston	1945	Ann Ayres, Ivy Charles, Ursula Frane, Pamela Laird, Clare Lee, Winnifred McCann, Dorothy Munro, Lena Page, and Peggy Reedhead, members
	ESWIC Club **	Ottawa	1945	Betty Ulrich, founding President Jean Spear, founding member, record keeper
	Mountbatten Club	Pelham area (near St. Catherine's)	1946	
	Ontario War Brides Association			Kay Mahon
	Picton War Brides Club (later became the Overseas Club)	Picton	1969-70	Kay Wright and Betty Payne
Quebec	Acorn Club		1947-1960s	Mrs. Aislet, Mrs. Pickup and Mrs. Thompson, founders
	Montreal Overseas War Brides Club (revival of the above)		1982	St. James United Church, Montreal
Saskatchewan	Overseas Wives Club	Saskatoon	1946-50 1971	Nan (Chester) Archibald was an early President 125 women from as far away as La Ronge SK, and Victoria BC met for a Reunion, hosted by Nan Archibald and her committee
	Saskatchewan War Brides Association		1975 1992	Gloria Brock, founding President Kay Garside, Secretary. Peggy Gliddon, President

231

International	Overseas War Bride's Parents Organization			This appears to have been a joint US/Canadian Organization set up to assist war brides with visits to their homelands
	Bring Back our War Brides Club			Based in the UK, parents and war brides could pledge certain monthly payments to this Club and have assistance with trips home (see text)
Holland				
	War Brides Clubs	location n/k	wartime	

* Dating from 1943, and 1943/1944 respectively, these are the earliest known clubs in Canada.
** ESWIC is the only club that has operated on a continuous basis from 1945 until the present.

Appendix VI: Glossary

"FBI, CIA, . . . we're all in the same alphabet soup."

The Professor, in Alfred Hitchcock's *North by Northwest*.

Acadia	Colonies of New France in Quebec, New Brunswick, Nova Scotia and Prince Edward Island. The expulsion of Acadians to New England and Louisiana (where "Acadian" became "Cajun") etc. was made famous by Longfellow's poem "Evangeline".
Air raid shelter, Anderson	Corrugated iron garden shelter, set into the ground. This proved to be safe from anything but a direct hit.
Air raid shelter, Morrison	Indoor table-type shelter with heavy wire mesh sides.
ATS	Auxiliary Territorial Service (women's section of the British Army).
AWL	Absent without leave. The US abbreviation is AWOL.
Battle Bowler	Steel helmet or Tin Hat.
Boffin	Technician; man in a white lab coat.
British Army	The British Army has no prefix: "Royal". The first British standing army was created during the Commonwealth rule of Oliver Cromwell after the beheading of King Charles I and before the Restoration of the Monarchy, and Brits are sticklers for tradition!
CB	Confined to barracks.
Canadian Divisions	1st Infantry Division (Red divisional patch) 2nd Infantry Division (Royal Blue divisional patch) 3rd Infantry Division (French Grey divisional patch) 4th Armoured Division (Green divisional patch) 5th Armoured Division (Maroon divisional patch)
Corvette	A small Canadian-built ship suited to coastal patrol. When used for escort duty it was a rough ride.
CPO	Chief Petty Officer.
CSM	(Canadian and British Army) Company Sergeant Major.
D-Day	The Allied invasion of German-occupied Europe, June 6, 1944. Code name: Overlord.
Demob.	Demobilize or release from military service.
Dependents	Wives, children and widows of Canadian servicemen,
Dhobey, dhobeying	(Royal Navy) clothes washing.
Dieppe raid	The disastrous Combined Operations raid on the French port of Dieppe, August 19, 1942 that resulted in high casualties (dead, wounded, and prisoners-of-war). The majority of the participants were Canadian along with small groups of British Commandos and Americans. Royal Navy crews manned the landing craft.
FANY	(British) First Aid Nursing Yeomanry (Princess Royal's Volunteer Corps).

Friday while	(Royal Navy) weekend leave, Friday to Monday.
Have a dekko	Have a look.
Heads, the; cleaning the heads	(Royal Navy) latrines. Cleaning the heads was an unpopular occupation and often used as a punishment. The person involved was known as "Captain of the Heads".
Jimmy the One	(Royal Navy) the First Officer.
Leathernecks	British Marines.
Long-johns	Men's long winter underwear, usually made of fine wool.
Matlot	British sailor (from the Fr. "matelot", pronounced mat-lo).
NAAFI	Navy, Army and Air Force Institute (the organization that ran the NAAFI canteens).
Natter	Talk.
NCO	Non-commissioned officer, for instance (Royal Navy) PO, CPO, etc.; (Canadian and British Army) Quartermaster, CSM, etc.
New Look	post-war style of women's clothing featuring longer, gathered skirts and many of the items forbidden in wartime: buttons, trimmings, pockets, etc.
Number One	(Royal Navy) First Officer (see also Jimmy the One).
Ocean going grocers	NAAFI staff on Royal Navy shore bases.
PO	(Royal Navy) Petty Officer.
Palliasse	Straw-filled mattress.
Pompey	(Royal Navy) Portsmouth.
Provost Corps	(British and Canadian) Military Police.
Pussers kye	(Royal Navy) Navy cocoa.
RAF	(British) Royal Air Force.
Rating	(Royal Navy) Another name for sailor.
RCAF	Royal Canadian Air Force.
RCAF, WD	Women's Division of the RCAF.
RCNVR	Royal Canadian Navy Volunteer Reserve.
RN	(British) Royal Navy.
RNVR	Royal Navy Volunteer Reserve.
Saturday while	(Royal Navy) weekend leave, Saturday to Monday.
Sawbones	Medical Officer.
Sky pilot	Chaplain or padré.
Sleeve lace	Gold braid near cuff, denoting a naval officer's rank.
Slop pail	(Canadian or British) container for waste fluids, often "grey" water that was recycled onto lawns and vegetable or flower beds. The pure soap of the time was a useful insect repellant.
Snowdrops	US Military Police, from the shape of their white helmets.
Sprog	New recruit (Royal Air Force).
Splice the mainbrace	(Royal Navy) issue of rum, neat for officers, watered (3 parts water, 1 part rum) for other ranks. WRNS were not included.
Take the can back	Take the blame for something.

Tannoy	Loudspeaker
Ticklers	(Royal Navy) issue tobacco.
Tiddly	(Royal Navy) clean, smart and ship-shape.
Trilby hat	A hat like a fedora.
Train smash	(Royal Navy) stew that included tomatoes.
Up the Smoke	To go to London.
WAAF	(British) Women's Auxiliary Air Force.
Wavy Navy	RNVR or RCNVR from the wavy gold braid (sleeve lace) denoting Volunteer Reserve.
WLA	(British) Women's Land Army.
WLA, Timber Corps	(British) branch of the WLA whose members felled trees and worked in lumber mills.
Wooden waistcoat	Coffin.
WRAF	(British)Women's Royal Air Force - the name of the women's section of the Royal Flying Corps in WWI. It was used for a time in WWII, before it was changed to WAAF.
WRCNS	(Canadian) WRNS.
Wren	member of the WRNS.
WRNS	(British) Women's Royal Naval Service.
WVS	Women's Voluntary Service. These British women who were not in the services for reasons of age, health, etc., drove ambulances, staffed canteens, distributed clothing, served tea and meals to those whose homes were bombed as well as to firemen and civil defence workers. Now the Women's Royal Voluntary Service (WRVS) the organization has just celebrated its 70th year (2008).

VII: End Notes

DEDICATION: v
1   This picture has been published without attribution many times since its initial
        appearance in 1940. It was clipped by Bill's mother.

PROLOGUE: xi - xvi
1   Undated memo from Kay Garside to the author.
2   Borden is a military camp in Ontario. Bordon in Hampshire, England has been
        associated with the Canadian Army in both World Wars.
3   Shukert and Scibetta, *War Brides of World War II*, 7.
4   Virden, *Goodbye Piccadilly*, 3, 88 (see 151 for extended source note).
5   Shukert and Scibetta, *War Brides of World War II*.
6   BCATP entry in *The Encyclopedia of Saskatchewan*.
7   Jarratt, Resumé of Marriages to 31 December, 1946 *War Brides*, 269.

PART I: British War Brides
CHAPTER 1: Future War Brides: The Phoney War and the Battle of Britain, 2 - 13
1   Blair, *Hitler's U-boat War*, 67-68.
2   Hibbert, *Fragments of War*, 11-21.
3   Retrieved June 18, 2008, http://news.bbc.co.uk/1/hi/uk/781858.stm
4   Waller & Vaughan-Rees, *Women in Wartime, The Role of Women's Magazines 1939-
        1945*, 10.
5   Calder, *The People's War*, 67.
6   Ibid., 331.
7   Jenkins, *Churchill: A Biography*, 558.
8   Thomas, *War Story*, 101.
9   Churchill and the Editors of *Life, The Second World War*, 112.
10   Owen, *The Voice of War*, 61.
11   Morrow, *This is London*, 113.
12   Hough and Richard, *The Battle of Britain, The Jubilee History*, 353.
13   The Royal Observer Corps covered the entire country working from posts that
        were manned day and night. The sight and sound of enemy and friendly aircraft
        were plotted and the information passed to Fighter Command. The 30,000-
        strong Corps was under the direction of the Air Ministry. Thomas, *War Story*, 84.
14   Johnstone, *Spitfire into War*, 148.
15   Ibid., 140.
16   Thames Television booklet "For Valour" 15.
17   Ibid., 15

CHAPTER 2: Future War Brides: The Dark Centre of the Tunnel, 14 - 29
1   McNeil, *Voices of a War Remembered*, 346.
2   Churchill, *Churchill, The Second World War*, Vol. 4, 53.
3   Lemann, *The New Yorker*, January 23, 2006.
4   Morrow, *This is London*, 70.

5   Tupper, "Subaltern Mary Churchill Thrilled to be in Service", *Globe & Mail* August 21, 1943.

6   Soames, *Clementine Churchill,* 356.

7   Ziegler *London at War, 1939-45,* 182.

8   Stursberg, *The Sound of War,* 54 -55.

9   Waller, *London 1945,* 162.

10   Gardiner, Juliet & Neil Wenborn, Eds. *The Companion to British History,* 464.

11   From the English cartoon character Tiger Tim.

12   The Ovaltine Company that advertised over Radio Luxembourg had a radio club for children, "The Ovaltineys". Birthday greetings for members were read over the air with this theme song as accompaniment.

13   Calder, *The People's War,* 54.

14   Robertson and Wilson, *Scotland's War,* 14.

15   Jarratt, *War Brides,* 201-202, and other sources.

CHAPTER 3: The Canadians in Britain: "We've come here to do a job . . . ", 30 - 51

1   Quoted in *The Canadians at War, Vol 1,* Reader's Digest Association (Canada) Ltd., 171.

2   Goralski, *World War II Almanac, 1931-1945,* 426.

3   *Hamilton Spectator,* May 31, 1945.

4   Wheeler, *Flying Under Fire,* 7.

5   Halliday, "Canadian Content in the RAF", *Legion Magazine,* January 1, 2005.

6   Hough & Richards, *The Battle of Britain,* The Jubilee History, 198.

7   Retrieved August 28, 2008, www.lancaster museum.ca/archives99_2.html

8   Peden, *A Thousand Shall Fall,* 109.

9   E-mail to the author, April 7, 2001.

10   Barris, *Behind the Glory,* back cover.

11   Ibid., 237.

12   Mackey, "Little Norway Remembered in Royal Visit", Heritage Perspectives, May 24, 2002.

13   Blackburn, *Where the Hell are the Guns,* n31.

14   Bercuson, *Maple Leaf Against the Axis,* preface.

15   Malkin, *True Canadian War Stories,* 69.

16   *Ottawa Evening Journal,* December 22, 1939.

17   Farren, *The History of the Calgary Highlanders, 1925-1954,* 57-68.

18   Ibid., 55.

19   Williams, *Far From Home,* 153.

20   Farren, *History of the Calgary Highlanders,* 60.

21   Warner, *World War Two, The Untold Story,* 290.

22   Farren, *History of the Calgary Highlanders,*70.

23   Ibid., 71.

24   Smith, *All Tanked Up.*

25   Stacey, *Six Years of War,* n29.

26   Correspondence with Annie's daughter, Valerie Bowden, August 2002.

27   O'Hara, *From Romance to Reality,* 26.

28   Whitaker & Whitaker, *Dieppe, Tragedy to Triumph,* 244.

29	Stacey, *The Canadian Army, 1939-1945*, 40.
30	Stacey, *Report No. 41,* 9 Aug. 1941, to the Director, Historical Section, National Defence HQ, Ottawa.
31	Lieut. Kenneth J. Rootes, Loyal Edmonton Regiment, in a conversation with the author.
32	Paudash, "I Married an Indian", Maclean's, December 1, 1951.
33	September 27, 2007, www.rbc.com/history/i_remembrance/london_branch-detail.html
34	Weinreb & Hibbert, *The London Encyclopedia*, 343.
35	Day, Spence & Ladouceur, Eds. *Women Overseas,* 154.
36	Ellis and Dingman, *Facepowder and Gunpowder*, 28.
37	Evelyn Clark, Canadian Red Cross, quoted by O'Hara, *Romance to Reality,* 54.
38	Day, Spence & Ladouceur, Eds., *Women Overseas*, 210.
39	Ibid.
40	May 2008, www.studios92.co.uk/info/BEO.htm
41	Day, Spence & Ladouceur, Eds., *Women Overseas,* 254.
42	Stursberg, *Sound of War,* 52-56.
43	Stacey, *Six Years of War*, 196.
44	*Globe & Mail,* Jan 20, 1940.
45	Ibid.
46	Day, Spence & Ladouceur, Eds., *Women Overseas*, 223.
47	Ibid., 197.
48	Ibid., 252.
49	O'Hara, *From Romance to Reality*, 237.

CHAPTER 4: Paths Cross, 52 - 59
1	Maclay, *Aldershot Canadians,* 97

CHAPTER 5: Wartime Weddings, 60 - 73
1	Maclay, *Aldershot Canadians,* 122.
2	This did not apply to RCAF ground crew overseas or aircrew anywhere, or to personnel of the RCN. Stacey and Wilson, *The Half Million,* 136. However there are in existence signed RCAF (Overseas) Permission to Marry forms.
3	Ibid., 136.
4	Personal knowledge and reports from many war brides interviewed.
5	Wicks, *When the Boys Come Marching Home,* 117.
6	Jim, a Fredericton, New Brunswick serviceman in Holland, took advantage of this offer. Shewchuk, *If Kisses were Roses,* 172.
7	Wicks, *When the Boys Come Marching Home,* 126, 128.
8	Windsor, *Blind Date,* 27.
9	Tania Long, *New York Times,* reprinted in the *Globe and Mail,* August 24, 1943.

CHAPTER 6: Curity® Diapers and Johnson's® Baby Powder, 74 - 79

--

CHAPTER 7: On to Victory: D-Day and Ever Present Dangers, 80 - 85
1   Retrieved May 1, 2001 (United States National Archives and Records
        Administration on line) www.archives.gov/research/
2   Retrieved Sept 27, 2004,
        www.eisenhower.utexas.edu/dl/dday/order_of_the_day_audio.html
3   Ziegler, *London at War 1939-1945*, 295-298.
4   Bercusen, *Battalion of Heroes*, 239.

CHAPTER 8: The War in Europe Ends: The Men Go Home, War Brides Wait, 86 - 89
1   Correspondence between Jane (Green) Brookes, and the author, July 17, 2008. The
        "abyss" mentioned is from Churchill's "Finest Hour" Battle of Britain speech: "Upon
        this battle depends the survival of Christian civilization. Hitler knows he will have to
        break us in this island, or lose the war. If we can stand up to him, all of Europe may be
        freed, and the life of the world may move forward into broad, sunlit, uplands. But if we
        fail, then the whole world, including the United States, including all that we have known
        and cared for, will sink into the abyss of a new Dark Age, made more sinister, and
        perhaps more protracted, by the lights of perverted science. Let us therefore brace
        ourselves to our duties, and so bear ourselves that, if the British Empire lasts a thousand
        years, men will still say, 'this was their finest hour!' "
2   Retrieved November 29, 2008, www.chu.cam.ac.uk/archives/churchill_chronology.php
3   Heathcote, *Testament of Honour*, 73.
4   Maclean's August 22, 2005 np
5   Shukert and Scibetta, *War Brides of World War II*, 57.

CHAPTER 9: Leaving Home, 90 - 94
1   Undated, uncredited newapaper clipping.
2   Ed Davis, attached to Canadian Wives Bureau, quoted by O'Hara, *From
        Romance to Reality*, 45.
3   Stacey and Wilson, *The Half Million*, 174, quoting NDHQ file HQ 650-124-
        33 RG24 vol. 6435.

PART II: **War Brides from Northwest Europe, the Rest of the World
             . . . and Newfoundland**
CHAPTER 10: Brides from Holland, Belgium and France, 96 - 105
1   Tassie, *Life in Holland Under German Occupation*, 1940-45, quoted by Kaufman
        and Horn, *A Liberation Album*, 11.
2   Stacey and Wilson, *The Half Million*, 138.
3   Telegram No. 3395, quoted in Department of External Affairs Canada letter
        dated January 8, 1945, Immigration Branch Records.
4   Kaufman and Horn, *A Liberation Album*,
5   Annual Report of the Canadian Red Cross, 1946.
6   Article, Anthony Sas, University of Maryland, Annals of the Association of
        American Geographers, Vol. 8, September, 1958.
7   Kaufman and Horn, *A Liberation Album*, 142.

CHAPTER 11: Brides from the Rest of the World, 106 - 113
1   La Doucier, Editor, *Blackouts to Bright Lights,* 159.
2   Shukert and Scibetta, *War Brides of World War II,* 123. (S and S credit Carl J.
        Friedrich and Associates, American Experiences in Military Government in World War
        II).
3   *Globe and Mail,* April 30, 1948.
4   *Hamilton Spectator,* February 18, 1948.
5   Stacey, *The Canadian Army,* 292.
6   Wicks, *Promise You'll Take Care of my Daughter,* 218-9.
7   Letter dated March 26, 1947, confirming Mrs. Wheeler's entitlement for free
        passage to Canada, Immigration Department Records.
8   *Globe and Mail,* April 14, 1947.
9   Shukert and Scibetta, *War Brides of World War II,* 270.
10   Yvonne Brown's obituary.

CHAPTER 12: Newfoundland, A Special Case, 114 - 121
1   Atwood, editor, *The New Oxford Book of Canadian Verse.*
2   Mowat, Claire, *The Outport People,* 28, 29.
3   Hicks, *Long Reach Home,* 32.
4   Correspondence with Memorial University, St. John's.
5   Retrieved August 9, 2008: Address to Kiwanis and Rotary Club of Grand Falls Windsor,
        December 2, 2003, www.mun.ca/govhouse/news-dec2_03.html
6   Stacey, *Six Years of War,* 550.
7   Roses and Thistles, a 1984 paper held by Memorial University, St. John's.
8   *Newfoundland Studies #2,* 1984, Memorial University, St. John's.
9   War brides, whatever their destination, were squeezed aboard any trans-Atlantic vessel
        which had some space.
10   Retrieved November 17, 2008, www.durham.net/kburt/ScreechStory.html
11   Retrieved June 11, 2008, www.cormack.netfirms.com/information/warbridestory/htm
12   Ladouceur and Spence, *Blackouts to Bright Lights,* 260-271.

PART III: On to Canada
CHAPTER 13: On Board Ship, 124 - 133
1   Jarratt, "The War Brides of New Brunswick", Master's Thesis, University of New
        Brunswick, 1995.
2   Correspondence from Department of Mines and Resources to Mr. Joliff, November 9,
        1944, Immigration Branch Records.
3   Quoted by Broadfoot, *The Veteran's Years,* 142.
4   The Boat Boards were lodged with the Ashton Museum, 724 Vanalman Avenue,
        Victoria, British Columbia after the Vancouver Island War Bride Association disbanded.
5   Jarratt, "The War Brides of New Brunswick", Master's Thesis, University of New
        Brunswick, 1995.
6   A zig-zag clock from the *Queen Mary I* is part of the museum exhibit "Cunardia" aboard
        Cunard's new *Queen Victoria.*
7   *Daily Sketch,* March 14, 1941
8   Thomas, *War Story,* 205-211.
9   Smith, *The English Companion,* 42.
10   Quoted by Parker, *Running the Gauntlet,* 150-1.

11	Pier 21 records.
12	O'Hara, *From Romance to Reality,* 131.
13	Quoted by Parker, *Running the Gauntlet,* 252.
14	Passenger Elsa (Bromley) Lintott.
15	Author's records.

CHAPTER 14: The Canadian Train, 134 - 143
1	Hibbert, *The War Brides,* 74-75.
2	Interview with Kay McCaskill, June 21, 2001.
3	Hibbert, *The War Brides,* 84.
4	Grizzle, *My Name's Not George,* 19.

CHAPTER 15: A Far Cry from Thornton Heath, 144 - 151
1	Morton and Granatstein, *Victory, 1945,* 165.
2	Retrieved July 26, 2007, www.vac-acc.gc.ca/general/sub.cfm?source-history/secondwar/diary/grandmother/crane
3	Tessier, Editor, *Beyond Bad Times,* 140.

CHAPTER 16: Happily Ever After?, 152 - 159
1	The late Canadian journalist, historian and media personality.
2	Retrieved July 23, 2007, www.archives.cbc.ca/war_conflict_second_world_war/clips/10322/
3	McNeill, *Voices of a War Remembered,* 231.
4	Ibid., 265
5	Wright, *The Canadian Encyclopedia.*
6	Hunting dogs kept by Tahltan People of NW British Columbia, *The Canadian Encyclopedia.*
7	Adapted, with permission, from Ivy Riese's contribution to *Voices in the Wind,* an anthology compiled and edited by Monica Crooks and Victoria Neligan, published Victoria, 2000.

CHAPTER 17: Crimes, Mischiefs and Misdemeanors, 160 - 165
1	Farran, *The History of the Calgary Highlanders 1921-1954,* 95.
2	*Time* magazine, September 24, 1945.
3	Ben Malkin, *Legion* Magazine.
4	"My friend Phyliss (sic) Binns Bailey . . . mentioned the long white envelopes held at the Red Cross tables until their arrival . . . " e-mail to the author from Kaye Edmonds, North Bay, Ontario, dated January 5, 2001.
5	Wicks, *Promise You'll Take Care of my Daughter,* 79.
6	Retrieved August 18, 2008, www.geocites.com/auntie982000/stowaway.html
7	*Toronto Star,* October 15, 1946.
8	*Kent Messenger,* April 5, 1946.
9	Barris, *Days of Victory, Sixtieth Anniversary Edition,* 357; and Sangster, *Regulating Girls and Women: Sexuality, Family and the Law in Ontario, 1920-1960,* 63.
10	Valee, *The Story of the Notorious Boyd Gang;* and Mackey column, "The Life and Times of Edwin Boyd", *The North Star Nugget,* May 11, 2002.

CHAPTER 18: Some *Really* Excellent Citizens, 166 - 177
1   Campbell, *Butter Side Up,* 6.
2   Ibid., 9,10.
3   Ibid., 198.
4   Linda and Bill Bonvie, "Flying in the Mist", *San Jose Mercury News,* July 17, 1994.
5   Gwladys (Rees) Aikens, letter to the author, June 27, 2001.

CHAPTER 19: War Brides Clubs and Associations, 178 - 185
1   Anne Harmsworth, Director, Kiss the Bride Productions, Ottawa. Premiered on History Television, February 14, 2001.
2   Saskatchewan War Bride Association estimate.

CHAPTER 20: The Next Generation, 186 - 193
1   Personal correspondence; July 18, 2006, CBC News Online: "Romeo Dallaire", www:cbc.ca/newsbackground/dallaire October 24, 2003; March 20, 2005, www.cbc.ca/story/arts/national/2005/01/30/Arts/dallairesundance050130.html
2   January 1, 2005; CBC Documentary, "The Unseen Scars, Post Traumatic Stress Disorder".
3   Article: "Filmmaker turns lens on his own family", Solange de Santis, *The Anglican Journal,* May 1, 2006; article "Filmmaker's last work left undone", Solange de Santis, *The Anglican Journal,* August 22, 2007; author's correspondence with Richard Stringer, October 2006, and his widow Carol Stringer, July, 2008.
4   David Clayton Thomas' website www.davidclaytonthomas.com/

CHAPTER 21: "She Remembers . . . ", 194 - 201
1   CD "She Remembers, The Best of Shari Ulrich", Esther Records, Canada. "She Remembers" was originally released on "One Step Ahead" by A & M Records of Canada, 1982. Excerpt of lyric reproduced by kind permission of Shari Ulrich, Juno Award-winning Canadian singer.
2   Clipping from a Lethbridge newspaper dated December 16, 1945; reprinted from an earlier *Vancouver News-Herald* story.
3   Catherine Ford, "Why No Parades for War Brides?", *The Burlington Spectator,* January 29, 1996, B3.
4   From his CD "Fields of Dreams and Glory".
5   Now a Health Sciences Centre. Sunnybrook's veterans' wings are home to 500 veterans of World War II and later wars. Retrieved June 12, 2008, www.66.59.179.35/programs/aging/AgingHistory
6   From Barbara's biography, Memorial University Collection, credited to "What's Happening", December 5, 1992.

CHAPTER 22: Failure to Communicate: War Brides, Citizenship and Passports, 202 - 215
1   Jarratt, *War Brides,* 250. Mrs. Walshe's citizenship has since been restored.
2   Speech, following presentation of the Freedom of the City of Aldershot to the Canadian Army, Mclay, *Aldershot Canadians.*
3   Reported in news media and by many war brides who were on that sailing.
4   Brochure, "Dock to Destination", Department of National Defence, copy in Melynda Jarratt's possession.
5   Stacey, *Six Years of War,* 425.

6   Telephone interview with Audrey Waddy, May 3, 2005.

7   Jarratt, *War Brides,* 23.

8   CBC Archives on line: "War bride loses then recovers Canadian citizenship", broadcast August 2, 1994. www.archives.cbc/war_conflict/second_world_war/clips/a03351

9   Interview with Joe Taylor's mother, June 2, 2004.

10   Day, Spence and Ladouceur, *Women Overseas,* 276..

CHAPTER 23: Betty's Story, 216 – 221

--

POSTSCRIPT: Unification or Schism?, 222

1   Granatstein, *Who Killed the Canadian Military?*, 81.

2   Ibid, 81

APPENDIX I: Names of War Bride Ships, 223

1   data gathered from interviews and historical data. Note: Capt. Hubert Hall advised Melynda Jarratt that ARIA and SITMA may not be valid names as he could find no record of them.

2   data gathered from interviews; O'Hara, *Romance to Reality*, 305; Capt. Hubert Hall corrected spelling of "TETELIA" to "TETELA" .

3   spelling of IVERIA corrected to IVERNIA by Capt. Hubert Hall.

APPENDIX II: Number Crunching, 224

1   World at Arms, Reader's Digest Association, 485

2   Ibid.

3   Ibid.

4   Ibid.

APPENDIX III: World War I Brides, 225

1   "A Plain Account of the Demobilization of the Canadian Expeditionary Force", information from Annette Fulford.

VIII: Bibliography

World War II

Addison, Paul	*Now the War is Over: a social history of Britain, 1945-51*, Jonathon Cape, 1985.
Aikens, Gwladys M. Rees	*Nurses in Battledress*, Nimbus, 1998.
The Air Crew Association, Vancouver Island	*Air Crew Memories (Sixty-five stories of service with the Royal Canadian Air Force and the Royal Air Force in war and peace)*, Victoria Publishing Company, 1999.
Allison, Les	*Canadians in the RAF*, self published, 1978.
Allison, Les and Harry Hayward	*They Shall Grow Not Old, A Book of Remembrance*, Commonwealth Air Training Plan Museum, Inc., Brandon, Manitoba. Second printing 1996.
Andrews, Allen	*Brave Soldiers, Proud Regiments*, Ronsdale Press, 1997.
Atkins-Sheldrick, Coreen	*In our Defense: The Veterans and Military Heritage of Historic Osgoode Township*, self published, 2 vols., 2007.
Barrett, Barbara and Eileen Dicks, (war brides), editors	*We Came from Over the Sea, British War Brides in Newfoundland*, ESPress, Newfoundland, 1996.
Barris, Ted	*Behind the Glory: the plan that won the Allied War* (The British Commonwealth Air Training Plan), MacMillan, 1992.
"	*Days of Victory, Sixtieth Anniversary Edition*, 2005.
Beavis, Debbie	*Who Sailed on the Titanic?*, Ian Allan, 2002.
Bell, Ken and Celia Franca	*The National Ballet of Canada, A Celebration*, University of Toronto Press, 1978.
Bercuson, David L.	*Maple Leaf Against the Axis*, Stoddart, 1995.
Betjeman, John	*London's Historic Railway Stations*, Paperback Edition, John Murray, 1972.
Bishop, Edward	*Their Finest Hour, the story of the Battle of Britain, 1940*, Ballantine Books (Battle Book No. 2), 1968.
Bisset, Alex ed	*Oxford Canadian Dictionary*, OUP, 2004
Blackburn, George G.	*Where the Hell are the Guns? A Soldier's Eye View of the Anxious Years, 1939-44*, McClelland & Stewart, 1985.
Blair, Clay	*Hitler's U-Boat War, The Hunters, 1939-1944*, Modern Library Paperback, 2000.
Blythe, Ronald, editor	*Private Words: Letters and Diaries from the Second World War*, Penguin Books, 1993.
Braynard, Frank O.	*Lives of the Liner*, Cornell Maritime Press, 1947.
Briggs, Susan	*The Home Front, War Years in Britain 1939-1945*, American Heritage Publishing, 1975.
Broadfoot, Barry	*Six War Years 1939-1945, Memories of Canadians at Home and Abroad*, Paperjacks, 1976.
Broadfoot, Barry	*The Veterans' Years: Coming Home from the War*, Douglas and McIntyre, 1985.

Bungay, Stephen	*The Most Dangerous Enemy, A History of the Battle of Britain*, Aurum Press Ltd., 2000.
Byers, A.R. editor	*The Canadians at War 1939/45*, 2 vols. Reader's Digest Association (Canada) Ltd., 1986.
Calder, Angus	*The People's War, Britain 1939-1945*, Jonathan Cape, 1969.
Campbell, Gray	*Butter Side Up*, Horsdal & Schubert, 1994.
Chartrand, René	*Canadian Forces in World War II*, Osprey Publishing Ltd., 2001.
Christie, Carl A.	*Ocean Bridge, The History of RAF Ferry Command*, University of Toronto Press, 1995.
Churchill, Winston S.	*The Second World War, The Commonwealth Alone*, Vol. 4 of twelve, Cassell, 1949.
Churchill, Winston S. and the editors of *Life*	*The Second World War*, Time Incorporated, 1959 edition.
Cockett, Olivia Robert Malcolm, editor	*Love and War in London, A Woman's Diary, 1939-1942*, Wilfred Laurier University Press, 2005.
Collier, Richard	*Eagle Day, The Battle of Britain, August 6 - September 15, 1940*, J.M. Dent & Sons (Canada) Ltd., 1998.
Controller of His Britannic Majesty's Stationery Office	*Front Line - The Official Story of the Civil Defense of Britain*, J.M. Dent & Sons (Canada) Ltd., 1943.
Costello, John	*Love, Sex and War, Changing Values 1939-45*, William Collins, 1985.
Dallaire, Roméo	*Shake Hands with the Devil, The Failure of Humanity in Rwanda*, Random House, 2003.
Day, Spence and Ladouceur, editors	*Women Overseas, Memoirs of the Canadian Red Cross Corps*, Ronsdale Press, 1998.
Dear, I.C.B. and M.R.D. Foot, editors	*The Oxford Companion to World War II*, Oxford University Press, 1995.
Deighton, Len	*Blood, Tears and Folly, In the Darkest Hour of the Second World War*, Jonathan Cape, 1993.
Demarne, Cyril, OBE	*The London Blitz, A Fireman's Tale*, Battle of Britain Prints International Limited, 1991.
Dewar, Jane, editor-in-chief	*True Canadian War Stories, Selected from sixty years of Legion Magazine*, Lester & Orpen Dennys Limited, 1986.
Dixon, Ann	*Silent Partners, Wives of National Park Wardens*, Dixon and Dixon, Publishers, 1985.
Donovan, Rita	*As for the Canadians, The Remarkable Story of the RCAF's "Guinea Pigs" of World War II*, BuschekBooks (sic), 2000.
Dundas, Hugh	*Flying Start, A Fighter Pilot's War Years*, St. Martin's Press, 1989.
Dunmore, Spencer	*Wings for Victory (the story of the British Commonwealth Air Training Plan)*, McClelland & Stewart, 1994.
Dunmore, Spencer	*Above and Beyond*, McClelland & Stewart, 1996.
Dunmore, Spencer and William Carter	*Reap the Whirlwind, The Untold Story of 6 Group Canada's Bomber Force of World War II*, McClelland & Stewart, 1991.
Ellis, Jean M. (with	*Face Powder and Gunpowder* (The Canadian Red Cross), S.J.

Isabel Dingman)	Reginald Saunders & Company Limited, 1947.
Fallows, Carol	*Love & War, Stories of War Brides from the Great War to Vietnam*, Bantom Books, 2002.
Farran, Major Roy, DSO, MC	*The History of the Calgary Highlanders, 1921-1954,* Bryand Press Ltd., 1954.
Fee, Margery and Janice McAlpine	*Guide to Canadian English Usage*, Oxford University Press, 1997.
Fitzgibbon, Constantine	*London's Burning, Ballantine's Illustrated History of World War II,* (Battle Book No. 17), 1970.
Fleming, Peter	*Invasion 1940, An account of the German preparations and the British counter-measures*, Rupert Hart-Davis, 1957.
Fodor, Jenis J. and the editors of Time-Life Books	*The Neutrals,* World War II, Time-Life Books, 1982.
Francis, Daniel	*A Road for Canada,The Illustrated Story of the Trans-Canada Highway*, Stanton Atkins & Dosil Publishers, 2006.
Fussell, Paul	*Wartime, Understanding and Behaviour in the Second World War*, Oxford University Press, 1989.
Goddard, Lance	*Canada and the Liberation of the Netherlands, May 1945,* Dundurn, 2005.
Goralski, Robert	*World War 2 Almanac, 1932-1945,* Putnam, 1981.
Granfield, Linda	*Brass Buttons and Silver Horseshoes, Stories from Canada's British War Brides,* McClelland & Stewart, 2002.
Grant, Doris	*Feeding the Family in War-time*, George G. Harrap & Co. Ltd., nd, but obviously published early in the war.
Granatstein, J. L.	*Who Killed the Canadian Military?*, A Phyllis Bruce Book, 2004
Grizzle, Stanley G.	*My Name's Not George, The Story of the Brotherhood of Sleeping Car Porters in Canada*, Umbrella Press, 1998.
Grogan, John Patrick	*Dieppe and Beyond*, Juniper Books, 1982.
Harding, Stephen	*Great Liners at War*, Motorbooks, 1997.
Harrington, Michael and James K. Hillier	*The Newfoundland National Convention, 1946-48,* Montreal: McGill-Queen's University Press on behalf of Memorial University, 1995.
Harrison, Tom	*Living Through the Blitz*, Penguin Books, 1990.
Heathcote, Blake	*Testament of Honour, Personal Histories of Canada's War Veterans*, Doubleday Canada, 2000.
Hibbert, Joyce, (war bride) editor	*The War Brides*, PMA Books, 1978.
"	*Fragments of War*, Dundern Press, 1985.
Hines, Sherman and Donald Cameron	*Outhouses of the West*, Nimbus, 1988.
Holmes, Richard (Professor)	*In the Footsteps of Churchill, a Study in Character*, Basic Books, 2006.
Hough, Richard and Denis Richards	*The Battle of Britain, The Jubilee History,* Hodder & Stoughton, 1989.
Howard, Leslie Ruth	*A Quite Remarkable Father,* Longmans Green, 1959.

Howard, Ronald	*In Search of my Father,* St. Martin's Press, 1981.
Infield, Glen B.	*Disaster at Bari*, Macmillan, 1971.
Jarratt, Melynda	*War Brides, The stories of the women who left everything behind to follow the men they loved,* Tempus, 2007.
"	*Captured Hearts, New Brunswick War Brides,* Goose Lane, 2008.
Jenkins, Roy	*Churchill, a biography,* Plume, a member of the Penguin Group, 2001.
Johnstone, Air Vice-Marshal Sandy, CB, DFC, AE	*Spitfire into War,* Grafton Books, 1988.
Kaplan, Philip and Jack Currie	*Convoy, Merchant Sailors at War 1938-1945*, Naval Institute Press, Annapolis, 1998.
Kaufman, David and Michiel (sic) Horn	*The Liberation Album, Canadians in the Netherlands, 1944-45*, McGraw Hill Ryerson, 1980.
Kee, Robert	*We'll Meet Again, photographs of daily life during World War II,* Dent, 1984.
Keefer, Ralph	*Grounded in Eire*, McGill University Press, 2001.
Kokin, Morris with Ian Walker	*Women Married to Alcoholics*, William Murrow, 1989.
Konings, Chris	*Queen Elizabeth at War, His Majesty's Transport 1939-1946,* Patrick Stephens, Wellington, 1985.
Kozar, Judy	*Canada's War Grooms and the Girls who Stole Their Hearts,* General Store Publishing House, 2007.
Ladouceur, Barbara and Phyllis Spence editors	*Blackouts to Bright Lights, Canadian War Bride Stories*, Ronsdale Press, 1999.
Latta, Ruth, editor	*The Memory of All That, Canadian Women Remember World War II,* General Store, 1993.
Longmate, Norman	*How We Lived Then, A history of everyday life during the Second World War*, Arrow Books, 1971.
"	*The G.I.s, The Americans in Britain*, Hutchinson, 1975.
McBryde, Brenda	*A Nurse's War*, Chatto & Windus, 1979.
McIntosh, Dave editor	*High Blue Battle, The War Diary of No.1 (401) Squadron RCAF*, Stoddart, 1990.
Maclay, Mark	*Aldershot's Canadians: in love and war – 1939-45,* APPIN Publications, 1997.
Major, Kevin	*As Near to Heaven By Sea, A history of Newfoundland & Labrador*, Viking, 2001.
Marteinson, John	*We Stand on Guard, An Illustrated History of the Canadian Army*, Ovale Publications, 1992.
Miller, William H. Jr.	*The Great Luxury Liners, 1927-1954,* 1981, Dover Publications Inc., 1981.
Mitic, Trudy	*Pier 21, The Gateway that Changed Canada*, Nimbus Publishing, 1997.
Mollo, Andrew	*The Armed Forces of World War II, Uniforms Insignia and*

	Organizations, Greenwich Editions, 2000.
Morton, Desmond	*Victory 1945 - Canadians from war to peace*, Harper Collins, 1995.
Momathuk, Yva, and John Eastcott	*This Marvellous Terrible Place, Images of Newfoundland and Labrador*, Firefly Books, 1998, second printing.
Mosley, Leonard	*Backs to the Wall*, Random House, 1971.
Mowat, Claire	*The Outport People*, McClelland and Stewart, 1983.
Murrow, Edward R. Elmer Davis, editor	*This is London*, Schocken Books, NY, 1940.
Nicolson, Harold, Nigel Nicolson, editor	*The War Years: Dairies and Letters, 1945-1962*, Atheneum, 1971.
Owen, James and Guy Walters, editors	*The Voice of War, The Second World War Told by Those Who Fought It*, Penguin, 2005.
Peck, Ira	*The Battle of Britain*, Scholastic Book Services, 1970.
Peden, Murray	*A Thousand Shall Fall*, Stoddart, 1998 edition.
Rains, Olga (Dutch war bride)	*We Became Canadians*, Overnight Copy Service, 1984.
Robertson, Selena and Les Wilson	*Scotland's War*, Mainstream Publishing, 1995.
Sangster, Joan	*Regulating Girls and Women: Sexuality, Family and the Law in Ontario, 1920-1960*, Toronto OUP, 2001.
Saunders, Andy	*Bognor at War*, Middleton Press, 1995. (This book is distinguished by the fact that it has only two references to the multitude of Canadians in the area defending the south coast including Bognor's beaches.)
Shewchuk, Helen	*If Kisses were Roses*, Shewchuk, 1996.
Smith, Frank	*A Genealogical Gazetteer of England*, Genealogical Publishing Co., Inc., 1977.
Smith, Godfrey	*The English Companion, An Idiosyncratic A-Z of England and Englishness*, Penguin Books, 1984.
Soames, Mary	*Clementine Churchill*, Cassel Ltd., 1979.
Southern, George	*Poisonous Inferno, World War II Tragedy at Bari Harbour*, Airlife Publishing Ltd., Shrewsbury, England, 2002.
Stacey, Colonel C.P., OBE, AM, PhD	*The Canadian Army, 1939-1945*, The King's Printer, Ottawa, 1948.
Stafford, David	*Ten Days to D-Day, Countdown to the Liberation of Europe*, A Little, Brown Book, 2003.
Strachan, Tony	*In the Clutch of Circumstance, Experiences of Canadian Prisoners of War*, Cappis Press, 1985.
Stofer, Ken	*The Biggs Boys*, Kenlyn, 1995.
Stursberg, Peter	*The Sound of War, Memoirs of a CBC Correspondent*, University of Toronto Press, 1993.
Tassie, Vicki (war bride)	*Life in Holland Under German Occupation*, (Privately printed) quoted in *The Liberation Album, Canadians in the Netherlands, 1944-45*, McGraw Hill Ryerson, 1980
Taylor, A.J.P.	*English History, 1914-1945*, The Oxford History of England, Sir George Clark, Editor, Oxford University Press, 1965.

Tessier, Vanna, editor	*Beyond Bad Times*, Chapbook, Snowapple Press, 1993.
Thomas, Ethel	*War Story,* self-published, 1989.
Townsend, Peter	*Duel of Eagles,* Pocket Book editon, 5th printing, 1972.
Tubbs, D.B.	*Lancaster Bomber,* Ballentyne Books, 1972.
Valee, Brian	*The Story of the Notorious Boyd Gang,* Doubleday, 1997.
Waller, Jane and Michael Vaughan-Rees	*Women in Wartime, The Role of Women's Magazines, 1939-1945,* Macdonald & Co. (Publishers) Ltd., 1987.
Waller, Maureen	*London 1945, Life in the Debris of War,* St. Martin's Griffin edition, 2006.
Warner, Philip	*World War II, TheUntold Story,* Cassell Military Paperbacks edition, 2002.
Weinreb & Hibbert, editors	*The London Encyclopaedia,* Macmillan, 1983.
Wells, Captain John	*The Royal Navy, An Illustrated Social History 1870-1982,* Wrens Park Publishing, an imprint of W.J. Williams & Son Ltd., 1999.
Wheeler, William J., DSO, DFC and Bar, W/C RCAF (Ret.)	*Flying Under Fire, Canadians Fliers Recall The Second World War,* Fifth House Ltd., 2001.
Whitaker, Brigadier General Denis, DSO, CM and Shelagh Whitaker	*Dieppe, Tragedy to Triumph*, McGraw-Hill Ryerson, 1992.
Whitcombe, Fred and Blair Gilmour	*The Pictorial History of Canada's Army Overseas, 1938-1945,* Whitcombe, Gilmour & Co., 1947.
Wicks, Ben	*When the Boys Came Marching Home, True stories of the men who went to war and the women and children who took them back,* Stoddart, 1991.
"	*Promise You'll Take Care of my Daughter,* Stoddart, 1992.
Williams, Jeffery	*Far From Home, A Memoir of a 20th Century Soldier,* University of Calgary Press, 2003.
Windsor, John	*Blind Date,* Gray's Publishing, 1962.
Wright, Glen T.	*The Canadian Encyclopedia,* 1985.
Wright, Michael, editor	*The World at Arms,* Reader's Digest Association, 1989
Ziegler, Philip	*London at War, 1939-1945,* Alfred A. Knopf, 1995.
anon	*Wartime Recipes,* Jarrold Publishing, 1998.

Booklets

anon.	*For Valour,* Thames Television, UK, nd.
Department of National Defence	*Dock to Destination,* 1946.
Department of National Defence	*Welcome to War Brides,* 1944.

Magazine articles

Halliday, Hugh	"Canadian Content in the RAF", Legion Magazine, January/February 2005.
Lemann, Nicholas	"The Murrow Doctrine", The New Yorker, January 23, 2006.
Paudash, Anne Rosemary	"I Married an Indian", Maclean's, December 1, 1951.

Newspaper articles

Mackey, Doug	" The Life and Times of Edwin Boyd", *The North Shore Nugget*, Ontario, May 11, 2002.
Tupper, Jan	"Subaltern Mary Churchill Thrilled to be in Service", *Globe & Mail*, August 21, 1943.

DVDs

Love and Duty, Canadian Red Cross Women in WWII	Director Shel Piercy, Produced in association with History Television, Infinity Films, a division of Infinity Filmed Entertainment Group Ltd., 2002.

Unpublished Sources

Memorial University	"Newfoundland Studies # 2", 1984.
Birch, Libby	"War and Peace" Thesis prepared for Kathryn Arnup, July 1990.
Forsyth, Honor Joan	"The Memories of 55 years Together", nd
Jarratt, Melynda	Master of History thesis, "The War Brides of New Brunswick", New Brunswick University, 1995.
Spergel, Estella	Master of History thesis, "Topics in Canadian Social History: British War Brides, World War II, A Unique Experience for Unique Immigrants - The Process that Brought Them to Canada", Toronto University, 1997.
Stacey, Col. C.P.	Report No. 41, August 9, 1941: "Movement of Second Canadian Division to South Coast."
Wiseman, Yvonne	"The Story of a War Bride", nd.

World War I

Abraham, Dorothy (war bride)	*Lone Cone, A journal of Life on the West Coast of Vancouver Island*, B.C. Paperback, 5th edition, privately printed, 1961.
Holmes, Peggy (war bride)	*It Could Have Been Worse, (WWI war bride memoir)*, 1980.
Knott, Grace L. (war bride)	*English Smocking*, Thomas Allen Limited, 1957.
McKenna, M. Olga, SC, Professor Emeritus, Mount Saint Vincent University, Halifax, NS	*Micmac by Choice*, Formac Publishing, 1990.

IX: Permissions

I am grateful to: Joan Bowles for providing her wedding photograph for the cover; the late Gray Campbell who gave his permission "willingly and enthusiastically" to use material from his book, *Butter Side Up*; The Canadian Government for permission to use a small amount of material from their website: *Native Soldiers, Foreign Battlefields*; the late Roy Farran, DSO, MC, for permission to quote extensively and use photographs from his book, *The History of the Calgary Highlanders*; The City of Edmonton Archives for permission to reproduce the photograph of the 1940s Edmonton Public Library; Kay Garside for permission to reproduce the war bride brooch symbol which has been adapted for this publication; Leah Halsall, Red Cross Escdort Services for permission to use her picture abord the *Lady Rodney*, Eric Hibbert for permission to use material from Joyce Hibbert's book, *The War Brides*; Diane Hicks, for permission to reprint a stanza from her poem, "Newfoundland Warbride", originally published in "Long Reach Home"; Susan Lyster for permission to use her photograph of John Ralston Saul taken at the Canadian Ambassador's residence, Santiago, Chile; Nimbus Publishing for permission to use the Aubrey Jeffries quote from Mike Parker's *Running the Gauntlet*; Peggy O'Hara and the Highway Book Shop, Cobalt, Ontario, for permission to use war bride names, places and the names of ships from Peggy's book, *From Romance to Reality;* Harry Palmer for the special permission to use his photograph of Betty Oliphant; Ken Stofer for permission to use text and photographs from his book, *The Biggs' Boys*; Shari Ulrich, for permission to reprint part of her song, *She Remembers*; and the late Ben Wicks for permission to use material from *Promise You'll Take Care of My Daughter*. Other credits are noted on photographs and illustrations.

X: Index

Some items are listed under headings such as CANADIAN REGIMENTS and WAR BRIDES. Indented items relate to the un-indented item heading above them. War brides are listed under their married names (capitalized) with their maiden names, where known, in brackets. Hyphenated surnames are alphabetized by the last surname.

256

257